From Bricks to Clicks

5 Steps to Creating
a Durable Online Brand

Serge Timacheff
Douglas E. Rand

McGraw-Hill
New York   Chicago   San Francisco
Lisbon   London   Madrid   Mexico City   Milan
New Delhi   San Juan   Seoul   Singapore
Sydney   Toronto

Library of Congress Cataloging-in-Publication Data

Timacheff, Serge.
    From bricks to clicks : five steps to creating a durable brand / by Serge Timacheff and
    Douglas E. Rand.
        p.   cm.
    Includes bibliographical references.
    ISBN 0-07-137189-3 (hc.)
    1. Brand name products.   2. Advertising.   I. Rand, Douglas E.   II. Title.
        HD69.B7 T55 2001
    658.8'27—dc21

                                                                                2001018017

McGraw-Hill

*A Division of The **McGraw·Hill** Companies*

1 2 3 4 5 6 7 8 9 0   DOC/DOC   0 7 6 5 4 3 2 1

ISBN 0–07-137189–3

Printed and bound by R. R. Donnelley & Sons Company.

McGraw-Hill books are available at special quantity discounts to use as premiums and sales
promotions, or for use in corporte training programs. For more information, please write to
the Director of Special Sales, Professional Publishing, McGraw-Hill, Two Penn Plaza, New
York, NY 10121-2298. Or contact your local bookstore.

This book is printed on recycled, acid-free paper containing a minimum of 50%
recycled de-inked fiber.

To Tim and Rebecca,

for their vision,
support, and encouragement

Contents

Foreword

Life and death. It doesn't get any more black and white than that when you're talking about emotional connections. And emotional connections are *the* essence of branding.

Strangely enough, as we've imprinted LapLink's brand on file-transfer, synchronization, and remote-access products over the last 14 years, we've learned just how closely software is linked to many personal career life-and-death stories.

I heard one of my most memorable LapLink stories from a mid-level product marketing manager for a large company. He had a high-impact presentation to make to senior management, and one PowerPoint presentation had the potential to catapult his career or, alternatively, cripple his chances for advancement. Not surprisingly, he poured a lot of time into the presentation and saved it to his notebook computer.

As luck would have it, things went haywire an hour before the meeting.

His computer screen was black. He could hear the processor churning but he couldn't see the display. And he couldn't get it to project onto another device. He was frantic when he called our com-

LapLink, formerly Traveling Software, has been a solid brand at the product and corporate level since the 1980s. The founder, Mark Eppley, is himself a well-known brand in the technology industry and a frequent speaker and participant in many industry events. In adapting and evolving with the New Economy, and now on into the "Customer Economy," the company has experienced a profound brand transformation, and the LapLink story is one of the most notable case studies we've encountered.

pany. We calmly walked him through the steps to hook a LapLink cable to his notebook, run our LapLink program on the "dark" computer, and copy the PowerPoint file onto another computer. The presentation came off without a hitch. And from the looks of it his career seems to be doing just fine. He's now a senior executive.

I've lost count of the number of times I've heard similar stories during my travels. Customer awareness of LapLink, and the passion, appreciation, and enthusiasm the software often generates eventually led us to rename our company and create our current corporate identity. Like essential overnight delivery, faxes, and email, LapLink has even vaulted to "verb" status. People now say "I will LapLink a file to you."

From Bricks to Clicks describes the method, creativity, and business acumen required to build and extend the brands that successfully attract, engage, and hold onto passionate and loyal customers.

It's a challenging undertaking. The Internet certainly changes how businesses interact with customers. But the Web, on its own, is not powerful enough to change the emotional relationship between a brand and its customers.

Many have tried, and failed, to extend or establish their brand onto the Internet.

Methodology is critical. To do it right, you must intimately understand the emotional connection an existing brand has with your clients no matter where they are, who they are, or what they are doing. And, for new brands, it requires that you have that magical foresight to correctly foretell future emotional ties.

To me, the key is leveraging what you know best.

In our case, that's file transfer. Want to transfer files from one PC to another? We like to think we make it easy, which is a big part of our appeal. Try it on the Web. Just try. Attach some files or, better yet, images from your last vacation to an email message. I can predict the nightmare you'll experience trying to get that email elephant down the throat of the pipeline python.

We're taking our file-transfer solutions to the Web; LapLink will become a verb for a whole new generation on the Internet. Yes, the Internet as a medium is new, but the reason for our success is as old as our company: When customers cry out for a simpler way, we've already got an answer.

Whether you're a bricks-and-mortar Old Economy company in a state of migration or a pure Internet play moving beyond the New Economy to the Customer Economy, applying what your corporate team knows to this new medium is not only wise—it's been done and is being done by John Deere, Singapore's Great Eastern Life, AT&T, Ariba, Palm, Germany's Mediantis.de, IBM, Yahoo!, Microsoft, Cadillac, AOL, Volvo, Avaya, Kmart, NetRadio.com, Wind River, Brazil's iG.com, and even by pop stars like Denmark's Marie Frank, as well as countless other people and organizations discussed in this book.

These companies and the people behind them have walked the same tightrope. To grow and thrive, you've got to evolve and do it a step ahead of the changing market. You've got to widen your viewpoint to embrace a global marketplace. But no company can afford to become such a chameleon that its own customers no longer recognize its core strength—the brand that earned it all of those loyal fans to begin with.

Mark Eppley
CEO, LapLink.com Inc.

Preface

And on her lover's arm she leant,
And round her waist she felt it fold,
And far across the hills they went
In that new world which is the old.
   —Alfred, Lord Tennyson,
      Locksley Hall, 1842[1]

The first official board meeting of the Desmond Tutu Peace Trust took place one steamy June 2000 day in Manhattan at St. James Cathedral: a two-hour meeting packed with potentially world-changing agenda items being decided upon by global leaders, academicians, theologians, and philanthropists. Blessed by Nobel laureate Archbishop Desmond Tutu, the newly formed Tutu Peace Trust, headquartered in Capetown, South Africa, with a U.S.-based foundation headquartered in Seattle, was faced with a daunting task: to speak to spirituality, equality, scholarship, world peace, and the general human condition.

Ten minutes seemed hardly long enough to explain to the board why branding and the Web would be at the heart of the effort's potential success. Yet the approach taken was one to which board members could relate, and it got their attention. There exists a similarity between the Internet and Africa. Both are growing out of control, both are plagued with viruses, both are chaotic and disorganized, both are of critical concern to the entire globe, and both have the potential to bring the world to its knees. Yet both offer incredible hope, profound opportunity, a medium for common interest and community, and an entirely new way to communicate.

The board members had not thought about the Tutu organization in the context of a brand, nor had they fully realized the impact the Web could have on building their brand to help quickly and successfully achieve global recognition and staying power among nonprofit organizations. This was a new and fresh approach, the right thing to consider for an organization being formed at the turn of the century.

It's been said that the eyes are the window to the soul. In the same way, the Web is the window to the brand. A brand isn't something tangible; just like a human spirit, only its physical manifestation is visible. But without a spirit, a body would be mere flesh, and, without a brand, an organization is mere bricks and mortar.

Theologians continue to struggle, as they have for centuries, to explain concepts like "spirit" and "soul." They're tough concepts, and trying to explain branding is the business equivalent of explaining the human soul. Marketing executives across six continents labor to get the concept of branding across to CEOs, who—understandably—listen and question something they can't directly see, demanding tangible methods and results with predictable costs and revenue potential.

Where religion and branding diverge is in process. Religion is based on faith, which, by definition, requires people to believe in something they can't necessarily touch or see. But a strong business-based brand cannot be based on faith. It must be the result of a process, one with a strong foundation and framework that has been clearly defined, developed, and managed. CEOs presented with a logical process—tied to virtually every aspect of the company from sales to administration to marketing to the Web—as part of developing a brand begin to realize that even the elusive concept of "brand" can provide tangible results.

Many venture capitalists today question their money-hungry applicants—especially ones intending to make the Web a strong part of their business—about the attention they've paid to building a brand as part of their business model. Arguably a company's most significant asset—especially in the New or Customer Economy—a brand is as important as product quality, technology, and a financial plan. A strong brand makes the difference between success—securing partners, financing, media coverage, and customers—and failure. More important, it means emotional attachment and repeat business—the intangible factors that make a company win in any highly competitive, overcommodified market.

* * * * *

Today it's a *new,* New Economy. Chastened by battered stock portfolios and failed dotcoms, those fortunate enough to survive the rigors of a softening economy are realizing that perhaps the bricks-and-mortar companies haven't been eclipsed and forgotten as the world has gone virtual. A single good idea, a great technology, an alluring brand name, and even a fat checkbook aren't enough individually to ensure business success. Lured by the sirens of the Internet, many a company has been dashed on the rocks of cyberspace, leaving the litter, perhaps, of great ideas that lacked solid business planning. Technology for the sake of technology is falling by the wayside, and technology for the sake of the customer has taken its place.

It may surprise many readers to learn that branding is more about solid business planning than it is about creative naming or logo design. Branding efforts must employ "business empathy," an "I've walked in your shoes" approach from which a solid solution to a well-articulated problem flows naturally. Business today is justifiably resistant to pouring money into any effort that has failed to provide foundation, structure, and tangible results.

This back-to-basics approach resides at the heart of this book. When pioneering in new territory, it's the wrong time to experiment with untried tools and equipment, and doing so increases risk, exponentially. *From Bricks to Clicks,* instead, emphasizes a thoughtful integration of Old Economy business and marketing principles with New and Customer Economy acumen. Neither pop marketing nor pure philosophy, it is a book about an extensively field-tested, methodical approach adaptable to virtually any business problem involving brand development, complemented by commentary from people who understand its implications.

From Bricks to Clicks also emphasizes the crucial role that globalization plays in building brands on the Web. Brands are being built in every corner of the world, and they are becoming increasingly interconnected. Building brands offshore—wherever "onshore" might be—is becoming more and more of a competitive asset as well as a business challenge. Firms that prepare themselves for the coming wave of globalization will hold one very important key to success as business continues to evolve.

The Web has carried many aspects of traditional business across a new threshold. The way the world finds information, buys products and services, and communicates has been augmented, and in some cases changed profoundly, in a matter of a few years. But, in many cases, business has stuck with old ways more than the average Internet executive might like to believe. Adapting to how business and the Internet interrelate has involved branding at a fundamental level.

Things are still changing fast, especially in the realms of business-to-business transactions, commerce opportunities, and globalization. As various markets become highly commodified, with literally hundreds of new entrants to the world of ecommerce, differentiation will become increasingly challenging. Extending and leveraging strong brands on the Internet is critical to building and retaining a strong and loyal client base, as well as to attracting partners and investors. According to an ominously timed January 2000 article on branding in *Red Herring,* "It sounds straightforward enough, but in pursuing brands these nascent companies are trying to attain something in a matter of months that took companies like Coca-Cola, Ford Motor, and even IBM and Microsoft decades to establish."[2]

In this fast-changing economy, companies not only have to be able to change or grab market share quickly, but to communicate an established brand. Clients beg branding firms to make them look "established," "partnerable," and "bigger than life" within a much shorter time frame than it has taken to grow a traditional brand to maturity. Today, many of the big brands are using that maturity effectively, like patient parents who know their teenagers will realize one day that they don't actually know everything there is to know.

At the heart of the brand that wins the venture capitalist's heart and pocketbook, and, down the road, the hearts and pocketbooks of clients and customers, is the right combination of brand and business savvy, process, creative abilities, and strong execution. Building brands on the Web isn't just about being able to understand the New Economy, although that helps. It's about being able to combine tried-and-true methodology with a contemporary understanding and vision of business today and where it's headed. It's actually very good news that many of the same factors that enable bricks-and-mortar businesses to stand strong can be effectively leveraged into a Net economy. Moving from bricks to clicks is every bit as much about the bricks of the past as it is the clicks of the future.

Acknowledgments

The vision for *From Bricks to Clicks* required an effort far beyond what two branding and communications consultants pontificating on theory and spinning personal anecdotes could produce. Depth and meaning could only come from the support of numerous business and industry associates, acquaintances, and friends, as well as a tremendous network of new contacts around the world that included corporate executives, branding experts, musicians, professors, marketing gurus, entrepreneurs, designers, physicians, historians, venture capitalists, priests, journalists, software developers, and artists.

We are indebted to these people for their contributions, which collectively begin to define what branding means and will continue to mean in the New Economy as it matures and comes to no longer be "new." It is, in fact, through the good work and vision of these and many others that the New Economy is indeed evolving, focusing much more on business collaboration and customer benefit, than on mere technology and get-rich-quick schemes. Tried-and-true marketing and brand principles continue to prevail, and our message of applying "method to madness" was validated with the help of many colleagues and friends around the world. Through the process of research and writing this book, our understanding of what brand development means today has been vastly enriched, hopefully for the benefit of anyone who might wish to read further.

In addition to all those interviewed and named in this book, we would like to thank several key people who provided us with on-going or specialized support:

Our families and friends, Amy, Sheri, Jennifer, Reagan, Bink and Lou, Donna, Tatyana, and Alexander, especially for their patience, quiet support, and ability to keep home fires burning; Bill Smith, for foresight and encouragement (Doug); Mark Wilson, Bob Angus, Alan Zeichick, Rob Calem, and Carlos Gutierrez, and in particular Yeo Toon Joo in Singapore for his support and introductions in Asia (Serge).

The Garrigan Lyman Group, www.glg.com, the entire "Solution Branding" team, for their great talents, support, and spirit, especially Jennifer Winegardner, Amy Brodie, Kelly Spencer, Tim Garrigan, Rebecca Lyman, Matthew Harper, Angeline Yeo, Doug Strohm, Bryan Cummings, Christine Garrigan, Merritt Etzel, Aly Prestel, and Chris "Whitey" Geiser.

Our guiding lights at McGraw-Hill, in particular, our editor, Michelle Williams, and her assistant, Sue Gerber, for everything they've done to enable a passion for both branding and writing to converge successfully. Finally, thanks to Ruth Mannino for a thoughtful, clean edit.

Waterside Productions, literary agents with the rare combination of both foresight *and* insight, especially, David Fugate, and Bill Gladstone.

If you would like to contact us, our email address is from brickstoclicks@hotmail.com. We sincerely hope *From Bricks to Clicks* provides you with a unique and new way to look at brand development, a logical insight into well-established methodology, and new tools for ensuring brand success.

Serge Timacheff
Seattle, Washington

Douglas E. Rand
San Francisco, California

1

The Complete Brand and the Web

Every intellectual product must be judged from the point of view of the age and the people in which it was produced.
—Walter Pater, *The Renaissance,* 1873[1]

Since its inception as a commercial entity, the Web has grown to be a viable communications venue for a brand. Today, potential employees, investors, partners, competitors, customers, and journalists often turn to an organization's Web site before any other form of marketing or communication to obtain substantive information. They may know absolutely nothing about the "brand"—having surfed to the site after first seeing the company name appear as a result on a search engine—or they may have heard of the company through an ad or word of mouth, or even in a news article. But the Web is now the primary source for in-depth information, far surpassing corporate brochures, annual reports, or telephone calls.

How did business ever survive without it? Today it seems ludicrous to wait a week for a corporate brochure to arrive in the mail or a sales representative or PR person to call with information, which is often incomplete at that. All it takes is simply typing in the company name, and *voilà!*—virtually unlimited corporate data, available to anyone.

All this has profound implications for brand development, one being that the past isn't as far behind as wound-licking dotcoms would lead the market to believe. The essential burden for a Web site is to accurately reflect the brand and bind itself to a business proposition.

"It's about setting expectations," according to Jerry Fiddler, chairman of Wind River Systems (www.windriver.com), the market leader in embedded systems technology. "You work to create a sense of who you are so that when anyone sees your name they get what they want, and the Web may be the only shot you get at that customer."

A company may have the greatest support team in the world, the best products, or the most fantastic service yet available. However, if the image presented on its home page fails to compel the viewer, if it looks cheap, if it's culturally insensitive, if it's impossible to decipher, or if it's really slow, the brand takes a direct hit amidships. Some theories of interpersonal psychology show that impressions made during the first few minutes of meeting someone really do count for the life of a relationship. That's exactly what happens when someone encounters a company for the first time via the Web: It's a first impression of vast proportion.

Brand Building with Power Tools

Companies today are still hitting the nails and screwing the screws they've always used to build their business, but they have some new power tools to aid in the effort. The Web provides a way for brands to be communicated and reinforced more quickly and more effectively. However, as with any power tool, damage can occur swiftly and severely. An ebrand, whether from a bricks-and-mortar firm or a raw start-up, claims specific differentiating factors:

- It provides limitless opportunities to engage audience members in direct communication, at their own pace and interactively.
- It allows audience members to experience a brand at all times, simultaneously, from anywhere.
- It offers extensive personalization.
- It provides an immediate and streamlined channel to information updates.

- It allows communication with targeted audiences, while being comprehensive for all audiences, speaking one-on-one and en masse at the same time.
- When managed properly, it greatly enhances, complements, and supports an offline brand.
- It can significantly cut the time needed to achieve high levels of brand awareness and recognition.
- It is immediately global.
- It provides a virtually limitless space to communicate in a cost-effective manner.

In spite of these advantages, it isn't easy for companies to short-cut well-defined business practices and grow a bumper crop in less than a typical growing season. In many cases, the Mother Nature of branding fights back and brings them down. While a company may be able to shorten the time it takes to create a brand, it can ill afford to skimp on brand process or business planning. Get-rich-quick schemes haven't worked—with a few notable exceptions—and won't work by simply adding ".com" to a name or assuming that hanging an Internet shingle will compel masses of buyers to flock to a site. First-to-market brands—such as eBay and Amazon—continue to dominate in spite of up-and-comers, naysayers, and challengers. While the New Economy nouveau riche may not have old-money brands like Coca-Cola or IBM, they are fervently advised to take "advice from Dad": Employ solid business plans, be early to market, build strong relationships, and focus on developing enduring brands.

Brand Gap

In the spring of 2000 it became evident that dotcom brands were not invulnerable, and success wasn't guaranteed by just any higgledy-piggledy branding effort mounted by a couple of technology retirees with more money and programming experience than marketing sense. A volume of urban business myths vanished overnight. Venture capitalists became more skeptical, and a "brand gap" (Figure 1.1) began to widen: Those with strong brands became stronger and

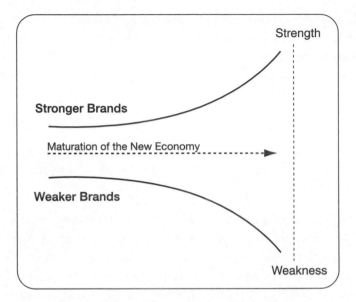

FIGURE 1.1. Notice the strengths and weaknesses through the maturation of the New Economy.

more able to secure financing, and those without strong brands became weaker, either dissolving or becoming easy pickings for corporate predators.

"The 'How can I be out of money? I still have checks in my checkbook!' mentality evaporated quickly," stated Heidi Roizen, venture capitalist, at International Data Group's DEMO 2001 conference that took place in February 2001 in Phoenix. It became clear that while the Web represented a revolutionary and unique medium for business and communication, tried-and-true branding methodology still applied. Business over the Internet is new, which doesn't mean every marketing method ever developed has to be tossed—the challenge is to consider and understand the New Economy and how it impacts business, and then apply branding and marketing practices known to work to the new business model.

Two primary requirements for building a brand on the Web fly high, above all others:

1. Understand and be able to apply traditional branding methodology and process, and look to the entire business to define the Web

brand, not the reverse—the concept is "bricks to clicks," not "clicks instead of bricks."
2. Understand and leverage the Web's effects on business and the New Economy.

The market is constantly evolving. In fact, the "New Economy" is today evolving into a "Customer Economy." This is simply because the Web, above all, gives companies the opportunity to adapt their brands to the individual customers in a mass audience, instead of forcing customers to adapt to them. A more relationship-oriented, collaborative approach to branding overall—including the Web—is the vision of thought leaders, analysts, and the media today.

Sounds reasonable and simple, right? Unfortunately, in practice, basic branding is neglected in myriad corporate business plans, in spite of its star status in popular business culture. Many companies hesitate to put concepts like brand into a business plan because it is difficult to explain and apply, and to show tangibly. Or they simply don't recognize it as an asset. Many people still believe "branding" just refers to a name or a logo, something relegated to marketers and designers.

The good news is the branding process is fundamentally easy to understand and apply to Web business. It doesn't require an economics or engineering degree to comprehend the principles of the New Economy, and the Internet still offers wildly exciting opportunities for all kinds of brands—whether it's Sunkist Oranges, Ariba, IBM, Yahoo!, Banco do Brasil, Oxford University, BMW, or even a photographer running a business from home.

Natural versus Forced Branding

More good news: Most marketers and businesspeople naturally have a good "ear" for branding without even knowing it. Believability and "natural" branding are perhaps the most important factors in building brand on any medium, Web or otherwise. Understanding a natural versus a forced brand can make the difference between success and serious brand erosion.

For example, *Forbes* named UPS "Company of the Year" in January 2000, stating "UPS used to be a trucking company with technology. Now it's a technology company with trucks."[2] Many fine brands have been tempted to jump on the Web brandwagon too energetically, only to take a hard fall. Should UPS, with its tremendous leadership in global transportation technology, reposition itself as a "technology company"? Why not?

A quick jump to UPS.com revealed it had effectively resisted the call of the technology wild: In the first half of 2000, the UPS home page simply sported a factoid stating "*Forbes* magazine named UPS 'Company of the Year' in its January 2000 issue." Kudos go to the UPS executive team for staying true to its brand and for not creating a new tag line or flashing a giant banner on its Web site saying "Now we're a technology company!" Since that time, the company has continued to tout its various technological achievements and offerings, but has remained true to its roots by identifying itself as a package carrier.

So, why not position UPS as a technology company with trucks? Simply because UPS is not a technology company, despite what *Forbes* has to say. UPS still picks up and delivers packages, a highly visible and immediately recognizable service that articulates the core of its brand. Were UPS to communicate to its vast client base that it is a technology company with trucks, consumers would rightfully cry foul.

Conversely, for a company like Amazon.com, faced with competition from book-selling behemoths like Barnes & Noble, to position itself as a technology company with books (and other things) may very well be the way to competitively differentiate itself against the big guys. No one believes Barnes & Noble is a technology company with books; the best bet for www.bn.com is to present itself as an established, bricks-and-mortar brand using technology to provide the best possible selection, pricing, and service available. Many people choose Barnes & Noble, in fact, simply because they can order a book online and return it around the corner, if needed, instead of going to the trouble of shipping it back. In other words, the strength and familiarity of the original brand—if any—have a profound effect on how the brand is portrayed in online business. For Barnes &

Noble, saying it's a technology company is neither natural nor believable and veers away from its core brand positioning and competitive differentiation. Further, it undermines Barnes & Noble's powerful physical presence.

What defines "natural" brand messaging, beyond a simple gut feeling that the branding effort is in line with the company and its personality and identity? As in the case of UPS and package delivery, a brand promise often has one primary benefit (in rare circumstances, there may be more than one) that needs to be focused upon to keep a trusted promise.

Over time, the brand promise will be "pulled" by the market and the company won't have to rely on the brand's "push" so much to continue to win audience favor. Audiences naturally expect their trust will continue to be enhanced by innovative enhancements, along with even higher levels of quality and reliability. As the brand matures and its promise is continually realized, marketing plans need to aggressively address how to take advantage of an expanded trust factor. Complementary positioning for the primary association can possibly be extended into separate product launches, taking advantage of the parenting and endorsing nature of the established promise (Figure 1.2). The primary association that was initially pushed and is now readily accepted should continually be nurtured and be allowed to expand naturally.

- *Impatience:* A premature extension to a brand, before the primary, competitive differentiating promise has been fully experienced, creates doubt in audiences.
- *Confusion:* Degrees of improvement in quality, innovation, and reliability must be obvious to reinforce the primary association. A straying brand leaves audiences wondering what to believe.
- *Inconsistency:* With the myriad promotional media, online, and advertising venues available, as well as potential differences in how disparate internal groups perceive which associations are primary and which are complementary, there are risks that a once-focused and concentrated message may be seen as inconsistent.
- *Promise dilution:* With a successful marketing-driven brand promise, there is the inclination to extend its believability across several,

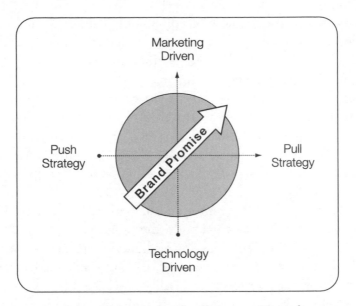

FIGURE 1.2.   From push to pull strategy. So, what
gets in the way of a natural brand campaign?

if not many, additional product/service offerings—thus diluting the
believability not only for the new offerings but also for the existing
ones. The risk is that if the primary promise becomes the most
believable factor in the extension because of weak and poorly supported subbrands, the established primary association will suffer
from overexposure and lack of focus.

• *Nonfocused primary association:* Audiences need to know consistently what to believe and what is complementary to the core belief. "If a brand doesn't take a stand, it stands for nothing."

Rafe Needleman, editor of *Red Herring Online*, emphasizes that
trust and expectations drive the best brands on the Web. "Take, for
example, Epinions.com versus ConsumerReview.com. In my opinion, Epinions has better branding," he said, "with an integrated
community that really highlights everywhere on the site member
opinions, pictures, what people think/feel, and which emphasizes the
whole idea of the 'Web of trust.' It's about product users or movie-
goers, restaurant patrons, and rating their experience for the good of
everybody—all presented very cleanly.

"ConsumerReview, philosophically, does the same thing, and they even have a better name, in my opinion—even though calling me a consumer is patronizing. 'Consumer review' is the expectation and the experience, is the promise, but is not as pervasive until you're off the front page. Instead, it's a more corporate design and the community content doesn't surface—which makes it less believable. The Epinions experience is more true to the brand."

Process resides at the core of analyzing and understanding the challenges of leveraging the core assets and branding personality and attributes of the company, and determining how the consumers, partners, press, and others perceive the assets, personality, and attributes.

Many people involved in building brands, however, simply lack the formal methodology and guidance that will make their brands shine. Highly experienced CEOs and marketing executives often meet branding agencies with skepticism, simply because branding is one of the most intangible "black arts" of marketing and business. Yet when they understand the inherent process—which can be explained conceptually very easily—they become believers, and understand why branding provides a cohesive bond between the various silos of marketing and communications tools, sales, and corporate messaging and strategy. With a strong brand, every employee becomes an ambassador of the company, and every sales representative is able to use brand to competitively differentiate products, services, and solutions from the competition. Branding becomes a competitive weapon and a driving spirit behind an organization, and the Web is at once the newest and sharpest arrow in the quiver.

Recognizing and Employing a True Brand Process

Setting expectations implies forethought and planning, which is all about process. Unfortunately, too often branding is considered to be more an art than a science, and less of a business activity than a chance for marketing people to get together over cappuccino for a creative break. Even worse, many agencies and consultants hired to develop a brand provide creative recommendations, but lack a process tying the various elements of marketing together with a branding constant, from the research and discovery stages all the way through execution. Most agencies specializing in branding incorporate some form of process, but often it's lightweight, more of a sales pitch than a deliverable entity. Ad agencies and PR agencies will sometimes claim to do branding, but beware: They either subcontract the work or do basic naming or creative treatment only, and team members lack the experience to truly understand brand process and method.

Marketing pros and agencies that really have a grasp of branding will rely on a process that contains a lot more than creative treatment. That's the fun part, which is great, but having *real* fun—meaning building a brand that will take the market by storm—takes foundation, structure, framework, project management, and logistics. All of the more creative services—from events to Web design—look artistic and fun-filled, and good implementers and professionals make it look easy, but, like a virtuoso guitar performance, it's not as easy as it looks.

The Five Steps to Building a Durable Online Brand

There are five essential stages of brand development, all of which directly relate to building a brand with a powerful Web element. Furthermore, the stages all tie in with one another, and everyone involved in each stage of the process must have strong exposure and involvement in the other stages to ensure seamless brand development, efficiency, and a high degree of brand consistency across any medium.

1. *Discovery:* This stage involves ensuring that everyone on the team understands the brand challenge and issues; the time lines involved; market/brand research; business plan analysis and its relationship to branding; competitive differentiation; visual brand analysis (logo, Web design, etc.); and name analysis (including tag lines). Here core messaging is evaluated, the "elevator speech"

is tested, and overall brand strategy is examined and developed. Many CEOs don't even realize they *need* a new name, tag line, or Web site until they've gone through at least an abbreviated form of this stage. It's not that they lack awareness or education; rather, once they understand how to clearly evaluate their brand, comprehend how vital it is to the success of their business model, place it into real context in the marketplace, and get a full grasp of the market opportunity a strong brand can garner, they experience an awakening. It's also in this stage that a focused effort is made to characterize the *problem*, not the *solution*. Too many companies eagerly jump to explain how what they have created will solve some vaguely defined global problem and forget to place it in the context of an already recognized problem.

2. *Framework:* This is the time for building the brand structure (a "branded house" versus a "house of brands"; see Chapter 3); brand mapping; understanding the parent brands as well as sub-brands; laying the foundation for future brands to be added; understanding the specific naming and design challenges; beginning to develop the site map for the Web site as well as analyzing any current site(s). At this stage the core message is finalized.

3. *Verbal articulation:* Here, the creative process kicks in: content development for the Web site, including outline and writing; content development for other marketing materials (brochures, advertising, white papers, etc.); naming of the URL, the company name, the products and services, and any other naming needs identified in stages 1 and 2; legal name acquisition; tag-line development. The seeds of design begin to sprout.

4. *Visual, physical, and sensory articulation:* In this stage, the creative process continues to flower. The look and feel of the brand, and the logo, are developed. Web design; collateral design; corporate colors; advertising design and development (including selection of media); and trade show booth design take place. Nonvisual sensory elements—such as sounds—are developed and put into use. For example, "You've Got Mail" is one of the strongest auditory brand labels on the Web today, as strong as the NBC three-bell chime was to television in the 1960s and 1970s. Increasingly, the Web is featuring sound as part of brand identity. Over time, other

sensory tools will be put into play, beginning with tactile feedback (touch) and, even further in the future, taste and smell. Certainly, today a challenge for companies producing foods with great tastes, products that "feel" good, or brands relying on smell as part of their selling proposition (colognes, leather goods, etc.) is how to accentuate some of their strongest marketing points when building a brand on the Web. Industrial design, or "physical branding," ranging from product design to packaging, also plays an extensive role at this stage.

5. *Execution*: In this phase, the developed brand is launched and presented to its target audiences. The URL and Web site "go live"; the advertising appears; collateral development is completed; business packages (stationery, business cards, logo, etc.) are completed; partner links are integrated into the Web; PR begins in earnest, educating the press and analysts; the trade show schedule begins, and so on. This stage fulfills the development of the first four, and, ultimately, becomes a lead-in to circle back to the beginning because at some point everyone wants to know how well the newly developed brand succeeded and has penetrated the market—which puts things back to "discovery." That's not to say the company is renamed, but there must be accountability for all the marketing activity that led to the launch of a major brand.

The brand process, and its various terms and concepts, is fully explored in Chapters 2 to 6.

Marines on the Beach

The difference between encountering a brand at a Coke machine, on a billboard, on a TV commercial, or reading a news article and encountering a brand on the Web is that the Web is completely interactive, and an organization is exposed beyond a simple slogan or opinion. Sitting down in a new car at a dealership is certainly an interactive experience. However, the consumer is also evaluating (at least subconsciously) the dealership and the individual car brand (not

General Motors), and has also probably experienced the car either in a brochure, a review, or on a Web site.

The brand on the Web—at least in part—is like the Marines on the beach: first in to establish the beachhead, securing it for the big guns to take over. If the Marines don't do their job, the big guns will not succeed and the troops won't be able to land. In addition, of course, the Web brand may, in fact, be the Army, the Air Force, and the Navy, or it may be none of those. Nonetheless, in all cases, it's the Marines.

It's the brand's responsibility to secure viewers' attention and emotion when they first come to the Web site and "meet" the brand. That meeting, until viewers go further, will very possibly represent the complete experience they have with a brand—so it had better be accurate. Today's Web mind-set is channel surfing on steroids—viewers who don't like what they see, or who aren't captivated, flip the channel. It's up to the program provider to ensure that the commercials aren't too long or boring and that the programming is tight, interesting, and targeted at the audience. Further, it's up to the program provider to ensure that unwanted viewers do lose interest and go away.

Audience Savvy: A Primary Key to Brand Success

There's no way to underestimate the importance of understanding the proper audiences for a business and consistently communicating a core message to them in a compelling and comprehensible manner. The core message remains the same, no matter who the audience, but the way it is presented—the "wrapper" put around it—caters to individual groups. Successful brands, such as IBM, Disney, Oracle, FedEx, Coca-Cola, Nestlé, Cisco, and Volvo—whether consumer or business-to-business, and whether or not they have flashy graphical intros to their sites—can all quickly communicate their core brand message and then route viewers to the area they need to reach. Whoever they are—an investor, a newspaper reporter, an interested customer, a non-English-speaking potential partner—if there's a place for them in the business model, the site gets them there, and fast.

Katie Hafner, in her online article, "Are Customers Ever Right? Service's Decline and Fall," states, "Phone systems and Web sites that are supposed to help can turn into infuriating mazes."[3] What was meant to be a marketing improvement and enhancement, and a golden opportunity for many company brands to shine forth, is being cast to the winds. The rate of brand deterioration on a Web site, if it is managed poorly, is exponentially more devastating to the overall corporate brand than an individual experience with a poor phone support person or a faulty product.

This means understanding who the audience is and being able to segment that audience appropriately, apply key goals and secondary messages for each audience member, appeal to each in the order of priority, and then service all of them quickly and efficiently—all beginning with the home page. Some audiences may appear identical on the surface, and only with significant analysis will key differences become evident. But this type of brand mapping needs to be done before the Web site is designed and the site is mapped. Web designers refer to "site mapping," which can take place logically only if the company knows what needs to go into the site.

The Virtual Corporate Campus

Frequently, corporations underestimate the detail and customization required to effectively reach individuals in today's Customer Economy in a compelling, unique, and customized manner. Site mapping is very much part of building a "virtual campus" out of a site—which means the site is like a university or a corporate campus with different locations for different people, all served by a central administrative location. Manufacturing and shipping may be located in a relatively distant location from the main campus, which is analogous to companies having Web sites that serve ecommerce needs literally separate from their corporate home sites. Business-to-consumer companies such as Amazon.com, Expedia, eBay, and Yahoo! all have broad virtual campuses spread over multiple sites and hundreds of pages, all designed to reach the right audience at the right time for the right reason.

Laying Foundations through Analysis, Mapping, and Process at Microsoft

Microsoft's Web solution platform, Windows DNA, holds a market-leading position against competitors such as Sun Solaris or Linux in terms of the sheer number of live Web sites worldwide using this technology. Yet when the audiences for the platform—Web and software developers, system architects, CIOs, and technical consultants—were asked, "What is Windows DNA?" they were hard-pressed to offer a meaningful answer. Even the average Microsoft employee had a hard time describing the meaning and definition of Windows DNA.

Microsoft asked what it could do to create a Windows DNA Web site to address this problem by clearly and thoughtfully explaining Windows DNA to interested audiences. As it stood, the site was a mix of technical and marketing information lacking coherent structure or context to help answer the key questions of what Windows DNA was or how it would benefit the audience.

The first thing needed to resolve the Windows DNA brand problem was to bring the team together for a session of brand mapping, laying the foundation to understand the potential audience and what the actual viewers of the Windows DNA site were doing at the site. It was clear that the average *home* Windows user, for example, would have no real need to go to the site. However, even the more technical audiences are highly segmented; so together with the Microsoft Web marketing team a brand map was built. The brand map consisted of an overview of the platform in a "Discover Windows DNA" section, with summary detail in other sections, to help people with various levels of technical knowledge create a mental map of the relationship between each piece and the value it would give them. Techno-gurus were then pointed quickly to Microsoft's main technical Web site, the Microsoft Developer Network (MSDN), to wallow in as much tech talk as they could handle.

What does that do for the brand? It immediately makes Microsoft more approachable, keeping it from appearing to be overly techno-cratic—a common image pitfall for Microsoft (as well as many other technology firms trying to appeal to increasingly nontechnical audiences). It allows viewers to take comfort in immediately finding what they need in order to use the site and get the information they need, yet it is consistent with the Microsoft parent brand.

But for people who really don't need to be reading about Microsoft Windows DNA (maybe they were searching the Web for something about DNA as the "building block of life" and accidentally found the Microsoft site), what is the effect? Microsoft has to gently let them know they're in the wrong place, but without being overbearing or intimidating (after all, they could be investors). And if another part of the Microsoft site attracts a visitor, the visit could very well turn out to be the person's first interactive experience with the Microsoft corporate brand. Even if the visit is not the intended one, it can nonetheless be critical to set the stage for the "brand experience." It's quite likely the viewer has heard of Microsoft before, and probably used a Microsoft product—and is in all likelihood using a Microsoft product, such as the Microsoft Internet Explorer, to see the site. But upon reaching the Microsoft Web site, the brand "meeting" truly takes place as the corporate personality, core messaging, and key company attributes become evident. (Microsoft has since announced the integration of the Windows DNA platform into the Microsoft.NET initiative.)

The Complete Brand

The Web site provides the sum total of the corporate brand and all its subbrands, personality, and attributes rolled into one. Even if a product or service isn't being used, there isn't a more complete and unrippled reflection of the brand anywhere but the Web site, which is another reason having a great Web site isn't an option—it's a requirement. One reason the New Economy has been able to take hold with such a global stranglehold, and the reason the brand gap continues to widen, is that there is no other way to so comprehensively and thoroughly provide information about a company or organization, with the ability to fully and completely control the brand image and tweak it on a moment-to-moment basis.

It's about control. An ad can't be controlled once it's out there.

The media can't be controlled (although they can be directed). Investors can't be controlled. A sales force can't be controlled as well as the sales VP would like. Customers can't be controlled. The market can't be controlled. But a Web site can be controlled. It can say exactly what the company wants it to, and position the brand exactly and precisely. And anyone who comes to the site expects just that, which is why it is essential that the Web site be as natural an extension and reflection of the brand as possible.

The downside occurs if the Web site is not controlled or if a company's Web designers fail to develop a Web site that accurately portrays the brand. If the "window to the brand" is cracked, tinted, or obscured; or too small to provide more than a keyhole effect; or gives a tramp-steamer image to a first-class cruise-ship company; or allows people who really shouldn't to look inside, then the brand begins to erode dramatically.

The complete brand is the one controlled as completely as possible. The good news is the Web provides that opportunity, in spades, and it's within reach.

What Is a Brand?

Brands can and have been defined in many ways, in many books, and by many people. It is not the intention of this book to define a brand beyond saying that it represents the complete experience anyone has with an organization, meaning its image, its service, its name, its people, its Web site, and its products. It is the spirit that gives life, in the corporate setting. Without a brand, a company is merely a collection of its parts with no cohesive element, much as a person's body is merely flesh and bone without a spirit to make it alive.

So the corporate executive who is building a brand is literally breathing life into his or her organization, which is what will make it compelling. Choose a topic and surf to four or five Web sites in a given market and it becomes obvious which brands have life and which do not. Typically, the more generic, off-the-shelf Web sites look and act robotic; while they may be representing a very spirited company, they are failing to communicate that spirit—the brand.

Brands are about differentiation. Branding cattle differentiates one rancher's stock from another. At www.investorwords.com, "the biggest, best investing glossary on the Web," the term *brand* is defined as "An identifying symbol, word, or mark that distinguishes a product or company from its competitor." Most dictionary definitions of brand resemble this one, relegating a brand to a simple set of marketing communications tools; the concept of differentiation, however, holds true at all levels. To be able to competitively differentiate one brand from another is essential in providing clients and consumers with choice, and with the ability to attach emotion to a product, service, or company. Nowhere is this more important than on the Web, a very linear medium where viewers see only one site at a time and must differentiate different brands by remembering them. This is why so many companies (often in an unbelievable, "forced" fashion) claim to be the biggest, the best, the leader, the authority, and so on.

A brand must be experienced to be understood, and it can no more be simply defined than the concept of "life" can be simply defined. Through understanding the process of brand development, and specifically branding on the Web, the overall concept of the brand, and how essential it is to success, becomes evident.

"What is a brand?" is a simple question without a simple answer. Branding firms and consultants are frequently asked this question, and it's clear that many people make false or shallow assumptions about the answer. Is it a name? Is it a product's packaging? Is it the CEO? The answer to these questions is "all of the above"—and a lot more.

A name is a part of the brand, but the brand isn't the name. The CEO's personality drives the brand personality, and the only way to ensure a consistent brand across all products and services is when the brand is driven and committed to from the top, but the president, CEO, or chairperson is *not* the brand. Packaging frequently communicates volumes about the product inside the box, but little about the corporation or anything else. Yet all these factors add up to a sum of experiences any one person has with an organization, which, for that person, represents the "brand." What ensures that any one of these factors is in sync with the others, so that no matter what a person experiences, the brand is communicated as fully as possible?

Many times what a company really needs is a *naming* strategy, as opposed to a *branding* strategy. Naming is of course *part* of branding, but it is more tactical than strategic. Often this is because a strong brand strategy is already in place and simply needs to be reinforced and complemented by a subbrand naming convention. The names Yahoo! Sports, Yahoo! Classifieds, and Yahoo! Auctions exemplify this phenomenon, in contrast to a dominant subbrand like Microsoft Encarta, which is individually held responsible for a financial return and essentially only supported by the Microsoft parent brand.

Companies often trot down the path of creating a brand or brand name, but ultimately customers and target audiences will determine whether or not a brand actually comes alive. This is especially true in the New Economy. With so many freshly cast online brands, companies are learning to demand increasing individual return from messaging elements. This necessitates their employing a serious brand management and brand promotion infrastructure.

The decision to create subbrands should be driven from the expectation that the individual product or service they represent does more than simply complement the corporate brand. The subbrand must have the promise of independently projecting a dynamic image that will create its own standards of differentiation among the targeted audiences. For example, it's more than Microsoft simply offering a word processing program, a spreadsheet program, or a streaming video application that augments an established brand. It's the appeal of touching, feeling, and interacting with a subbrand that represents functionality and consumption at the individual level and that is connected to a strong parent brand. There is broad variation in the interaction between a subbrand and a parent brand, and differing levels of emphasis are necessary by design as a direct result of a methodical branding process. In some cases, the parent brand will dominate, and in others the product/subbrand will take the lead (see the discussion of this topic in Chapter 3).

The Promise You Keep, Not the Promise You Make

If branding is about anything, it's about delivering what is promised. Many companies make bold statements, but how many of them back it up? In the software industry the 1980s and 1990s were all about vaporware: buggy, bulky software applications, elusive upgrades, and upgrades promised to fix earlier upgrades. Thin-client software— meaning users didn't need to load an application into their PC to run it—was the promise of the legacy enterprise software providers. The Web is much, much more than a device for capturing leads for new customers; it's about building a bold promise and backing it up.

Keeping Your Promise on the Web

A truly strong and growing Web brand mirrors all its offline brand attributes, combining them with the primary Web benefits of being immediate, convenient, interactive, and comprehensive. The strong Web brand is

- Always up and ready (as in Hewlett-Packard's "always on" concept)
- Always quick to reply
- Always raising convenience standards
- Always and immediately correcting flaws
- Always raising the audience experience
- Always rewarding the audience with something new and different

As the Web continues to influence industry, making just about everything thin-client—even having the power to transform Microsoft with its Windows orientation into Microsoft with a Microsoft.NET, Web/browser orientation—it continues to be the responsibility of each brand on the Web to ensure that people looking at it leave the site feeling better then when they got there. Dead sites, sites "under construction," bad links, poorly behaving ecommerce sites that take users through a purchase process only to fail in the final stages, no response to emails asking for tech support, and any number of bad experiences on the Web mean that the promise has not been kept.

The goal of every brand on the Web needs to be keeping promises, not making them.

Naming: Branding Figurehead

For many, a brand name is the most visible characterization of a brand. In fact, many people think a brand is a name. As stated previously, however, the name is merely a component of the brand—albeit a highly visible one. A person's nickname may seem to support that person's personality and perhaps some behavioral traits, but a name can only be a part of an individual. When the name "eBay" is said or read, it conjures up a specific image and set of services and characteristics, yet it is only one part of the brand. When the name "Amazon" was first launched as a corporate name, it was initially perceived in the context of the South American river, because that was the only Amazon anyone knew. As the services, products, Web site, and so on penetrated more completely, and as people came to understand and experience the brand, the name slowly took on a meaning: The first-to-mind thought was no longer the river.

A new brand name passes through several stages as it penetrates the consciousness of its intended audiences. Descriptive real-word names, or words that sound real (e.g., "Canon"), are at first taken and interpreted literally. Some of the following names are well-established legacy brands; others are still in their infancy. All are technology brands, but very few say technology in their name:

handspring.com	Network devices and software
hummingbird.com	Enterprise ebusiness tools
yipes.com	Optical IP networking
zephyr.com	TCP/IP host connectivity ("zephyr" means "gentle wind")
greatplains.com	Enterprise administration tools
bluestone.com	Enterprise interaction/management tools
flipdog.com	Online job search service

freeagent.com	Online administrative and human resources services for the self-employed
goship.com	Shipping services for online shopping
hearme.com	Live voice, via PC or phone

Each name creates an image in the mind of the person first experiencing the brand. The image is not that of technology; even if the name suggests some form of technology, it doesn't spell out what the company does. Without the dotcom, a name like "goship" could be confused with any local "Mailboxes etc." or, worse, with the word "gossip." "Yipes" seems to be attempting to express the speed of the technology. These are prime examples of why a sound brand methodology is so important in creating an enduring, compelling, and natural brand. There is no easy formula for the correct name for a company, and what works for one company might not for another. Only by thorough analysis and articulation can the brand be justified, explained, and supported.

Stages of Name Familiarization

Each of the above brand names, first encountered, leads the surfer away from the stodgy, acronym-laden world of 1980s and 1990s technology, creating a more interesting, and theoretically more memorable, name. The challenge for these brand names is to go beyond this first impression and to bond to the various other components of the brand: the service offered, the people, the personality of the company, and so on.

Brand names pass through several stages of familiarity on the road to completely integrating with the core brand. Various tools, such as tag lines and graphics, can be used to improve the speed at which a brand name progresses through these stages—and may sometimes circumvent the stages altogether. The second stage is one of exploration and understanding, or "discovery," where the interested viewer explores the brand after being led to it via the brand name.

It is at this juncture that believability and natural branding are fundamental. Suppose an enterprise IT manager goes to yipes.com, finds that it is an optical IP networking company, and wonders what in the world the name and the company have in common. What does that say about brand believability?

Stage One: First Encounter

On seeing a name like Amazon.com, which has nothing to do with the South American river, the viewer may do some quick interpretation ("Well, it's a big river, so I guess it's a really big collection of stuff like books and CDs), may think something slightly negative ("What's that got to do with books and CDs?), or—accurately—realize the name is there because it's memorable. On the other hand, for a nonconsumer, business-to-business (B2B) brand, a name like "Yipes" may come off as being memorable, but at the same time may be perceived as rather lightweight, and without the necessary endurance for a long-term enterprise brand.

Frivolous names, such as Yahoo!, Amazon, and Yipes, populate the Internet like seagulls on a shrimp boat, but a great number of them have been created with only the first stage of brand naming in mind. Once bonded with the brand itself, the name "Yipes" becomes silly and frivolous, too descriptive of an emotion when in reality the developer has created something nonfrivolous. On the other hand, product names like Java and Bluetooth, though common words, are sufficiently abstract to find endurance because they don't get in the way as the brand name bonds to the brand.

Nicknames for children often undergo a similar process. Many kids outgrow nicknames by the time they become teenagers. The names that stick are usually the ones that match the teen's personality, while babyish, cutesy names are abandoned in the face of school-bus ridicule. For corporate brands, however, getting rid of a cute name that has firmly attached itself to the company and core brand may not be so easy.

Stage Two: Overcoming the Brand Hump

For believable, memorable brand names, getting over the brand hump represents a critical milestone in successful brand naming. For example, once the average person, when queried in research, says that Amazon "means online books," the hump has been overcome. The name is well on its way to becoming a solid brand in combination with its core services, products, and overall brand identity. It is a bad sign when, six months to a year after being launched, a brand name still evokes the original meaning and cannot be easily matched to its core brand offering and company by members of its core audience; it means the name has been less than successful in bonding. Only qualified market researchers can truly determine why some names fail to get over the hump: poor marketing, a really bad name, lack of believability, overwhelming competition, ineffective business planning, or a combination of mitigating factors (see the discussion on market research in Chapter 2).

Stage Three: Changing Tools

Following a successful time period during which the name and the brand bond, initial branding tools such as tag lines can be changed. Strong tag lines complement the brand name, and the more unknown, abstract, and unfamiliar the name, the more descriptive the tag line should be. Although only successful common brands can really effectively use abstract tag lines with abstract names, this principle is violated frequently and often to the serious detriment of the brand. However, when a brand has spent a good time period establishing itself, and is relatively common and well known to its market, tools such as advertising message, Web site headlines, and tag lines can be changed and more assumptions can be made. At this level, the brand can be called the "adolescent brand," and some of the constraints inherent to a launch can be eased.

Caution is still advised, however. Some companies loosen the restraints a bit too much and lose some ground in believability. Others do not move beyond the constrained mode, failing to fully explore their ability to become strong, leading brands (the "wallflower" theory).

Early on, it was in this stage that many dotcoms set their sights on going public, a move they thought would propel them to the next stage: full maturity. They believed money was the answer, in lieu of establishing sound business practices, including that of building a strong brand. Some matured, and some didn't. Only the ones able to build customer bases, establish brands, deploy products, and position themselves as strong partners had enough appeal to the marketplace and investors to become strong "adults."

Many more abstract brands with overly complex business models never gained enough momentum to garner customers or establish their brands in spite of sound, highly developed technology. The irony of the successful Web brand is that it isn't always the most whiz-bang technology that gets the brand into the limelight.

Brand Equity

Brand equity, a term that has been used in traditional branding for decades, has come to mean the value a brand has attained over time. Many dotcom brands that quickly attained high market values lacked strong brand equity, which is what made them vulnerable to market shifts such as the one in the spring of 2000.

"Early on it was really cheap to build a brand on the Web, and today it's expensive," said Jerry Fiddler, chairman, Wind Rivers Systems. "Many of the strongest brands existed before the Internet, such as Oracle, although a few of the enterprise brands are strong today, such as Commerce One. The old way was to establish a brand and then be rewarded by it. Today, people build brands and then introduce them. While there was actually a window of time where VCs pumped money into Internet companies, that time is over. The dotcom crash was an indicator it was over. Companies without profits and business models aren't getting market cap any more. Today, we're back to rational valuation of companies based on profits, business models, and brand equity."

Brand equity, like any other form of equity, takes time to grow and build if it is to have endurance. There is a widening brand gap between companies with shrinking brand equity and companies with growing brand equity; the latter are those which understand profitability and the value of building a strong brand and integrating it into a sound business model. This is why venture capitalists today are no longer just looking at great ideas for the Web, but for the ability of the company to manage a business profitably and to build a brand effectively.

"When evaluating brands, we look for ones that are creative, recognizable, and easily remembered, and that generate interest and curiosity from the target audiences," said Scott Cordell, managing director and co-founder of Vantage Capital Advisors, Inc. (www.vantagecapital.com), a firm based in Bellevue, Washington, that provides investment banking and strategic business development services to technology companies. "We believe a strong brand foundation, method, and commitment is invaluable for all companies, whether or not the company sells goods directly to consumers. A brand can be one of a company's greatest assets in the information age. Take Yahoo!, for example, a company with few physical assets. Its tremendous market capitalization is owed in large part to its brand. Information assets, like brands, are extremely important elements to a successful business model."

It's critical to remember that venture capitalists look at literally hundreds of business plans. "For an early-stage company that is considering private equity funding," said Cordell, "it is important to establish as early as possible the right brand and brand strategy. To maximize your chances of getting noticed and financed, entrepreneurs need to make branding a high priority in the formative stages of the company."

David Aaker, in *Managing Brand Equity: Capitalizing on the Value of a Brand Name,* defined brand equity as "a set of brand assets and liabilities linked to a brand, its name and symbol, that add to or subtract from the value provided by a product or service to a firm and/or to the firm's customers." He further grouped the assets and liabilities of brand equity into five general categories: brand loyalty, name awareness, perceived quality, brand associations in addition to perceived quality, and other "proprietary brand assets," such as patents, trademarks, and channel relationships.[4] Other observers, such as market research firm DSS Research (www.dssresearch.com), say brand equity is directly measured by a brand's monetary value, intangible values, and perceived quality.

These perspectives apply favorably to Web branding, albeit with the caveat that the amount of time available to create ebrand equity, compared to the amount of time available to create Old Economy, legacy brand equity is dramatically compressed.

Brand equity is measured by the strength of the brand as indicated in market research, market leadership, sales growth, and brand recognition. These various factors can be combined into an index of brand equity, comprising a series of points shown as a compound result that has predictive value especially when compared with the brand equity of competitors, or with itself, over time (providing the factors are controlled so as to be relevant, meaning that in order for data to be meaningful, it must be controlled across samples and over time so that consistent and similar factors are examined).

The Integrated Brand and the Web

A strong brand, and consequently a strong company, integrates a powerful core message with well-articulated brand personality characteristics and attributes into the business model and plan. The brand is not a creature hiding in the marketing department, or a label slapped onto the company, its products, or its Web site by a creative agency. It is integrated at the epicenter of the corporate or organizational model, affecting sales, product development, support, services, administration, human resources, executive management, distribution, partnerships, and all other components. It cannot be extracted from the company because it *is* the company.

Companies that go through renaming exercises—AirTouch, GTE, and Bell Atlantic all changing to Verizon, for example—can do so because they realize the brand extends far beyond the name. A common misunderstanding is that a company name change is a brand change; nothing could be further from the truth. Although the brand name is changing, the characteristics of the brand must hold even steadier than usual to withstand any market confusion that might ensue from the change.

Companies with poorly bonded brand names and brands are at a high degree of risk if a name change isn't managed properly and combined with an effort to ensure that the core message is well articulated. However, a company with a poor name, one that seems forced or lacks credibility, can put itself on a strong path to increased brand equity and profitability if the naming exercise focuses on tying the brand name more closely and believably to the business model and aiming for higher degrees of credibility with its target audiences. Effectively integrating the brand name more closely with the business model makes the brand stronger overall.

The Web can be a powerful tool to emphasize, measure, and ultimately accelerate the brand change and the increased integration. Infinite, a Maryland-based telecommunications company developing wireless gateway communication, is more than 10 years old and has developed numerous products and services. Yet only recently was it able to acquire the "infinite.com" URL. When the URL became available, due to changes and corporate developments at the hands of its previous owners, Infinite purchased the infinite.com name and quickly put itself on the track of resolving a number of years of confusion resulting from a broad mix of products and services being associated with a mismatched URL.

"We've had close to 30 products, but they've not been closely tied to the company name and we were hesitant to do too much around 'infinite' since we didn't have the URL," said Brett Warthen, Infinite's CEO. "We reevaluated our branding process, we were able to get the name, and now we have a tremendous opportunity to build a strong brand."

In this instance, tying the brand name into a strong, core business model and a believable and memorable URL allowed the company to place itself directly in line to build business globally in wireless telecommunications—a market fraught with gaggles of products and services that are difficult to combine and connect. Using the Web as a tool for the brand, the entire company has been able to organize and rally behind the name in support of the brand. Early in 2001,

Infinite was purchased by Captaris corporation, a further testament to Infinite's ability to effectively develop a market-worthy brand.

The Brand Continuum Framework and the Web

Building natural links between and among product names that tie equally naturally to a corporate brand is often referred to as product naming convention, product branding delineation, or simply a brand strategy. Its goal is to create viable associations with a consistent and reinforced corporate message, and at the same time to allow differentiating elements to validate the unique qualities of the individual product or service. There are several methods various companies commonly use to achieve this goal:

- *Word-part consistency.* Sun Microsystems' use of the "J" and four-letter combination with Java, Jini, and Jiro.
- *Theme carryover.* Sun Microsystems' consistent use of Solstice and Solaris subbrands to the Sun brand.
- *Corporate brand combined with descriptive subbrand that cannot be trademarked.* Microsoft Exchange, Microsoft Word, Microsoft Access, or even IBM eBusiness. This can also be done with a dominant product brand.
- *Visual icon consistency.* Nike Swoosh. This is especially appropriate when the graphic representation has matured and built its own levels of recognition.

The motivation behind building a cohesive brand strategy is, simply, to leverage and extend overall believability, to immediately substantiate a new product's existence as part of a larger whole, and to justify the individual promise the new product offers as a part of the broad corporate offering.

How does the Web alter brand continuums? It allows companies to bring together all their products and services in a concentrated venue much more easily than with offline methods. A Web site can address different audience needs from the main page by speaking directly to the specialized interests of the different audiences. An affected subbrand can be quickly summoned by an effective navigation system, leveraging the primary Web strength of personalization, and the audience member can be seamlessly directed to his or her particular area of interest.

Companies also have the option of devoting a particular promotion to a subbrand's message by simply aligning its URL to the corporate domain, separating it by either a dot or slash:

www.companyx.com/brandx
www.brandx.companyx.com
www.companyx.brandx.com

Most companies prefer the slash differentiator, but the dot method is a plausible alternative, depending upon the stature of the subbrand and the goals of the company. Thus, because of the immediacy and comprehensive experience the Web offers, a subbrand need not necessarily have an obvious relationship to a parent brand.

Many times, subbranding means aligning a company's well-known brand with one that is less known in order to leverage audience loyalties. An example of this is the Kleenex brand appearing on Huggies packaging. Although facial tissues and disposable diapers share only general sanitary associations, Kimberly-Clark's strategy maximizes the fact that the company owns a leading brand identifier, universally accepted for quality and softness.

The art of successful subbranding, on the Web or off, is founded upon illustrating the proper amounts of association and disassociation among company brands. Microsoft faced this issue when it built its leading portal (www.msn.com), partnered in the television field (www.msnbc.com), and designed a program specifically for the developer audience (www.msdn.microsoft.com). It decided to build a Microsoft "bridge" using the "MS," which does not prominently display the Microsoft brand, but offers a logical, recognizable, and familiar link.

Should a URL be owned for a subbrand so it can act as a referral to the corporate site when its address is entered? While optimal, it is not always necessary—and is likely not to be possible, especially considering the preponderance of unavailable domain names and the fact that purely descriptive elements, often desirable for subbrands, cannot be trademarked. It is becoming obvious to audiences that access to all company products and information begins with the corporate name. It is then imperative for effective ebranding to have an exemplary navigation system in place so audiences can quickly access the information pertinent to them.

So what's the optimal way to subbrand on the Web? Following the path of Yahoo! is a good model, where Yahoo! Auctions, Yahoo! Sports, Yahoo! Financials, and so on, share a simplified yet effective corporate and descriptive continuity, but is only possible because Yahoo! has built its brand around the themes of portals, instant access, and brand experience. It would be much more difficult, for example, for eBay to offer eBay Sports or E*TRADE to offer E*TRADE Auctions because of their established and primary vertical associations in auctions and stock trading, respectively.

Perhaps Amazon.com will ultimately realize its believability as the largest Web retail center, but the firmly established association of the name with "online bookseller" will take a considerable effort to expand upon, and at the same time niche retail sites specializing in other Amazon.com offerings—such as home repair products and sports equipment—will continue to attract clients with the "we're specialists" angle. Despite all it can do, the Web does not supplant the tried-and-true principle of sticking to accepted, natural, and believable brand associations. It does, however, allow for much faster expansion of general brand believability, providing enriched experience and personalized quality.

Winning CEOs with Process

The black art of branding looms as one of the least tangible business activities and one of its most alluring pitfalls. "We need a name for the company. Why don't we just huddle in a conference room, throw some names on the white board, go to register.com and check for available URLs, call the lawyer, and call it done?" With such words, or words like them, naïve CEOs have launched the end of many a fine company, product, service, and brand. They assumed the branding process is simple and, because it is one of the more "touchy-feely" tasks, relegated it to just another corporate brainstorming session, treating branding as a recreational break from finance meetings and sales projections. The only trouble is, that amounts to treating it as a frivolous, superfluous activity.

Branding, while it surely can be a break from the tedium of finance or business planning, is neither shallow nor to be taken lightly. In fact, it has a greater impact on financial and sales performance than perhaps any other single factor in a business, and the touchy-feely side of it is merely its most visible characteristic.

At its best, branding is a finely honed process, driven by logical thinking, skilled creativity, purposeful harmony with a business plan, and clearly defined strategy and goals. It can succeed only if it is based upon a strong core message and a solid framework, much as a house can be decorated and sold only after the framing and Sheetrock have been put into place according to an architect's plan and a contractor's execution.

Many books on branding, and many branding agencies, lack a tried-and-true process and instead rely on theory and shoot-from-the-hip techniques. Consequently, many brand books on the market today feature great thoughts and ideas but don't tell how to use them in an orderly fashion or how to communicate branding simply and easily to a tough client. Some present the process as so complex as to be overbearing or "canned"—not adaptable to individual problems. Like the process of therapy, branding is a facilitative one that if performed properly, allows the client to discover truth and direction from within. However, the process, while relatively opaque to the client, is always at work in the mind of the therapist, and is critical to ensuring a positive outcome.

Solution Branding

Solution Branding, a proprietary method the authors were instrumental in developing, integrates the branding process, creativity, and development of a customized collection of marketing and business services for any client—ranging from a two-person start-up looking for a corporate name and URL to a Fortune 500 company that needs to develop a brand strategy to drive its next major trade show event. Solution Branding was trademarked by the Garrigan Lyman Group (www.glg.com), a creative services and branding firm based in Seattle.

The term *solution* has been vastly overused in the language of the New Economy. A journalist-founded site dedicated to identifying and ridding the industry of overused terminology, www.buzzkiller.net, puts "solution" at the top of its list of offending terms. One freelance writer said his editor at *The Wall Street Journal* issued an edict that "solution" should be used only if it refers to a chemical process. Nonetheless, the term is highly useful if it means the following: "a group of services and/or products that are custom-fitted and unique to the needs of a given customer."

Solution branding specifically addresses the needs of any organization and its specific branding and creative issues by applying established, tried-and-true principles of business development, marketing, and best practices. By necessity, it requires that very specific and methodical steps be taken to evaluate the business situation logically and thoroughly before undertaking any creative effort. As a result, it is efficient, completely customized, and able to be deployed in virtually any industry anywhere in the world, with a company of any size.

Great branding, and especially successful branding on the Web, involves a combination of skilled creative services, extensive design and development abilities, strong and organized project management, and a commitment to adhering to a logical and useful process. The brand process serves as the essential element in the many components of branding, and it provides the way to integrate the parts and pieces of marketing communications traditionally isolated and siloed away from one another. Often, there is little connection among business planning, market strategy, brand development, PR, collateral design, Web design, logo development, advertising, events, and market research. The brand process ties these activities together, streamlining the time it takes for them to connect with one another and providing seamless transition—resulting in a perfectly matched image and identity (Figure 1-3).

As discussed earlier in the chapter, the brand process contains five essential parts: discovery; framework; verbal articulation; visual,

FIGURE 1.3 Ultimate brand strategy goal: to perfectly match image and identity consistently and coherently.

physical, and sensory articulation; and execution. A variety of ways exist from agency to agency to define the process, but in order to truly understand and manage a brand, a branding effort needs to include all these components, which are discussed one by one in the next five chapters. It is incumbent upon every marketing and corporate executive to understand the process (which is really quite simple) and to apply it effectively (not quite as simple). People involved in one part of the process need to ensure that effective communication and transition take place between stages.

Many agencies and self-proclaimed brand experts provide only a simple, superficial form of branding—such as naming or design—but ignore the essential (but often more boring) aspects such as framework or messaging as part of strong verbal brand execution. Ultimately, this costs the client money, time, market share, and, in some cases, the entire business or product line.

Other agencies, still high on the adrenaline rush of the client pitch and winning the business, take clients through a quick but effective discovery process, only to hand them off to team members with less brand experience to develop a Web site or a logo. This effectively destroys everything they've worked to "discover," since none of the people actually building, articulating, or executing the brand benefits from the discovery. If they're lucky, they receive a discovery briefing document; at worst, it's left up to the client to try to explain what happened during discovery and use it during the subsequent stages.

The secret of the brand process is that no matter what it is labeled, the process takes place naturally. Similarly, a person's hair grows naturally, but hair left unmanaged will ultimately be neither controllable nor attractive.

Because it is a necessity for every business today, a brand, unmanaged or not, will still be developed, a Web site will be created, marketing materials will be produced, and the product and company will be launched. Numerous companies in the pre-dotcom-crash era, before April 2000, thought they could launch and employ a get-rich-quick exit strategy in the absence of a business plan, profitability, or a well-developed brand.

Many of the have-nots on the poorer side of the brand gap suffer from brands without process: they are the tangled, knotting hair of the business brand world, and the longer they fail to attend to the brand, the more gnarly it will get. By combining a strong process with the unique opportunity the Web presents to fully develop and exploit every possible part of a brand, even companies whose brands have become weak or are clearly failing to perform can be revitalized. The Internet Age is still only Stone-Age-old, and the next five years will see thousands of companies worldwide competing for space, especially in business-to-business marketplaces. Services and products will continue to become highly commodified, and, just as with software and hardware in the 1980s and 1990s, Web branding will be the key differentiator to rein in clients, investors, and partners to favored business models and offerings.

2

The Discovery Stage

Building a Common Point of Origin

What we have to do is to be forever testing new opinions and courting new impressions. —Walter Pater, 1873[1]

Solving a problem requires understanding it. Because branding and the Web are moving at Internet speed—meaning development and marketing cycles are highly accelerated—there is less time available to devote to really understanding the intricacies, goals, and fine-level details of a business plan. Although it's in the nature of the well-educated CEO to encourage the executive staff to labor intensively over long-winded business plans (which may exceed 100 pages of text, graphs, forecasts, market justification, and other traditional components), today's venture capitalists often encourage start-ups to submit plans of fewer than 20 pages, about the size of the traditional business plan's executive summary (which is often what the team submits in lieu of the entire plan, thus avoiding a massive and painful rewrite).

The branding effort often involves a group of professionals and executives: the CEO, the marketing VP or an outside consulting firm or individual, and the marketing communications team. The mistake many companies make is to assume branding is separate from business planning, when, in fact, the two are forever intertwined. Whoever is involved must have a good grasp of the company mission, goals, and business mode, and must also be able to make command decisions for the company. It means understanding the core brand the company is attempting to build and what that will represent to the various audiences, from investors to clients.

Companies need to decide earlier rather than later that branding is essential—at the outset of the business planning process, if possible. The CEO who understands that she or he is building a brand as a core component of the business is ahead of the game when it comes to succeeding in today's economy.

Brand Discovery, Defined

The discovery process ties the brand promise, the core message, and the business plan together to ensure that strong branding resides at the core of the business. It is, in fact, the most critical of all the stages because it lays the foundation upon which the brand will be built. To stand firmly, the brand must have a solid, cohesive, and well-defined base.

Often the marketing people—internal or external—move quickly into the more creative stages of branding, such as naming or Web design. Equally frequently, that's OK with the CEO because it means a shorter time to market with a ready-to-wear brand. Unfortunately, this myopic approach results in a poorly defined brand that is out of sync with the core business plan and message, and, in fact, ends a year or so later with the executive team back in the brand-planning stages—often without the planned revenue to adequately address the problem. This doesn't mean the brand discovery stage is long. Sometimes it's a day, sometimes it's six months, depending on scope, launch timing, complexity, budgets, and myriad other factors. The discovery stage differs for every branding situation, and, as mentioned above, can be dramatically different in time, cost, and results depending upon the business model, brand strategy, and amount of information the company may already be able to provide.

What it does mean, however, is taking the time to fully understand many things about the brand effort facing the company:

• The existing company name
• Any existing corporate Web presence and its level of consistency with any other visible aspect of the company visibility—collateral,

advertising, direct mail, telephone service, building design (yes, even building design)
- Any existing products or services
- The core message and "elevator" speech of the company
- Competitors and their positioning
- External and internal brand visibility, perception, and awareness
- Market viability of the product and/or services
- Competitive Web sites and how they position competitive brands and how in sync they are with the corporate brands
- Corporate "personality" versus "attributes"

Examining the various factors of the brand, analyzing them, and creating a strategy for building a strong brand that is founded in or, at the least, tied very closely to the Web presence is called brand mapping (see "Brand Mapping," in Chapter 3).

Finding Qualified Web Brand Services

Branding and marketing people aren't in the business because they love project management, business analysis, and long-term strategizing. It doesn't come naturally to them, which typically is what makes them brilliant creative minds. However, it's a red flag if there isn't an effort underway to build structure and process into the brand effort but instead a plethora of white-board, conference-room brainstorming sessions, which provide more fun for the executive team than qualified branding results.

Brand consultants abound, as do books on branding. It's easy to find a branding firm, but it's not easy to find one that will ensure a great, enduring brand, one with a defensible brand process that extends beyond simple naming and logo design. Large, multinational branding firms provide as much process and service as a company is willing to pay for, but the typical start-up gets sticker shock quickly from the likes of a Landor or an Interbrand branding firm. For a Lucent, FedEx, or SGI brand, it makes sense to pay sky-high branding fees to these types of firms, because the fees represent a fraction of the companies' ad budgets—and it's worth it to have an attentive, professional team watch-dogging the brand.

However, the giant branding firms may be more than the small-to midsized company needs—even a well-established $300- to $500-million firm. The branding firm may end up putting relatively junior people on the account (a lot of junior people on a large team won't do the job, either). Further, if the client company is in a location distant from the branding firm headquarters, the client will be paying a premium rate for the services of a small, regional office of the brand firm, and junior people will attend the account from a distance.

Finding the right firm for a brand effort is essential. Interview several firms; quiz them about their brand process and the elements listed in the branding firm checklist. Don't be unduly influenced by size—a brand firm being too small or too big—but generally beware of the very small shops (they lack the ability to effectively manage and provide comprehensive services), the regional offices (unless they can positively guarantee and provide references to prove they can manage the account), and the giant firms (unless they are small, comprehensive teams capable of managing the effort from soup to nuts). Check references. Hold them accountable at each stage. Don't be afraid to ask questions.

Be extremely wary of the brand firm that takes direction and then disappears for a few weeks. Branding with a company is an interactive process that demands frequent involvement from both sides. Likewise, the intelligent brand firm will be wary of the client lacking senior executive involvement. If the person who drives the dominant personality and attributes of a company's brand, often the CEO, is not involved in the brand process, it's doomed to be tossed out of the boardroom when presented, no matter how tremendous the effort has been. This isn't true for a simple product naming effort, but in the New Economy, simple product naming efforts are falling by the wayside, yielding to brands more uniquely tied to the core business model of the company.

Think of it as similar to finding a wedding planner: There's one shot at success. Once a new brand and Web site goes live, that's it. Going back to the drawing board is next to impossible, and exceedingly costly, especially when it means executive-team-intensive activities such as corporate naming.

The big question remains, however, does the branding firm—whatever its size—guarantee to provide the following full range of services backed by a strong, established process?

Branding Firm Checklist

What should a company look for in a qualified branding firm? Refer to the following checklist:

- *In-depth research.* Be sure the agency has the ability to conduct, manage, and interpret in-depth research, even if actual research work is outsourced.
- *Related experience.* Be sure the agency has worked with similar clients: technology, company size, mission, timing, budget, etc.
- *Strategy.* Does the agency have experienced, qualified senior strategists who truly understand business planning and brand strategy?
- *Senior-level involvement.* Once through strategy and discovery, watch to ensure that the agency doesn't drop the project in the lap of junior people. There needs to *always* be a senior brand strategist involved in all aspects of the effort, no matter what size the client company or project.
- *Project management and phase transition.* There need to be strong project managers dedicated to keeping the team organized, on track, and on budget, and to ensure smooth transition between phases.
- *Creative verbal skills.* There should be a history of effective naming projects, mounted by great writers, and a staff who understand that naming is only a part of branding, and who aren't simply combining random word-parts to find available URLs.
- *Creative design/visual/sensory skills.* Does the agency have designers who can create world-class logos, and a Web design team containing programmers and developers, creative designers, writers, and project managers who know how to map, design, write, and execute a world-class Web site?
- *Execution.* Be sure the agency has the ability to execute an established brand, whether it's through advertising, PR, events, or other launch activities, either in-house or outsourced. The bottom line:

No matter what the process has been, the brand effort must never leave the executive team "hanging" without an easy transition to the launch of the brand.

Finally, the firm needs managed research to fully understand and exploit the success of what it has created. In addition, consider the following factors:

- Time requirements
- People who will actually be working day-to-day on the project
- History of achievement
- Methodology
- References
- Full-service portfolio
- History of partnering with other agencies
- Quality of presentation
- International reach through offices or partnerships
- Best example of the agency's work, or the biggest example of disappointing work experience
- Examples of past working relationships with PR and advertising agencies
- Explanation of standard fee structure—that is, retainer-based or project-based—which must correspond to a closely monitored timeline
- Explanation of how the agency manages its finances and projects

Gary Tripp was founder of Driveway.com (before the company was named "Driveway"). The 360 Corporation (www.360.com), which Tripp founded after leaving Driveway.com, is a growing and up-and-coming enterprise Web brand providing a unique way for any site— from search engine to government intranet—to search and index 100 percent of any Web site on a frequent and automatic basis—a true business-to-business infrastructure Web brand and service. Tripp, who has been through the proverbial wringer, comments on how solution branding and the brand process finally yielded success:

"The name they would have liked to see us called was 'blue scooter'—a name that didn't fit our criteria, not one with which you could partner with IBM or which denoted a sense of technological superiority or completeness. It was frivolous, and would make a great portal or consumer name—but that's not us. We're a technology company with a B2B/infrastucture business model. . . .

"The brand process only works if it is completely integrated with the business and all the parts of marketing, and if the people who analyze and build the brand to begin with stick with the effort all the way through to a launch."

Brand "Therapy"—Key to Successful Natural Branding?

Why use an outside agency at all, especially when the core executive team probably understands the business model and marketing plan better than anyone else? Quite often, the brand session with outside agencies deviates from core branding activities, simply because it's one of those rare places where executive staff members can roll up their sleeves and talk about non-day-to-day issues in a facilitated, comfortable environment.

After selecting a brand firm, the executive team will, most commonly, find itself in several closed-door sessions as part of the discovery and framework stages, in particular. Prepare for these, allow the right amount of time: Two hours per session is about right; any more than that and the team will begin to lose concentration and focus. The number of sessions depends largely on the nature of the branding problem, the amount of research being undertaken (which can significantly lengthen the discovery stage), and the size of the team. However, the sessions and discovery stage shouldn't go on too long; if they do, it's hard to maintain a strong, cohesive thought process. Besides, business conditions change rapidly, so if too much time elapses between discovery sessions, the business model may change, and each time that happens everyone has to be brought back into sync again.

Like marriage counselors, brand consultants often find themselves not so much giving advice to the executive team but as facilitating and providing the ability for the group to come up with its own answers and thoughts. This is an essential element when it comes to a brand effort being able to effectively yield natural, believable results—precisely because the answers have come "from within."

For this reason branding groups frequently want the brand team to meet at least several times during the discovery and framework stages, so that team members can get comfortable, understand how the dynamics work, and get in touch with their "inner brand selves." Sometimes this is what it takes for the team to really see and understand the brand personality. The brand personality is very much a reflection of the executive team in the branding session. It is essential for a CEO or another driving corporate personality to be directly and actively involved in branding. A portrait painted from life, with the subject sitting through the portrait sessions, while more tedious and time-consuming than painting from a photograph, will always look much more natural and realistic.

Prepare to devote focused time to the branding effort, even if only for a short period. Good brand consultants will not cram brand theory or ideas created in a vacuum down the executive team's throat; and if they do, stop the branding effort. Don't feel bad about cutting the brand sessions short if they don't feel natural. Remember, the best, most natural brands come from within.

Getting to Know a Brand and a Company

At the risk of sounding Zen-like, the brand and the company must be whole and "one." The spirit has no tangibility without the body, and the body has no life without the spirit. Likewise, the company has no life without the brand, and a brand without a solid company beneath it will wither away.

The discovery stage makes it possible for a company to understand what a brand that accurately represents it will look like, and to do everything possible so the company business model can succeed. At this stage any existing brand visibility is analyzed—especially if the company has an existing Web site—and it is determined whether the body and spirit seem to be in harmony. Further, getting to know the company means understanding how the company is currently positioned versus where it wants to be, as well as knowing its competitive environment (see "Competitive Differentiation: Unique Web Believability" toward the end of the chapter).

Brand Attributes versus Brand Personality

Brands—on the Web and off—exhibit two primary types of characteristics: attributes and personality. Think of it this way: A person has both a personality and a set of behaviors. The personality might be extroverted or introverted, funny or dull, energetic and "type A" or passive and sensitive. Personality traits typically do not change; they're built into the core of the person's psyche, and are unwavering and distinctive.

A person's behavior, on the other hand, tends to be habitual: walking fast, speaking loudly, fidgeting constantly, interrupting others' conversations, dressing conservatively, exceeding the speed limit. These and other behavioral traits can be changed. While expressive of the personality (for example, an energetic, aggressive person typically walks fast), they're not so embedded that they can't be changed (although it can be difficult!).

Brands also have personalities and behavior traits, or attributes. Microsoft is a good example: Its personality is widely known to be energetic, aggressive, and arrogant. Corporate brand personality is frequently a strong reflection of its corporate leadership, typically the CEO or founder. Bill Gates and Steve Ballmer both fit the Microsoft brand personality to a "T." As long as the management personality remains the same, so does the brand personality—and it's tougher than grabbing a fish with bare hands to change it. Oracle is led by Larry Ellison, and its brand personality, a reputation for being high-flying, arrogant, and "pushy," reflects Ellison's flamboyant personality.

In contrast, Dell, the online/mail order PC giant, garnered huge success by reflecting the personality of its leader, Michael Dell, who although highly driven and achievement-oriented is a gentle and relatively quiet person. Dell had to be highly responsive to its customers and at the same time easy for vendors to partner with—which all benefited the company in its 1990s climb to peer-level competition with the likes of Compaq and IBM.

It's critical in the brand discovery phase to understand the difference between brand attributes and personality factors, and to understand what can be changed or leveraged. Attributes—such as being more responsive—can be addressed early on, and capitalized on in advertising or online as key points of differentiation and market leadership.

Personality factors can't be changed easily, so being aware of them is essential. If the company CEO is arrogant, a substantial effort must be made to ensure that the sales staff, tech support people, and business development team understand the personality and how it affects the business model. That doesn't mean staffing the company with arrogant, difficult people; it does mean that evaluating and communicating the style of the company as strong-willed in such activities as sales negotiations and partnerships will make a tremendous difference, both for the staff and for the outside contacts. It also means that the person or team in charge of branding must be able to effectively communicate the meaning of brand personality to the person who drives it—typically the CEO—which, in the case of a difficult personality, can be a challenge until the driving personality realizes the benefits the corporate image, brand, and success stand to gain.

Staying aware of both attributes and personality during the brand discovery phase, articulating the factors, and keeping them handy during the entire process will produce a more natural, effective brand. The Web can serve as a great "leveler" in helping communicate a brand naturally; it can, however, be out of sync with the brand personality, and the best time to find that out is in the brand discovery phase.

For example, a first-class hotel, such as the Ritz-Carlton, needs to have a Web site that caters to its intended clientele; this is reflected in attributes such as the partners it keeps and displays on the Web, the colors and images in its Web design, the services it offers online, the advertisers (if any) it permits on its site, and so on. (As it turns out, www.ritzcarlton.com really does feel first-class.)

A surprisingly high number of premium brands have chosen to ignore the advantages of the Web as anything more than "brochureware." Brochureware is a common Internet term referring to Web sites with little or no interactivity, providing nothing much beyond what would be in a corporate brochure. Companies producing brochureware are considered behind the times, lacking in New Economy savvy. Porsche is a first-class brand, but although the Porsche site looks first-class, and there is some interesting information online (such as news, events, and a few other goodies), the company has made a conscious decision not to use the Web as a tool for locating dealers, selling products (including cars), or generally making use of ecommerce capabilities. Instead, the site features prominent listings of Porsche clubs and news about Porsche rallies in exotic locales.

Market Research

The decision made by Porsche's executive team that the market wouldn't be able to use the Porsche Web site for anything more than basic information cries out for a clearer understanding of the New Economy market and where it's headed. The Web is neither a "digital blue-collar" entity nor is it a tool of the elite. The fact that a driver can purchase a Saturn online would in no way taint Porsche if the company decided to offer online sales, nor would it mean that Porsche was mingling among the "riffraff." If the Web is about anything, it is about taking service and vendor-customer communication and understanding to a new level—to the advantage of both.

Saturn's primary site and its "shop&buy" capability (click "shop&buy" on www.saturn.com) extends the brand to anyone who wants to understand anything about the cars, from exploring various options to calculating monthly lease payments. This means buyers are more educated about the brand, more emotionally attached, and much closer to the company than they would be if they merely received the digital version of the car brochure available in the showroom. The number of options for exploring the Saturn brand online abound on its site (as well as the options provided to communicate with the company and "attach" to the brand). Porsche has really missed a world-class opportunity to reach its target clientele. Saturn did its homework.

The World's Most Valuable Brands?

In July 2000 a survey conducted by Interbrand named the most valuable brands in the world, and the New Economy is definitely having a profound effect. While Coca-Cola still leads the brand list, Microsoft was only a hair behind the soft-drink giant, followed by IBM, Intel, and Nokia—all companies dedicated to aggressively building their brands online. The rating criteria used by Interbrand primarily emphasize current and future earnings and risk profiles.

Ford, GE, Disney, McDonald's, and AT&T completed the top-10 list; while 9 of the top 10 and 42 of the top 75 are U.S. companies, increasingly, these companies' business is coming from non-U.S. sources (more than 60 percent of Microsoft's revenue, for example, comes from outside the United States). Further, an increasing number of foreign brands are edging up the list; for example, in the auto sector, Volkswagen, Honda, and Toyota are all ahead of U.S. companies.

Interbrand's survey is not without flaws; it is more of an economic indicator than a true "brand perception" study. Further, it fails to discern between business-to-business and business-to-consumer brands, which is really where the major brand breakdown is headed today. Nonetheless, each of the companies topping the lists in its respective industry has a highly interactive, in-depth, and world-class Web brand presence. Coca-Cola, for example, realized early on the advantage of being a leader in New Economy brand presence, just as it realized years ago it could dominate world soda sales by being a major advertiser. In the past, staying on top as a brand in highly commodified markets (such as soft drinks) meant keeping exceedingly high levels of "mind share." By conducting extensive market research, Coke knew where its brand was strong and where it needed work. Why else would anyone see taxis on obscure islands off Hong Kong with Coke ads on their doors?

Coke and other brand leaders have taken this same approach to the Web, realizing through research that it is the new way to keep and increase its mind share. That might mean simply seeing www.cocacola.com on its cans, drinking a coke while looking at a Coca-Cola sign at an Internet café in Rio's Ipanema district while doing email, or surfing to the Coca-Cola site during an office break because it's refreshing and fun—just like the drink. Coke has combined contests, games, activities, and sound (the sound alone is worth a visit to the site) with information.

The AT&T site—and especially the AT&T Global part of the site (www.att.com/global)—is worth a mention because so much work has been done by AT&T to understand how U.S.-based callers use the site to understand rates and information about calling their home countries. AT&T went to great lengths in audience and brand research to determine how the site could be used, and how it could be differentiated from competitors such as Sprint and MCI by much more than just a rate listing. Right away, a visitor can choose a language—U.S.-based language and cultural localization is a completely new concept—and images and information are culturally sensitized through photos. The site even shows the current time in the country to be called. Simple tools to build a strong brand.

The Microsoft site is substantively different, but with the same level of depth and appeal based on what the company knows about its target audience—as broad as it is. Two brands couldn't be further apart in substance, products, and services than Microsoft and Coca-Cola—yet both know that domination of the New Economy and the Web mean brand domination, higher revenues, stock performance, and global leadership. Part of branding is about being seen everywhere in the world and in every situation where there's a possible fit for a product or service. Today that means the virtual world as much as the real one, and in order to effectively reach that market, it takes just as much research to understand customer habits and perceptions online as off.

Research provides information and data to the brand team so that the team can fully understand the general market and the external and internal perceptions of the company, its products, and its services, and be able to compare various audiences. It also serves as a benchmark, so that after the brand has been cast on the Web for a given time period, it can be repeatedly measured against previous results—yielding invaluable information about the parts of the Web site and the overall brand that may need to be changed, emphasized, or leveraged. Today, research is, to a degree, about asking people questions when they register for a product or a service, or simply tracking their buying and behavioral habits. That information can be used through online services to customize the Web experience on a particular site. Gathering and using research data is how, for example, Amazon is able to recommend books that a user likes (although this is also driven by publishers "pushing" their books through the channel), and how Victoria's Secret (www.victoriassecret.com) is able to keep track of women's lingerie interests and sizes—just as it does in its retail stores.

Nonetheless, traditional brand research provides vast opportunities for companies to understand what people are doing and what they think. There are three traditional forms of brand research:

1. Focus groups
2. In-person interviews (on the phone or face-to-face)
3. Mail-in surveys (using snail mail or email)

In 1995, when Chuck Pettis wrote his then-definitive book, *TechnoBrands,*[2] the people using technology and the way in which they were using it were substantively different. Although people were buying PCs for home use, the Internet wasn't their primary reason for purchasing a computer and the concepts of "business-to-consumer" and "business-to-business" had no real meaning in technology beyond computer companies that wanted to sell their products to offices or home users. There was no Internet business to speak of, and the vast majority of companies did not have Web sites. It was a different world. Still, Pettis accurately and articulately described the tenets of branding in a technology world (essentially fathering branding in the pre-Internet age), and stressed the importance of understanding the audience through research. The book is highly worth reading, especially the section on research (pages 81–105), which remains valid.

Each form of research provides unique benefits for Web branding, and determining which is right to use during the discovery phase (if any) depends on various factors such as time, money, existing available research, and whether the company is launching a business-to-business or a business-to-consumer model. If your brand firm is outsourcing the research (which is common), don't hesitate to ask for references from the research firm, including looking at samples of research results it has provided to other clients.

Combined techniques, involving both online and mail-in surveys, can take advantage of the strengths of both formats. For example, interviews can take place by phone while respondents are looking at pages on a Web site. Respondents can be recruited to look at a Web site in a focus group. Respondents can be mailed, on paper or on diskette, the same survey that is featured online, allowing them to choose a preferred option.

Focus Groups

Focus groups are small groups (usually fewer than 10) of carefully selected people in a given market segment and/or region. A facilitator leads them—often in a "blind" fashion, so that they don't know the name of the sponsoring company—in a discussion about the market and its various players. Members of the brand and marketing teams often sit behind a two-way mirror to observe the discussion.

Traditionally, a variety of discussions take place depending upon the interests and skills of the participants, and ads might be shown, as well as other visuals such as logos. Today, all focus-group facilities also provide online access so the facilitator can lead the group through various Web sites.

Focus groups are highly effective qualitative research tools, although they require time and effort to set up and to arrange so the entire team, whose members are frequently from many different cities or countries, can attend. On the downside, they can be commandeered by a strong participant combined with a weak facilitator, which can dramatically skew the results and opinions of the group.

Focus groups can be especially enlightening with business-to-business research because of the inherent complexity of today's New Economy B2B business models. While it is more difficult—and expensive—to get businesspeople to attend a focus group, it takes fewer of them to yield highly qualified information about a market and its products, services, and brands.

Even with businesspeople, finding truly Web-savvy participants can be a challenging task. While executives and professionals undoubtedly know the Web, they may not have a strong enough basic understanding of the New Economy. Obviously these issues will be influenced by the topic and level of discussion of a particular focus group: A group of IT managers will be significantly different from a group of marketing executives. Key to finding qualified participants in today's market is prescreening with New Economy knockout factors. Ask open-ended questions, the responses to which will reveal the person's comfort level with and knowledge of Web topics and an Internet orientation to business:

- Name three leading B2B brands.
- Define the difference between B2B and B2C.
- What does the term *New Economy* mean?
- Is the traditional "middleman" going away? Why?
- Why is it so important to partner in ebusiness?
- Define the importance of globalization in the New Economy.
- How can a Web site be used to the advantage of a nontechnology company?
- Define *ecommerce*.

There are a number of factors to have participants consider when evaluating various Web sites. Here are just a few:

- Navigation
- Ease and immediacy of understanding the company's business
- Naming and URL
- Partnership visibility
- Appropriateness to various audiences:
    Investors
    Press
    Clients
    Partners
    Analysts
- Ease of ecommerce infrastructure
- Overall speed of site
- Design quality

Focus group sessions last a few hours. A good brand/research firm will provide a detailed written analysis and presentation of the research results to the executive staff, compiling the outcome of all the various group sessions.

Marketing executives frequently debate the pros and cons of focus groups in general, and doing them online has added new dimensions to the age-old debate.[3]

Online focus groups can be good, because they:

- Bring together hard-to-find respondents from far-flung locations
- Require less time from the respondent, which, in turn, can reduce the incentive required to attract qualified participants
- Eliminate the cost of moderator and corporate "viewer" travel, re-freshments, hostesses, facility rental, etc.
- Can protect the anonymity of competitors so they can speak more frankly
- Are less likely to be dominated (in some cases, "railroaded") by one respondent

Online focus groups may also have drawbacks, such as:

- Less of the "group think" advantage which can really make in-person focus groups meaningful and helpful to brand develop-ment—the freewheeling, dynamic, interactive brainstorming of live groups
- Limited, abbreviated responses (most people don't type as fast as they talk—hence the chat-room abbreviations such as "LOL"— "laughs out loud")
- Comments that are out of sync and a conversation thread that doesn't flow smoothly (often due to typing delays)
- No real body language (except for "emoticons," such as ; } or :-) or UPPER CASE)
- Poor attentiveness (respondent is flossing, doing email in a separate window, talking on the phone, watching TV, or eating)
- A poor show rate (less of an issue if respondents are being paid or have volunteered)
- Having to acquire special software, services, or training, which re-duces choice of moderators

In-Person Interviews

Face-to-face and telephone interviews, ranging from shopping-mall surveys to dinnertime interruptions, have long stood as the workhorse of the research industry. Even with screening, this type of research often yields a low hit rate of qualified interviews yielding good information, but overall, in-person interviews can provide statistically significant, quantitative data. Interviews can be put together and executed relatively quickly, without the problem inherent to focus groups of organizing a meeting place, getting people scheduled, and herding executives of the sponsoring company to the sessions.

Telephone Survey Pros and Cons[4]

In-person interviews have the following advantages:

- *Less self-selection bias.* Phone survey respondents are randomly selected, so you hear from those who might not have bothered to reply to a mail or email request.
- *Complete data.* An interviewer can explain and probe, as well as push the respondent to reply in the appropriate format. With this format the respondent is less likely to terminate partway through.
- *Quotas.* Quotas can be set to represent the known profile of the response base.
- *Guaranteed sample size.* Interviewers keep calling until they get the required number of responses. You know your margin of error in advance, without gambling on response rates.
- *Speed.* Depending on the sample size, the survey may be in and out of the field faster than a mail survey (but not as fast as an online survey).

In-person interviews have the following disadvantages:

- High labor cost.
- No visuals. Respondents can't react to visuals (unless combined with a mail or Web survey).

In building a Web brand, in-person business-to-consumer research provides critical information and can be highly efficient, cost-effective, and revealing. For example, a company may wish to look at how people who own a PC, have an Internet connection, are over 20, and own a car are making purchases online and what they're buying. Such information can be particularly helpful to nontechnology companies: Kimberly-Clark, Nestlé, or Singapore Airlines all want to understand how people are—or may be in the future—using the Internet anywhere in the world to exercise brand loyalty. Are busy young mothers buying diapers online? Would people like free recipes from world-class chefs using Nestlé products? Are travelers looking at the Singapore Airlines Web site to schedule travel, or are they just buying the cheapest flights they can find on www.expedia.com—or are they still using a travel agent?

The speed at which Internet business is developing today requires every company to be much more visionary than in the pre-Internet age, which means understanding that consumer intentions can make the difference between success and failure a few short years out. It seems almost silly to still talk to people in person, with a tool like the Internet available. Chuck Pettis pointed out in *TechnoBrands* that research is much more useful if it is used to provide illumination, not just support. While it is important to approach a research audience with a hypothesis, the effort should not be undertaken just to prove a point. It needs to be directed toward understanding what an audience is thinking and, more importantly, what it is intending to do—especially on the Web.

If it's clear that 25 percent of mothers in Web-connected households with children under the age of one feel they have no free time, and if they think cloth diaper services cost too much, maybe they would like to be able to order diapers online, or find a delivery service close to their house. What about the latest advice on how to solve diaper rash? Maybe they'd like to discuss baby issues with other mothers and get free time-saving baby-care tips. Perhaps mothers-to-be would like to use a videoconferencing service which would allow them, for a reasonable fee, to order the hardware and services they need to show their new bundle of joy on a private TV network broadcast over normal telephone lines. (Check out the www.huggies.com site to see this actual service; Kimberly-Clark, the parent brand, is one of the most forward-thinking Web brands in the world today.) Never have diaper companies had it so good.

The point is, these companies aren't just putting brands on display with fun ideas they think will work. They're doing well-designed, quantitative research; they are continually examining and re-examining what's working and not working and reapplying their knowledge to make their Web sites increasingly useful and relevant for their target audiences. They understand the mind of the consumer and how consumers become emotionally attached to a brand beyond its design.

Make sure you allow enough time in the branding cycle to conduct initial consumer research, and look at the survey results exceedingly carefully. The initial survey should become the benchmark against which the brand will be measured in six months or a year. Try to get at the intentions of consumers, not just their habits. Find out whom they like, whom they don't, and why. Find out what they have, what they don't have, and what they'd like to have—from products to services to time and money. To build a world-class Web consumer brand, it's important to take world-class action. There's no exception: Understand the audience.

Snail Mail or Email?

Surveying an audience as part of a branding effort traditionally involves using direct mail pieces with an incentive (e.g., "fill this out and win a camera!") or asking for the relevant information on a product registration card. The New Economy term for the process of extracting knowledge from information is *data mining*. Data mining can mean anything from collecting leads through a proprietary lead-gathering system that was developed for use at exhibitor-only trade shows all the way to using extensive and complex database technology to track and analyze information about a given audience.

Data mining is used to gather large amounts of statistically significant data from a broad range of people. Like telephone research, data mining is a better tool for business-to-consumer than business-to-business branding efforts, because consumers typically respond to these data-gathering methods more readily—and are more likely to be attracted by the corresponding incentive—than busy workers or executives.

Because so much information is constantly being gathered, companies often have extensive data about various audiences, and coordinating with sales administration can often yield information relevant to branding, for example:

Competitors

Brand choices

Demographics: age groups and geographic locations

Names, email addresses, and phone numbers of people who were included in another form of research, such as a focus group or an in-depth telephone interview

The problem with using conventional, snail-mail methods to gather information during the discovery phase of branding is that they are very slow. Few organizations enjoy the luxury of having enough time in the branding process to compose a survey, mail it out, wait for results, compile them, and analyze them. Of course, if information gathered by snail mail already exists, it can be used. Otherwise, except in very specific situations, this method isn't useful—a victim of the New Economy.

Sending surveys via email can also be problematic: Today's users are highly annoyed by unsolicited invitations to fill out survey questionnaires. There are also legal implications. Further, the regulations governing unsolicited surveys vary from country to country, so if the survey is international, things can get even stickier. Germany, for example, strongly regulates "spam" and other forms of solicitation.

Placing a banner on a commonly used site or portal is undoubtedly the best (and safest!) way to accomplish "mail" surveys to large groups. Again, however, in a branding discovery phase only useful companies building significant business-to-consumer brands will need to collect extensive information on large audiences. Further, this method will yield information only about people already connected to the Internet. (Of course, this may, in itself, be a good filter.) For example, a business-to-consumer brand such as Honda Motorcycles may place a banner on Yahoo! saying "Click Here to Win a New Honda Motorcycle"; surfers who click on the banner have to fill out a survey before they are entered in the contest. Honda may analyze the survey results for information about consumers' awareness of or issues with the Honda brand, or may use the data in developing its next motorcycle's brand attributes.

The www.parenthoodweb.com site is dedicated to "helping families grow" and features everything from shopping to naming children to recalled kids' products to recipes to horoscopes. In the surveys section of the "community" part of the site is a statement that "At the heart of the ParentHoodWeb lies our 'I Wish I Knew' surveys." The information provided by site visitors is fed into other survey results, and, presumably, yields information about how the visitors perceive the site. This section may also be used to gather leads, but this is optional. This type of survey is becoming increasingly common in consumer sites as an inexpensive data-gathering device to monitor the brand, find information it can publish, and generally keep track of the mind-set of the audience.

Dr. Yardena Rand, a research specialist with Sage Research (www.sageresearch.com) of Natick, Massachusetts, believes strongly in the importance of online research initiatives and their benefits to both researcher and the respondent:

"They're much more convenient for our participants. They have great usability and branching opportunities, while you can conveniently rotate questions. They also have the important added piece of allowing the participant to open up a browser and evaluate something, whether a design, advertisement, multimedia presentation, or something else from which you would like to receive the participant's critique." Rand also says that she typically recruits respondents by mail for online research, and normal response rates among technology professionals is as high as 8 percent, with consumers running at a whopping 20 percent—both phenomenally high, as compared with Old Economy research methods.

In November 1999, Nabisco released results of an extensive survey about how a number of Internet-based leisure activities—such as gaming—are being used as breaks at work, replacing the water cooler as a common gathering place. In the press release, Tom Hernquist, senior VP of marketing for the Nabisco Biscuit Company, said "Nabiscoworld.com combines the two most popular ways to take a break during the work day—snacking and surfing the Web."

As a result, Nabisco now features myriad games, promotions, and contests at www.nabiscoworld.com to promote the overall Nabisco brand and to encourage consumption of its subbranded products such as Oreos, Ritz, Triscuit, Chips Ahoy!, and others. While most contests are used to gather basic lead information (name, address, email address, phone), some are used—at the company's discretion—to gather more significant marketing and brand data.

The most significant point, however, is that Nabisco specifically changed its Web brand presence and the way in which it interacted with site visitors based upon an independently commissioned online survey that asked 1000 adults and 1000 teenagers about online activities and habits.[5]

Although Nabisco may not have had time to build this survey into its initial Web development, as the site became more mature, the type of information obtained through the survey was invaluable to promoting the Nabisco brand—as well as the sale of its consumer products—through the Web.

According to Chamberlain Research Consultants Inc. (www.crcwis.com), self-administered surveys—both the mail and online varieties—are very attractive to many companies looking for feedback, but also have drawbacks and need to be evaluated for "quantity versus quality" factors. The following are some advantages:

- Labor costs are lower, since it is not necessary to hire interviewers. While some respondents are difficult to reach by phone, they do read their mail and email.
- These surveys are well suited for asking complicated questions requiring the respondent to read detailed descriptions or review and look at examples, and then make thoughtful choices.
- Respondents who find phone calls intrusive can complete a self-administered survey at their convenience.

The following are some disadvantages:

- The data returned may be incomplete. Self-administered surveys are often returned with skipped questions, illegible answers, comments instead of numerical ratings, etc. If respondents don't understand a question, they may answer inappropriately or not at all.
- There is a built-in self-selection response bias.
- Setup and data handling may cost more than other formats.

Mail-in surveys have their own, unique pros and cons, especially when compared directly with online methods. The following are advantages:

- They are lower tech than online surveys and don't require the respondent to have any special equipment. A mail survey can be completed anywhere, any time: on a bus, in bed, or while waiting for a Web page to download.
- It's easier to find mailing lists than email lists for a sample you can trust to be representative of the general population.
- The setup costs are lower than for an online survey, and a technical specialist isn't required, as it is for a Web-based interactive survey. Hence for small samples, snail mail surveys are more cost-effective than online surveys. (Phone surveys are probably somewhere in the middle.)
- The overall cost of a mail survey is usually lower than the cost of a phone survey, provided that printing costs are low and that it yields a high first-mailing response rate.
- Distribution of mail surveys can be piggybacked onto other contacts with the respondent pool, for example, they can be enclosed in a bill or printed in a magazine. This can improve saturation and reduce costs.

The following are disadvantages:

- As with any self-administered survey, the data returned may be incomplete, and there is self-selection.
- Penetration is unreliable. If the envelope is perceived as junk mail, it may be discarded without being opened.
- Some studies indicate that return rates for mail surveys are dropping every year as the public grows less willing to cooperate.

Online surveys, while all the rage in the New Economy, also have distinct pros and cons. The following are advantages:

- With a high-quality list (accurate addresses for people who are truly representative of a target universe) and a short survey, they represent the quickest, cheapest, and most flexible data collection technique.

- Data compilation is likely to be quick and simple, because a properly set up survey will yield data that can be dumped directly into data handling software.
- International surveys are usually simpler and cheaper to administer online than by phone because it is not necessary to find and pay interviewers in each language.
- Currently online surveys project a high-tech image, and are probably particularly effective with audiences looking for high-tech information, who may prefer this format and be more likely to respond than to phone or mail surveys.
- Once a good panel is developed (that's the hard part), niches can be reached more easily (CIOs in Fortune 500 companies involved in agriculture).

Email surveys are very inexpensive to distribute. If the panel is the company's own, once the setup is paid for, it costs about the same to send 100 as 100,000 (If the panel is rented, there's a unit cost.) The cost savings compared with postage or long-distance telephone can be large for a domestic survey, and even more dramatic for an international survey.

The following are disadvantages:

- There is a built-in sample bias. Fewer than half the general public in the United States, and an even smaller number in other countries, have email, and people with email tend to be the wealthier, whiter, male part of the population. Even with a good panel, the sample is likely to have slightly different characteristics than people with a similar demographic profile but no email.
- Connection speeds can be a problem. People with slow modems don't want to wait for a lot of pages to load, and even high-tech respondents with high-speed connections are surprisingly unwilling to spend much time with a survey. Volunteer or paid panelists may hang in there longer, but, in general, companies need to think seriously about using a different format for anything more than 10 questions.
- Online surveys are often returned half-finished (unlike mail surveys, which may not be returned at all). This makes the sample size for each question erratic, which affects reliability, and it also

requires extra administration to decide whether to keep or toss a partly completed survey.

- Online survey respondents are more likely to return duplicates (it's easy to hit the wrong button accidentally), and it takes extra steps to catch and eliminate these from the data set.
- Unsolicited emails are looked upon with disdain, and penalties for sending them are severe in some countries.

The availability of consumer panels is improving every day, but that of business-to-business panels is lagging far behind.

Competitive Differentiation: Unique Web Believability

The discovery stage of brand development is about more than understanding just the company and its personality and attributes so that they can be displayed on the Web. It's about understanding the company's existing or intended market so that the company brand can stand out in the pack, attract people, and help them become emotionally attached to the brand in addition to finding that it is a useful and productive tool.

Competitive differentiation is a concept developed by the authors to use differentiation within a highly competitive market to a company's brand advantage. It is especially useful for new entrants to a market (e.g., start-ups) or those redefining or rediscovering a brand.

Obviously companies want to differentiate themselves from competitors; however, in the last several years there have been so many new ideas thanks to the New Economy that having a unique idea can actually work against a firm. Venture capitalists, journalists, and industry and financial analysts have learned—often the hard way—to remain skeptical about companies that claim to offer a service online "that no one has thought of" or "that nobody has done yet." At this point, several years into the New Economy, it may very well be that anything that radically different may not have been done for a very good reason. Even if an idea is truly unique—and viable—skepticism will abound when the developer tries to sell it. A typical red flag for venture capitalists or journalists is when they ask "Who are your competitors?" and the response is "We don't have any . . . yet."

Another type of red flag is the one signaled by a company that is entering a sea of competitors without any uniquely different business proposition. Simply providing better service or pricing isn't enough to draw users to a new brand or to bond them emotionally. It's like moving to Seattle (home to Starbucks) and opening a new coffee shop—with nothing more compelling to offer than a slightly cheaper mocha or a prettier cup. When there is a plethora of choices, differentiation is a necessity, and differentiation is a key to brand equity. Companies entering a highly commodified market have to have something more, which is where the concept of competitive differentiation comes in. The process is remarkably simple, but powerful (see Figure 2.1).

Literally hundreds of press tours, branding sessions, and analyst meetings have demonstrated that the best way to position the company for the best reception by any audience, online or off, involves two steps during the discovery stage, which will carry through in all stages of brand development and will be made very clear on the Web site. The following two-step exercise can be conducted in a boardroom, or it can be distributed to individuals on the brand team to be completed and then discussed.

Acknowledge that the company has competitors. Identify them, determine what things make them unique as well as what things they have in common with the company being branded. Chart those factors. If possible, segment brand personality characteristics, brand attributes, and product/service offerings.

Now, on the same chart, mark the factors of the companies that make them unique—what does each offer that the others don't? In what way(s) does each do business differently?

The unique factors appearing as a result of this exercise are the desirable ones to analyze. For example, using NetRadio.com, a popular online music service, as a case study,[6] the company's unique properties might be the following:

- It provides exceptionally clear online broadcasts.
- It offers access to multiple multimedia players from a single location.

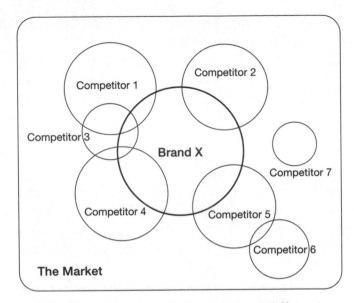

FIGURE 2.1. The concept of competitive differentiation. For a company to create a truly believable, successful, and unique brand, the brand must not only be legitimized by its being in an existing, recognized market but must also provide key points of differentiation from its competitors.

- It allows listeners to see the current and previous tracks at the same time.
- It allows listeners to rate tracks instantly, resulting in better play lists.
- It allows users to instantly purchase a CD of the music to which they're listening.
- Audible advertising is limited to station promos only.
- It provides interesting, well-written articles about music by musicians and music-industry professionals about topical areas (for example, clicking on the "electronica" music area will produce an article written about that genre of music by someone who knows what he or she is talking about).
- It offers 120 channels, all free, clearly marked, and instantly accessed.

These attributes differentiate NetRadio from competitors, such as online versions of actual airwave radio stations and other online radio services, which subject listeners to advertising, have clarity problems, are difficult to navigate, show only one song at a time, don't sell CDs, have limited variety, and don't make it easy to give feedback on play lists.

These points of competitive differentiation allow the company to legitimize its business model because it is in a known market: the online audio/radio market. However, when a company like this speaks to potential partners, investors, analysts, or the press, it can say, "We have a number of competitors, including conventional radio stations—who are broadcasting both online and off—as well as Internet-only radio stations, such as those you find promoted on www.windowsmedia.com. However, we don't compete with them exactly one-to-one, because we provide access to multiple players, instant purchase capabilities for CDs (we sell them ourselves), as well as the ability to see current and previous tracks and to rate them. We also offer 120 channels—significantly more than any close competitors—and they're really easy to access. We're similar, but not exactly; the way in which we're different, in our opinion, makes us a better choice for listeners."

Analysis like this lets the audience being addressed see that the market opportunity is real for the company: The company is in an existing and established and growing market, and yet provides a unique twist with clear revenue potential. Those are the marks of a strong brand with a great future.

How, then is this information, garnered in the discovery stage, used to build the brand on the Web? First and foremost, NetRadio blatantly capitalizes on its points of differentiation on its site by offering "Listen," "Learn," and "Buy" buttons for direct and immediate access to the reasons the vast majority of listeners come to the site. In addition, the company essentially uses a double tag line on its Web site (see the discussion on tag lines in Chapter 4 for information on developing tag lines): Its corporate tag line is "The Net Generation of Radio," while the "Listen," "Learn," and "Buy" words are used in a rotating banner, with accompanying text ("Listen: 120 Programmed Music Channels," "Learn: About Music and Artists," and "Buy: Choose from 250,000 titles").

The company has taken its most valuable and unique points of differentiation and used them to its advantage to transcend market clutter and and at the same time use a strong market to its advantage: NetRadio's Web site is competitive differentiation at its finest.

Business Plans and the Brand: Strange Bedfellows?

The business plan represents everything the company is and will be, covering virtually every aspect of the firm from sales and marketing to finance and administration, evaluating market conditions, and describing the executive team and their backgrounds. Everything in the business plan can and should be evaluated and written with the notion in mind that the company is building a brand. Again, to measure the company as an overall asset is to measure the brand; the two are bound together permanently, and when one changes, so does the other.

Frequently business plans lack "life," merely offering a collection of parts and pieces formulating yet another document tossed onto the venture capitalist's or banker's desk. Venture capitalists see as many business plans as journalists see press releases, and are equally disdainful of a lifeless, uninteresting read. With a mind to brand, brand process, and the elements of how the business will address the concepts of the New Economy, executive teams can breathe life into a business plan and optimize the chance that the plan will move to the top of the stack on the venture capitalist's desk.

During the discovery phase, the business plan needs to be read by all members of the brand team. If it is only in a developmental stage, as is frequently the case with start-up firms going through a branding exercise, then the business plan and branding as part of it need to be addressed. Typically the brand team is not considered to be an essential element of the business planning team, although members of the team may be involved in the branding effort. Including a section on "The Brand" in the table of contents of the business plan immediately suggests to investors that the team has thought of more than just the corporate structure and sales plan. Then, by articulating the framework of the brand and how the brand will be executed, within the business plan text, the company telegraphs its intentions to do more than just jump onto what seems to be a new revenue opportunity.

Addressing brand—and the brand strategy, in particular—in the business plan also encourages the executive team to actually think through the branding process. If as much time was spent building a brand as is spent building a revenue model and a sales channel, more companies would realize business reality radically more quickly.

How does the business plan relate to the Web? The Web is a reflection of the business plan, being the most visible and complete window into the business, and it is where the business plan and the brand meet, head-on. The business plan needs to address comprehensively virtually all elements of the business, including describing the brand attributes and personality; the Web site, in turn, must be in sync with information and planning stated in the business plan, and accurately portray the brand as described in the business plan.

Often the results of branding exercises become buried in the marketing communications department, a tool used by graphic designers, Web developers and Web masters, marketing staff in advertising and PR, and creative writers. While these staff members certainly need to have an in-depth understanding of the brand, they work with the tactical side of branding—colors, logos, name treatment and usage, proper tag-line usage in ads, and so on. The strategy of the brand, including the brand attributes and personality, core messaging, the elevator speech, and a map of the brand (see Chapter 3 for more on brand mapping) are invaluable tools that frequently don't make it into the company "brand" document, and certainly aren't perched high atop a senior executive's desk alongside the business plan—or as part of it.

Further, the brand strategy is what truly drives the development of the various marketing elements. If it is clearly stated and described in both a branding marketing document, containing comprehensive descriptions of both the brand strategy as well as how the brand is used tactically, as well as in the business plan, then the marketing and executive staffs stand a much better chance of being in harmony with how the Web site, the corporate intranet (the internal Web site), and all physical manifestations of the company appear—from trade show booths to annual reports to product packaging. Often the biggest disagreements in corporate life come when the CEO or VP of marketing reviews new ad designs, Web designs, and collateral documents and they fail to meet his or her expectations. If both the executive staff and those implementing the brand tactically are working from the same checklist, foundation, strategy, and framework, much time and money can be saved and surprises can be kept to a minimum.

The business plan is the most strategic and central document for an organization, and, as such needs to include strategic brand information. The following excerpt from a hypothetical table of contents of a business plan shows how the brand can be addressed as an individual section of the business plan:

4.0   Branding
    4.0.1   Introduction
4.1   Corporate Brand Strategy
    4.1.1   Brand Strategy Checklist
    4.1.2   Brand Attributes
    4.1.3   Brand Personality
4.2   Brand Visibility
    4.2.1   Corporate Web Site
    4.2.2   Service Web Site (for ecommerce)
    4.2.3   Company Intranet
    4.2.4   Partner/Vendor Extranet
    4.2.5   Partner Web Sites
    4.2.6   Annual Report
    4.2.7   Collateral
    4.2.8   Advertising
    4.2.9   PR
    4.2.10   Events
4.3   Corporate "Elevator Speech"
4.4   The Brand as an Asset (Here, the concept can be introduced that the company has value as a brand, articulating that the name, its visibility, and the subbrands can actually be measured in sync with the overall valuation of the company.)

By integrating the concept of "brand" into the business planning process, the company has automatically set the course for branding to be employed throughout the entire company. It won't simply be relegated to the marketing department, or subject to the whims of a maverick CEO. Instead, everyone from designers to customer service agents, from the PR manager to the HR trainer, can legitimately make use of a strong brand and thus ensure its successful deployment in the market.

Visual Brand Analysis

Analyzing a corporate brand during the discovery branding phase means looking at it visually in conjunction with words such as the name, the tag line, and the corporate message. It also means comparing the visual elements of competitive brands to understand how the market is represented visually and what the company faces in its efforts to build a strong brand.

Some markets are relatively immature in their visual identities: Recently, HR Services (now Cobos Group), a company in Seattle that outsources professional human resources managers to a wide variety of companies in the Pacific Northwest, engaged the Garrigan Lyman Group for a branding exercise designed to provide an understanding of how its brand was represented through its name, its tag line, its business materials (collateral, etc.), and its Web site. During the brand discovery and framework (brand-mapping) phases, the brand team looked at the various competitors in the market and their Web sites, as well as that of the HR Services existing site. The HR Services site was similar, in many ways, to the competitors identified in the discovery stage, in that—like many "vertical," nonconsumer sites—it was relatively simple and lacking design, developmental, and navigational sophistication. (See the sidebar below, "Vertical Markets: A Big Boon for Small Brands.) Only one site was significantly better, and even that site lacked a high-end look and feel. (See Chapter 5 for more on Web design.) So the good news was that, through visual brand analysis, HR Services had a great opportunity to build a much more powerful Web site to be used as a competitive advantage and to differentiate itself from the others.

Vertical Markets: A Big Boon for Small Brands

A vertical market is one that is specific to a given industry, for example, banking (as in a site specifically for bankers, not consumers), heavy-equipment shipping and transportation, organizations of oral surgeons, and plastics manufacturing, as opposed to horizontal markets, which address the consumer and business markets without regard to a specific industry or special interest group. Various Web sites and portals address vertical markets specifically, as opposed to portals such as www.yahoo.com or www.localbusiness.com. (Note that www.localbusiness.com is semivertical, in a sense, because it is a business portal addressing specific regions—so it is geographically vertical but horizontal in business focus.) There are a number of interesting vertical Web sites, even for nonmarket members, which do a great job of addressing a specific market. Often these sites are available by membership only, and can be structured as "extranet" sites.

The interesting thing about vertical markets and the Web is how the latter has created such an unprecedented venue for communication within these groups. Particularly for geographically challenged organizations (say, for example, hematologists, maritime attorneys, or Civil War aficionados), the opportunity to trade information, exchange goods and services, and find resources and people is invaluable. For companies addressing vertical markets, such as Cobos Group, following the basic tenets of the brand process has a dramatic effect on their ability to compete within the market; basically, the company is acting like a global organization in how it addresses its brand, which directly benefits its image in its target (albeit small) marketplace.

"The experience was very eye-opening, and really called things to home," said Victoria Cobos, Cobos Group principal and founder. "We were truly, for the first time, looking at the big picture, especially for a company in a niche market. We could see how far we had come over 13 years, which also showed how much we needed to change it.

"Besides the verbal part of the branding exercise, it was very enlightening that on the visual side there was so much opportunity for growth.

A decade ago that might not have been such a big issue, but in today's world to be in business you have to consider the visual element, especially how it's represented on the Web as well as the whole picture."

Visually analyzing the various brand sites using a brand mapping analysis tool (see "Brand Mapping" in Chapter 3) quickly shows which sites are deficient and which are strong, areas to avoid, and components of sites worth developing. It also becomes clear that various sites are out of sync with a brand personality or attributes for that industry, or for the existing corporate culture. For example, one Cobos Group competitor looks and feels as if it were a law firm, which is not the image that human resource service companies want to project in this day and age; even though the market they address is extremely corporate, they generally want to be much more "human" and less stodgy. That does not mean, however, that they want to go in the other direction, with sites that are so homey that they seem to be frilly, nonprofessional, and frivolous (and the Cobos Group analysis identified some of these, as well).

Furthermore, visual brand analysis in the discovery stage involves examining the physical materials a company and its competitors have: corporate brochures, annual reports, trade show booths, and the like. Often it becomes clear that these elements have been designed in marketing silos, without regard for brand consistency among the components. While corporate colors may be the same and the logo is cast correctly, things often diverge from there: The brand personality and attributes may vary wildly, simply because those brand-strategy elements have neither been established nor communicated. This can result in clashing elements and a confusing presentation to clients, partners, and investors.

Visual analysis allows brand teams to objectively compare and set standards, as well as to begin the work necessary to create a solid framework for the brand.

Core Messaging

A company's core message is the statement and group of words that define its business in a proverbial nutshell. It states the purpose of the company, its mission, and its goals, providing a foundation upon which the framework and creative elements of the brand will be built. No matter what audience encounters the company and the brand, the core message is so deeply embedded into the company that it permeates every activity and representation.

Where is the core message stated? First, in the business plan, which needs to state the core message at the outset. Part of brand discovery is to read the core message in the business plan—or to write the core message—at the outset of the branding effort. Often, before the first branding/discovery session takes place, and in the case of companies lacking business plans or core messages in the business plan, the executive team receives a document asking that each member articulate the core message of the company. Even if the company has a stated mission, executive team members frequently come up with dramatically different versions of the core message. During brand discovery, it is essential that all members of the team settle upon a core message, so that each member understands and buys in to what the company is doing. "A house divided cannot stand" applies directly to this stage—often the company that cannot agree upon a core message, or "agrees to disagree," creates a division that only widens into a "brand division" that causes serious problems as the company grows.

This is not to say there will not be customized messages for individual target groups: sales, marketing, finance, corporate communications, purchasing, and recruiting will all have their own way of stating, explaining, justifying, and publicizing the core message. Whether it's in a sales pitch, an annual shareholders' meeting and report, a press release boilerplate, the Web site, or a trade show presentation in German at CeBIT (the huge annual European technology trade show in the spring in Hannover, Germany), the core message can be identified. Further, all members of the executive team must be well versed in the basic points of the core message so they can express them at every opportunity.

The core message is essential to building a strong corporate brand. While the statement may not appear verbatim on the Web site, anyone who hears the core message or knows it should be able to see it reflected in the Web site's design, information, navigation, and services. For companies going through a branding or Web design process, it is essential to articulate the core message of the company as part of the project to ensure that it is accurately and dramatically portrayed on the site.

Brand Strategy Finalization

The discovery stage of the branding process sets a solid foundation for moving ahead in building framework, creative, and execution stages. Without it, the brand lacks a firm footing and the points of consistency that will allow the brand, creative, and executive teams to move ahead as a unified group. Also, true to its name, this stage discovers and reveals facts about the brand, the core message, and the overall business strategy that may not yet have come to light.

In the context of the Web, discovery is essential if for no other reason than that the entire world is stepping to the new beat of the New Economy. As pointed out by Cobos Group principal Victoria Cobos, factors such as the visual elements of the brand have taken on entirely new levels of meaning and importance today. Company brands are being judged by different standards than they were even five years ago, and the Web accounts for a tremendous part of the change in standards.

For companies moving from bricks to clicks and that have an established brand identity and revenue stream, it means reevaluating the company business model, core message, and the way in which the brand is represented to all its audiences, both offline and online. Companies like Barnes & Noble can no longer count on physical book browsing in a pleasant atmosphere to generate a majority of its sales. The company must take into account that it, just like all of its competitors, is working to attract and keep customers via a two-dimensional screen lacking the sights and smells of a traditional bookstore.

In fact, a company of any type—start-up to established, business to consumer or business to business—must diligently use the discovery stage of branding to truly understand its brand, its market, and its audiences. What it "discovers" will have a profound effect on the success of its brand.

3

The Framework Stage

A Branded House or a House of Brands?

Form is the cage and sense the bird. The poet twirls them in his mind,
And wins the trick with both combined.
—Henry Austin Dobson, "The Toyman"[1]

The framework of a brand determines its architecture, places it firmly upon a strong foundation of brand strategy, and enables it to carry corporate, product, and services brands into the future. The Web provides the essential and ideal platform for the brand framework to stand strong, enabling a high degree of flexibility to support any type of brand and subbranding structure.

Virtually every company around the globe today faces the challenge of representing its brand on a Web site or group of Web sites. For a one-hit-wonder company, it's a simple proposition. However, for companies with large groups of products and services and with complex corporate structures (often resulting from mergers or acquisitions), building a framework for the brand and determining how it will appear on the Web site are daunting tasks.

Brand development teams with significant Web savvy approach this problem from a method-oriented, logical perspective, within the context of the overall brand process. The framework stage is notably devoid of creative sessions (such as URL naming or tag-line development), focusing instead on existing, known brand names (even though they may change in later stages) and placeholders for products or services yet to be named.

The framework stage, the second stage in building a Web brand, doesn't have to be lengthy—in fact, many executive teams insist that it be short and intensive—but it must yield tangible results and provide a crystal-clear brand map synchronized with the brand strategy and corporate goals. It also must involve the team members who will devise the site map for the corporate Web site, as they will contribute greatly to what does and doesn't make sense within the overall framework. A number of exercises and interactive sessions in this stage produce materials that will carry the brand forward into the creative stages.

Designing and Building the Framework

Every brand framework is like a corporate fingerprint, unique in design and structure. In the same manner in which a company organization chart is designed and articulated, so is a brand framework. As with an organization chart, the mere act of putting it into place drives a proverbial stake into the ground, immediately giving the company a higher level of formality and structure—often to its immediate benefit. In fact, a brand framework often looks similar to an organization chart: hierarchical in nature, with many dotted-line reporting structures and formal and semiformal relationships (see Figure 3.1).

This isn't to say that running out and buying a copy of Visio (popular software for drawing organization charts) will be any help in building a brand framework. Building a framework requires a concerted effort, taking the information gathered and explored in the brand discovery stage and pushing it forward. Further, a number of questions need to be addressed:

- Is the brand being developed a parent brand, a brand campus, a house of brands, or a branded house?
- What are the key differentiating overall brand factors to be incorporated in all the parts and pieces of the brand?
- Should these factors be communicated in the parent brand, the tag line, the subbrands, or other communication?

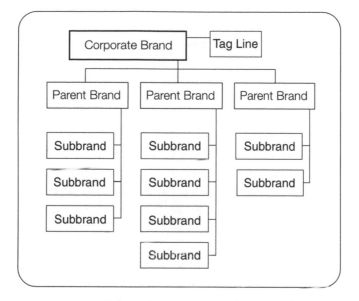

FIGURE 3.1. A brand structure can be viewed in an organization-chart context: driven by a single, high-level corporate brand, in a top-down fashion, to achieve high levels of consistency and brand management.

- What is the timing determining what brands and/or subbrands should be transitional or foundational?
- Which brands will fade away as a Web brand becomes more dominant, and which will become stronger?
- What branding measurement tools need to be put into place to ensure and maximize online and offline profitability and synergy, as well as essential communication goals?
- What type of naming should be developed in the articulation stage? Is the name descriptive, abstract, conservative, or progressive?

These are all factors to consider as part of the framework stage, and they all relate directly to how the brand and its various components will work together. The Web site must portray this structure accurately, and allow the brand parts to work both individually and as part of a broader strategy and structure.

Branded Houses and Houses of Brands

Compare two very different brands: Microsoft (www.microsoft.com) and Kimberly-Clark (www.kimberlyclark.com). Microsoft is a powerful parent brand, with many relatively generically named products underneath—a *branded house*. From its home page, Microsoft individual product subbrands are not visible, unless being specifically highlighted for a promotional reason or in a press release or news headline. From there, access to the myriad Microsoft products online is outlined. The brands are laid out logically into groupings of product families, services, and customer sites—essentially, the product brands follow users' general interests. Drilling down to the "Office" site, for example, yields another set of choices, which are once again all related to user interests as opposed to specific subbrand names.

At the top of the page is a choice to see "all products," which retrieves an alphabetical listing that provides the ultimate subbrands, such as Word, PowerPoint, or Publisher. The actual brand names of Microsoft subbrands are buried several levels deep in the Microsoft site. This is partly because there are many complex products that need much more definition and explanation than Microsoft can provide on the home page, or even on a secondary page. The site accurately reflects the Microsoft brand framework, with the application lying well below the level of the parent brand.

Someone interested in finding information about Microsoft Publisher, for example, needs a few extra clicks and page turns to reach the product and its information. However, the advantage is that when the desired section is reached, the amount of information about the product is comprehensive and detailed, with product downloads, support information, product FAQs, trial versions, and product tours. With such a complex application, the branded-house framework works effectively to provide users with the information necessary to make purchasing and business decisions.

The branded house is a frequently used framework in technology companies, for the same reason described for Microsoft: It is an effective way to manage and communicate a large set of complicated brands. Compaq, IBM, Oracle, Cisco, and Dell all use branded-house methodology, with slightly different spins evident for the brand frameworks and corresponding Web sites. Amazon.com, too, uses this method for its site: The powerful parent brand/branded house is the name, Amazon.com, and its subbrand groups—books, kitchen, auctions, software, music, video, etc.—have generic names. Amazon has put virtually no effort into subbranding, but much into framework.

The Kimberly-Clark Web site is one of the clearest examples of a *house of brands* found anywhere. In fact, Kimberly-Clark doesn't even refer to itself as a brand directly, but instead says "with some of the world's most respected brands . . ." Its brands, however, such as Kleenex, are household names the world over, first-to-mind consumer brands needing no introduction or explanation. Unlike the Microsoft products, no product tour, demo, FAQ, or download is necessary for facial tissue or diapers. The manner in which Kimberly-Clark markets its products, as stand-alone brands, thus becomes a much simpler proposition for presenting itself on the Web.

Or does it? For Kimberly-Clark an entirely new problem presents itself. Few will think "Word" is made by any other manufacturer than Microsoft, and the product is nicely nestled in the Microsoft site. Anyone interested in information on Microsoft Word will go to the Microsoft site and simply search for "word" on its site-specific search engine.

In the case of Kimberly-Clark, however, how many people know who manufactures Kleenex? How many people interested in looking for Kleenex on the Web think some other company manufactures Kleenex, such as Procter & Gamble? How many people simply don't have any idea?

The answer for companies like Kimberly-Clark is that they must, by necessity, create individual Web sites for individual brands. The first place interested parties turn to find information about Kleenex is www.kleenex.com, and the same is true for the other brands that Kimberly-Clark owns and manages: www.kotex.com, www.huggies.com, and www.depend.com.

So, instead of having a single site driven by a parent brand, as in the case of Microsoft, with a set of highly connected and complex products, Kimberly-Clark has a house of brands. Brands which are fundamentally simple and highly consumer-oriented, and which stand on their own with individual brand identity, are represented on the Web with their own Web sites. The house of brands relies much more heavily on the brand equity of the individual products or services than it does on the ability of the parent brand to attract and keep an audience.

Umbrella, Parent, and Subbrands

The process of building a brand requires defining a hierarchy to the brand structure, as pointed out in the organization-chart analogy earlier in this chapter. Brands under which other brands reside are referred to as *parent brands*. For example, Microsoft Office is a parent brand, with subbrands such as Microsoft Word, Microsoft Publisher, and Microsoft PowerPoint beneath it. The corporate entity Microsoft Inc. which is a parent brand to subbrands such as Microsoft Office and Microsoft Windows, covers such a broad set of brands that it is commonly referred to as a *corporate umbrella brand*, meaning that it encompasses a large set of complex brand structures. Not all umbrella brands are the overall corporation brand itself, although frequently that is the case.

General Motors is an umbrella brand, for example, with a complex group of parent brands underneath: Buick, Chevrolet, Cadillac, and so forth, as well as parts divisions. In turn, parent brands such as Cadillac have multiple subbrands beneath them, such as the Cadillac Escalade and the Cadillac Seville.

Likewise, *purebred* online brands have umbrella, parent, and subbrands as well, which may be service or product areas. A purebred online brand is one that exists only on the Internet, without a bricks-and-mortar presence. Amazon.com and Ariba are both purebred online brands, as opposed to BarnesandNoble.com and IBM.com—both of which are outgrowths of a traditional, non-Internet brand. In addition, as stated previously, Amazon.com has many generic subbrands underneath, such as DVD or Books. Some purebred online brands choose to create names for the parent and subbrands underneath the umbrella, and most, such as Ariba's "Buyer," "Marketplace," and "Dynamic Trade," are highly descriptive. Many common

		Yahoo! Auctions
CNNfn		Yahoo! Travel
CNNsi	entriOrder	Yahoo! Shopping
myCNN	entriConnect	Yahoo! Sports
CNN Europe	entriNumber	myYahoo!

FIGURE 3.2. Brand and subbrand hierarchies on business-to-business and business-to-consumer Web sites.

business-to-business and business-to-consumer companies have distinctive brand hierarchies (see Figure 3.2).

The Child as Parent: Dominant Subbrands

The house of brands is commonly an umbrella brand (like Kimberly-Clark) with several strong subbrands beneath (Huggies, Kleenex, etc.). A slight twist on this, however, is seen in the company with a subbrand that is so strong and dominant that it actually overtakes the company parent or umbrella brand. In effect, the child *becomes* the parent. This can happen when a product brand becomes so well known that it eclipses the parent brand, and the executive team makes a branding decision to allow the subbrand to become the primary corporate brand.

LapLink, one of the best-known utility products and brands in the personal computer industry, has been around since the 1980s. It consists of software that allows PCs to exchange data efficiently and quickly using a very bright and memorable yellow data cable. LapLink's former parent company, Traveling Software, was a strong and active member of the booming PC industry in the late 1980s and early 1990s. Mark Eppley, its president, CEO, and founder (who, incidentally, wrote the Foreword to this book), enjoyed a high degree of industry popularity, was frequently quoted in trade and business publications, and was often seen at industry events. Traveling Software even became notorious for its wacky and wild parties at Comdex, the huge computer trade show held every November in Las Vegas. Known as the "burnout party," the event took place on Thursday evening (the last evening of the five-day show), when everyone was celebrating the coming last day of a long week.

But the advent of the Internet Age posed a challenge for Traveling Software. People still needed to transfer data between PCs—especially when traveling—and Traveling Software's competitive differentiation focused around products that allowed people to manage and access information anywhere they went in the world. The Internet, however, was eating away at that identity, infringing on Traveling Software's ownership of the "go anywhere, do anything" brand attributes. Further compounding the brand-erosion problem was the fact that the name LapLink was substantially more well known than Traveling Software. Simple market research revealed a much higher level of awareness for LapLink as a recognizable name and brand than for Traveling Software; even people who recognized both didn't always know there was a connection between the two.

Eppley, returning from a hiatus of several years, took Traveling Software by the proverbial horns, reorganized, and set out to put the now struggling company back on its feet. After putting into place an entirely new management team, revamping the existing product line, adding new products which were very Internet-friendly, such as LapLink FTP, and generally overhauling the brand through intense discovery and framework efforts, Eppley was ready to put the final master's touch to his reworked brand: He renamed the company LapLink.com. This move, combined with Eppley's widespread industry recognition and appeal and the broad and global awareness of the LapLink name, received an immediate positive reception. Further, for people who had never known the parent name was Traveling Software, the brand change was transparent.

In this case, building a brand on the Internet meant capitalizing on brand strengths, seizing an opportunity, and leveraging public image to allow the naturally occurring brand strength of LapLink to lead the company into the next phase of its corporate brand.

For a company experiencing difficulties, discovery and framework often reveal this kind of brand opportunity as the answer to its problems. It is human nature to want to keep a subbrand from becoming dominant, because it seems as if the brand is controlling the company. In reality, of course, the client base and investors are the controlling force. For the CEO on a power trip, it might be hard to let the LapLinks rise to the surface—which could pull the entire brand under. The key is in listening to what the audience is saying and acknowledging the analysis and truths resulting from a good, solid branding effort. Even with the Internet, which is turning many businesses upside-down, a perceived challenge can sometimes yield a huge opportunity.

Leveraging Preexisting Brand Momentum on the Web

Companies that have shifted some (or all!) of their business to the Web (nonpurebred online brands), such as Dell Computer Corporation or Kmart, replicate their offline parent and subbrands on the Web, giving customers consistency and an easy way to find the product and service areas to which they were accustomed in dealing with the company off the Web.

Outlining and defining the brand hierarchy often dominate the framework stage of building a brand on the Web, and are essential to building an effective and enduring brand overall. Further, during this stage any considerations for future brands that have yet to be developed can be identified. Imagine, for example, if at the start-up Amazon.com had thought it would sell only books online, and didn't foresee selling videos, DVDs, kitchen products, auction services, and so on. It might have decided to simply call itself "booksonline.com," and since books were to turn out to be only a dominant subbrand of Amazon overall, this would have wreaked havoc—at least for naming efforts—and limited the ability of the brand to grow, expand, and diversify.

It is also during the framework stage that the house-of-brands versus branded-house structure is taken into consideration, allowing the umbrella brand to be identified as dominant or not.

For nonpurebred Internet companies, ensuring that the existing bricks-and-mortar brand infrastructure is accurately reflected on the

Web site can prove a daunting task, especially if a brand hierarchy has not been well defined. The brand hierarchy often proves to be a substantial element in the Web site map, and has tremendous impact on site navigation. The Microsoft Web site, for example, had to make sure that the Microsoft Office products were all properly mapped under the Microsoft Office parent brand and that the various services and resources—some of which were specific to individual subbrands and some which were common to all—appeared in a logical and expected location. The same was true for the various Microsoft Windows products, MSN, and so on.

In existence before the Web site age, Microsoft had to carefully map its existing bricks-and-mortar structure to a Web-based representation so that it could be in sync. The external visibility of the hierarchy was relatively limited; for the most part, people bought Microsoft products off the shelf at stores, it came bundled with hardware, or it was recommended and provided by a reseller or IT manager.

For a company like Kmart, the task was entirely different from that of Microsoft. Instead of replicating a large group of products and services which only existed on paper and, for the most part, didn't need to be broadly defined and mapped for a customer, Kmart essentially had to recreate its store online—and people had to be able to find the various departments, services, and products just as easily as if they were walking through the store. Kmart, Wal-Mart, and Target have addressed this effort with everything from virtual store maps to clear identification of easily found company brands, such as Target's "Honors" clothing brand.

Interestingly, Kmart's online brand is www.bluelight.com and typing the URL www.kmart.com redirects to BlueLight—a separate company formed in 1999 by a venture between Kmart and Softbank Venture Capital and based in San Francisco (Kmart is headquartered in Michigan). The only way to find information about Kmart Corporation, in fact, is by first going to the BlueLight site and clicking on "about Kmart," which yields a separate browser window under the www.bluelight.com shadow.

According to Kmart and BlueLight, "In the 1970s, Kmart had a vision of shopping that combined entertainment and value. Its vision came alive with a concept you may remember called the 'Blue Light Special.' At that time, Kmart had a blue light mounted on every aisle and would announce special sales on products—extra-low prices for a limited time—by turning on the blue light. We're dedicated to delivering special deals to you wherever you are, and we chose our name to convey both the sense of fun and the commitment to low prices that Kmart pioneered."[2]

While this strategy gives Kmart the ability to separately brand its company with a more "clicks" than "bricks" brand, it requires, at least initially, an uphill climb to build recognition, trust, and traffic to a site which is clearly *not* the Kmart that in-store shoppers have come to know. How many people really associate the "Blue Light Special" with Kmart? With www.Target.com, the site that comes up is very clearly the same brand as that of the store down the street.

Wal-Mart, another competitor of Target and Kmart, has been later to market in developing a site that allows customers to find what they need with ease, despite having relocated its online headquarters to California and hiring top-notch development talent. Despite press speculation about Wal-Mart's future, the company operated much of the time in stealth mode, frequently refusing to speak with the press about Wal-Mart's plans for the site. This approach was out of sync for the high-tech industry and frustrating to the press, to analysts, and to customers. Early on the site featured a photo and first name of a Wal-Mart "greeter," for which the stores have become famous, but there was little else to distinguish it from Target.com or a host of other online retailers. While the greeters have provided moderate to significant brand appeal in the physical stores, their two-dimensional online counterparts don't have the same warmth or effect. Today, making them even less differentiated, they have dropped online greeters altogether. Of the three companies—Wal-Mart, Kmart, and Target—the most unusual and interesting Web brand is Kmart's www.bluelight.com. Target and Wal-Mart are simply online brand extensions of the stores, neither being a particularly remarkable online brand experience. As thousands of retail opportunities continue to come and go online, it will be several years before it is clear which strategy and profits will be the strongest.

Companies like Kmart/BlueLight have thousands of products and numerous departments. In migrating its corporate (umbrella) brand, parent brands, and subbrands to the Web, the framework had to precisely map the retail-store structure—if for no other reason than to ensure that its own staff would be able to manage the two-headed bricks-to-clicks beast. In fact, Kmart is one of the few examples of an established brand that has extended itself onto the Web with a wholly different name—a near-impossible feat for most bricks-and-mortar brands.

This is why Web design is much more than just coming up with a great-looking design—even if it does precisely reflect the corporate brand personality—and dropping it into a Web site. It involves intricate navigation, development, efficient use of graphics, double- and triple-checking information such as pricing, and exhaustive testing to ensure that navigation works—and that's not even counting a tremendous ecommerce infrastructure to manage the thousands of online transactions. The best-looking Web site in the world will lose brand attachment at an alarming rate if the navigation leads to dead ends, if the transaction machine fails, or if promises are made and not kept. One DSL service, for example, promised to return calls within 72 hours when a request for a sale representative to call was made online, yet most people *never* received a return call, even after a few months. Brand equity is all about keeping promises.

The essence of keeping the brand promise is building a Web brand that is organized in a logical and meaningful manner and delivers what it promises. This means identifying how the complete brand is structured, laying it out as part of a brand-mapping exercise (discussed below), and then applying it in the articulation and execution stages.

The hierarchy is a critical element of the brand framework; it needs to be kept handy at all times and provided as a tool for the entire brand team to reference. If the hierarchy changes, the hierarchy document needs to be changed. A brand management person or team needs to "own" the document to ensure that it is always current.

Great Email, Bad Branding?

One of the more notable and widely reviewed but poorly branded sites is the free email service offered by www.usa.net. Actually, the email service that is free to users is www.netaddress.com, which is part of the Colorado Springs–based www.usa.net virtual campus. However, the two sites are so radically different in terms of colors, design, and navigation that the potential for confusion is high.

Little is done to communicate or connect the usa.net site, which is the corporate/parent brand. Connecting netaddress.com and usa.net is hardly obvious or intuitive; in fact, it seems they have deliberately been made disparate. While a user can click on a usa.net logo before logging in to his or her email on netaddress.com, once in the email service the usa.net logo will not allow the person to connect to that site. The www.usa.net site does use www. netaddress.com as a subbrand for the email service, and the www.usa.net site to show other services for businesses such as ISP and enterprise email capabilities. But since the suffix on www.netaddress.com emails is "usa.net" (e.g., johnsmith@usa.net), why have netaddress at all? Further, the two sites couldn't look more different. In fact, usa.net staff members who were approached about the issue at a trade show in early 2000 acknowledged that the sites and branding were confusing.

Using framework brand methodology is the way to avoid this type of poor branding. Standards can be set which will work even in the case of a subbrand that is operationally very different from other services in the company.

The email service has done well in reviews of its quality of service, although it remains a relatively obscure name in comparison with other, highly branded, free email services such as Hotmail (which falls under the Microsoft umbrella). Usa.net has a good product. The question remains what the company might achieve if it also had strong, consistent branding.

Branding the Virtual Campus

A virtual campus, as described in Chapter 1, is actually a group of Web sites all under an umbrella brand, sometimes reflecting a physical infrastructure. It gives the brand and executive teams perspective and helps them understand the layout of the Web site in a very visual

manner, one which has a great deal of relevance to the existing facilities and operations of bricks-and-mortar companies. The virtual
campus is a branding tool used in the framework stage as an intellectual aid to building a strong, logical Web site with enduring brand
consistency.

A front-page article of the "Money" section of *USA Today* titled
"Many Companies Kicking the Bricks-and-Mortar Habit"[3] highlighted how companies in general are shedding their bricks-and-
mortar skin in favor of a virtual environment. The article, which is
about true virtual companies, where the staff telecommutes via the
Internet, opens with "Technology is dismantling offices to such a
degree that a growing number of firms now have employees, pay-
rolls, and clients but no building to call home."

While it's true that the number of virtual workplaces is growing
quickly, employees and companies nonetheless need structure and
will find it however they can. During the brand framework process,
as companies build their Web sites—both internal and external—the
need to create the virtual campus as a structural tool becomes increasingly important. In fact, one of the people interviewed in the
USA Today article admitted to needing more structure than a completely virtual company can provide. One answer to the problem of
how to combine the demand for working virtually with the need for
structure is to make the virtual campus an integral part of the brand
strategy.

A good example of a relatively simple virtual campus is the ecommerce site www.nordstrom.com, where, after clicking to the Web
site, one of two basic types of activities can be pursued: shopping
for merchandise or for information. Shopping for "things" is the
default site when the basic URL is entered. For investors, the press,
or others interested in information about Nordstrom *the company*,
clicking on "about Nordstrom" at the bottom of the home page takes
the visitor to an entirely different set of information and navigational
options. In the corporate section, for example, current stock performance, press releases, and company history appear—hardly interesting for someone just looking for a great pair of shoes.

What this means is that during a framework branding phase,
Nordstrom's faced and met the challenge of how to allow people
seeking information, merchandise, or both to easily access their sites

of interest from a common URL, www.nordstrom.com. The people shopping at a Nordstrom's store don't care about wandering into administration and seeing buyers, PR people, or financial administrators. They just want shoes! How can the way that the "real" Nordstrom's bricks-and-mortar business is operated and built be replicated on the Web? First, a choice has to be as to whether it's more important to get shoppers into product areas quickly or to get the information seekers to what they're looking for. For a retail operation like Nordstrom's, the answer is clear: shoppers take precedence, and so merchandise is displayed on the home page and shopping can begin instantly. Investors have to click an extra click to get to their information—but, in theory, they don't mind because every shopper who shops increases the value of their investment.

For a business-to-business brand like Ariba, the story is a bit different. Look at the myriad options available from its home page at www.ariba.com—including a proprietary supplier log-in, a partner button, a buyer log-in, and corporate and media information. Essentially, anyone who needs to get to any type of information or service can do so conveniently and directly from the home page, although many of the links actually go to completely separate Web sites and subnavigational systems.

"Virtual campuses" like these Web sites are necessary for organizing and managing a complex umbrella brand. During the framework stage, companies often work on individual parts of a virtual campus, for example, revamping the corporate site but leaving the ecommerce site intact save for minor brand modifications which may have to be reflected in the other parts: logo tweaks or changes, name changes, etc.

To the users, the experience needs to be seamless. No matter what they do, or wherever they surf on the site, the brand must be the same and the way in which the site operates must be similar.

A number of various virtual "facilities" can appear on the brand campus. Some of these might be on the corporate intranet, and not visible outside the company; others might be on a corporate extranet and available to partners, suppliers, and vendors:

- Administration
- Shipping and packaging

- Finance and operations
- Sales
- Marketing
- Retail operations
- Technical support
- Sales support
- Dealerships
- International offices
- Investor relations
- Corporate communications
- Accounting
- Human resources
- Recruiting

Every company is organized differently, and so is each virtual campus. Microsoft is one of the most rigorous brand management firms anywhere, adamant that changes to any part of the virtual, global campus adhere to well-established standards. Changing notable characteristics such as color and, say, the "file-folder tab" look and feel isn't an option. By methodically and obsessively working to ensure that the site branding is consistent throughout, the branding effects are profound and the integrity of the brand is virtually guaranteed. The experience for the user is one of a completely seamless operation, without surprises or confusing or conflicting information.

Changing a virtual campus to reflect a new brand can be daunting, especially if the brand development effort involves a new name or logo. Name and logo changes had a profound impact on pre-Internet companies, as well, but typically those dealt with packaging, collateral elements, and product labels. To save money, many companies would cycle old products and materials out, replacing depleted stock with newly branded items.

With the Web, this is not an option. A new Web site can ill afford to contain disparate logos or names. In the event of a companywide name or logo change, a plan must be made for changing over the entire virtual campus within a short time period. That means that the new site designs must be ready to go, and on a given day must immediately be cycled in to replace the old ones—lest site visitors see the old *and* the new name or logo and be confused.

For minor logo changes, or even a new tag line, the challenge is less critical, and the change can take place over a period of days or even weeks without much worry about clients or others catching on. Essentially, the more significant the change, the more urgent it is that the change be quickly reflected throughout the site.

The advantage of viewing a complete site as a virtual campus is that it provides a context for the entire site; gives designers, employees, clients, and others perspective; and helps them understand the site. It is a *true* "site map"; but instead of dividing the site into sections of usability or functionality, it gives the site a direct relationship to the bricks-and-mortar side of the operation. Obviously, this is less useful for purebred technology companies, but it can be extremely helpful for larger bricks-and-mortar firms with a significant physical infrastructure.

The virtual campus may be a tool to be used by the executive and marketing teams during the branding process; it may be an illustration distributed to employees and others; or it may be replicated on the Web site itself.

Brand Mapping: The Right Direction

With a strong grasp of the company's core messaging, brand strategy, and brand hierarchy, a brand map developed during the framework stage provides a plan of action, identifying some of the more intangible brand factors, combining them with the brand hierarchy and strategy, and setting sights on the goals to be achieved in the branding exercise.

Every branding effort differs from all others in how the brand map is developed and drawn; however, certain elements remain constant. Mapping can differ according to the complexity of the brand framework, the amount of time the team has available, and various competitive factors. The goal is to complete the brand-mapping effort with several clear, deliverable end results:

- Identifying the brand (including the various umbrella, parent, and subbrands) according to specific brand personality characteristics
- Understanding the dominant and subdominant brand strategy

- Reviewing and stating brand attribute goals, especially focusing on unique attributes to be used to competitively differentiate the brand
- Mapping the competitive landscape
- Filling in the broad brushstroke beginnings to the Web site map
- Listing the various tactical components to be developed, such as corporate brochures, trade show properties, etc.
- Identifying the various markets to be addressed: vertical, horizontal, and geographic (including international)

Armed with this "brand map," the brand team is properly equipped to begin addressing the creative elements of branding, such as naming and design, and to ensure that the structure and framework of the brand will be intact far beyond brand launch and execution.

Identification of the Brand According to Specific Brand Personality Characteristics

Mapping company personality traits visually can be a highly revealing exercise for an executive team and can yield powerful results when a brand is being developed on the Web. The process also has direct benefits to creative naming efforts in the verbal articulation stage, and provides an analytical tool to understand where the company exists vis-à-vis its competitors. It also clearly indicates where the company would like to move its image, driven by creative brand efforts and positioning.

The brand personality map comprises four quadrants; the horizontal axis goes left to right from "abstract" to "descriptive" and the vertical axis goes top to bottom from "progressive" to "conservative" (see Figure 3.3). During the exercise brands are located on the map according to their personality characteristics. The primary reason that the quadrant exercise is in the framework stage, and not in the verbal articulation and naming stage, is that the exercise is designed to provide insight into the type of name and creative positioning the brand personality is to take on. The actual name to be changed,

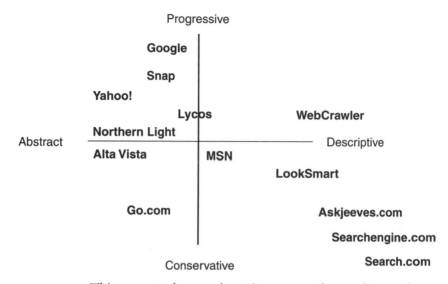

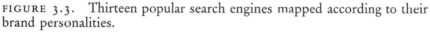

FIGURE 3.3. Thirteen popular search engines mapped according to their brand personalities.

created, or validated will be driven by the exercise. Creative development is essentially not an issue at this stage, although having a sense of the creative direction a company wants to move in is.

It's important to remember that the personality of the brand, unlike the brand attributes, is not something that changes frequently or easily. However, what often becomes evident from this exercise is that the brand personality is out of sync with the actual name(s) being used by the company. Fortunately, this exercise also often reveals that competitors are facing similar brand disparities.

Where a company is on the conservative-progressive axis speaks much about the corporate culture. For example, financial Web sites, such as www.fidelity.com or www.smithbarney.com, or legal Web sites, such as www.lawyers.com, are highly conservative; a flashy or design-intensive Web site for either would look unprofessional and would fall under the category of forced branding. Conversely, a site such as www.fabrica.it, a highly forward-looking, cutting-edge design firm in northern Italy that develops fashion, music, film, and other creative services, flies off the progressive end of the axis.

The abstract-descriptive axis differs from the conservative-progressive axis in that a personality—especially as represented by a name—can be very descriptive yet progressive at the same time. For example, the www.fabrica.it name is both descriptive (the company is a design firm and works frequently in fashion) and highly progressive (the name "fabrica" sounds very futuristic).

The URL name for Kmart, www.bluelight.com, is both abstract and conservative. It evokes certain images, such as "blue light," "blue collar," or "blue plate special"—but says nothing that specifically suggests "budget-priced department store." These images are not, however, progressive; Kmart is a conservative company that appeals to middle-American conservatism, and the "bluelight" name is essentially conservative.

Figure 3.3 shows a group of popular search engines positioned on the brand-mapping matrix described above. This exercise can be used to map brand names populating the competitive landscape in any target market, for corporate names and business, and for competitive products or services.

In the figure a name like WebCrawler appears in the progressive/descriptive quadrant because the name is extremely descriptive and the look and feel of the Web site is somewhat (not entirely) progressive. Google's site is very simple, with no news, games, auctions, or any other distractions; consequently it can be considered progressive; further, it is on the line between abstract and descriptive because the word has meaning but the meaning is not well known. (A "googol" is the largest number with a name—a one with 100 zeroes.)

AltaVista and Go both appear in the conservative/abstract quadrant because their names are mildly abstract (although "go" and "view at a high level" could both lead a person to "search engine"—but not directly), and their sites are relatively conservative.

The quadrant can be evaluated in a number of ways, and debated endlessly, but the exercise often shows that the name of a company or product and its actual brand personality and attributes are not in harmony. In fact, in this example, although the URL names are dissimilar, the search engines all provide extremely similar services, and what is found on one search engine is remarkably similar to what can be found on the others. The difference between the service offerings of the sites, while laid out differently and with slightly different emphases, is minimal: most offer a variety of search options, news, shopping, auctions, and the like. Google is the most differentiated from the others; it provides search options only and focuses on high quality. LookSmart also differentiates itself through quality—touting itself as "the quality Web directory"—and is the only engine in the group with immediate access to global city and search directories in Europe, Australia, Asia, North America, and elsewhere. Searchengine.com is regionally specific (primarily United Kingdom and Germany) with a generic identity. The intent of this analysis is not to claim perfect brand positioning for any of these search engines. That would provoke a never-ending discussion as heated as any barroom argument about politics or religion. It's meant to highlight two important facts:

- Mapping brands shows clearly how name and service offerings frequently differ, and why some brands are strong and others are not.
- The quadrant exercise is an excellent tool for understanding competitive differentiation, identifying who's doing it right, and indicating pockets of opportunity

Often at the beginning of the brand framework stage, each member of the executive team is given two sheets of paper, one with a conservative-to-progressive line and the other with an abstract-to-descriptive line. Each is asked to position, somewhere on the two lines, all brand entities—the company name, brand, and any branded product or service—as they stand today and as the person sees them becoming through the branding exercise.

After that, the group compares notes. The results—the positioning of the different brands—are mapped on the quadrant diagram, on a white board (it's often useful to use a different color for each person). The differences in how the various members of the team perceive the various entities can be dramatic.

At this point, the team, still as a group, positions the competitors they have identified in brand discovery. Through the exercise, it becomes clear whether the intentions of the group individually or collectively are correct as to where the brand(s) needs to be directed, as well as how harmoniously the brand components of the company work together.

Once mapped, the brand attributes of the company and its competitors can be discussed; it can be determined whether they appropriately match the positioned personalities, and the competitive differentiators can be highlighted. Of the search-engine companies in the example, LookSmart and Google both differentiate themselves using quality, while others use shopping, news services, brand sponsorships (such as NBC sponsoring Snap, etc.), and so on.

Mapping more focused brand offerings is actually much easier. Sites such as search-engine portals, which frequently have a plethora of consumer or business offerings, experience a "regression to the mean," homogenizing effect; they all offer highly commodified information that is really just about the same on each site, albeit organized and displayed slightly differently. New entrants to markets such as these must exercise extreme caution to not end up looking just like everyone else. Building a Web brand that would fit into a cluster of competitors without any significant competitive differentiation is a surefire formula for disaster.

A direction to avoid, or at least along which to proceed very carefully, is toward areas devoid of any competitors; frequently, there's a good reason that the area is sparsely populated. Few if any search engines hoping to attract mainstream Web surfers position themselves as highly abstract and progressive entities because credibility and the ability to be located are of utmost importance to them—neither of which is supported by being too wild or too difficult to recognize or remember.

After mapping the various brands, consider and discuss several issues:

- What are the points of competitive differentiation between the various brands?
- What are the areas devoid of brands? Why?
- What areas are highly populated? Why? Do the players in those areas have a way of differentiating themselves?
- How strong and recognized are the brands?
- Rank the brands in order of market recognition and brand strength. How does that relate to their position on the quadrant? What stands out?

- Which brands have significant differences between their mapped personalities and mapped names? Why?
- Where would the brand(s) being developed most likely have success in the quadrant? Does that mean the brand(s) needs to become more or less conservative, abstract, descriptive, progressive? Position the brand as it *needs to become* on the quadrant and reevaluate what that does to the competitive landscape.

List the issues which need to be addressed to effectively move or position the brand into the target areas on the brand map: perhaps the name that will be created needs to be emphasized, services need to be more accessible, or personality factors or attributes need to be highlighted on the site (responsiveness, creativity, partnerships, etc.) at higher levels.

Web Site Beginnings: Broad Brushstrokes

The verbal and visual stages of Web brand development determine the verbal and visual design content of the Web site according to the brand framework and strategy. However, in the framework stage, the Web site begins to take form at a high level. It's a good idea to involve senior designers from the Web development team at this point so they can understand what is being created, and why. Even if the company doesn't yet have a name, or it's about to be changed, the personality and character attributes, as well as the brand framework and mapping, will have been established, and the designers can use this information as they begin to craft a site.

There are three primary considerations:

- Is the Web site being created from scratch or is it a makeover of a current site?
- If it is being created from scratch, does the site need to reflect a bricks-and-mortar organization, such as the Kmart example?
- If it is a makeover of a current site, is it significantly changing the site map and existing Web hierarchy, or is it simply changing the look and feel and some basic naming?

This book is not about designing or developing a Web site, but rather about building brands on the Web. Two excellent texts about Web site development, *Designing Web Usability: The Practice of Simplicity*[4] by Jakob Nielsen and *Secrets of Successful Web Sites*[5] by David Siegel, cover the vast, growing, and intimidating area of Web project management, design, and development. Siegel briefly addresses the topic of branding in his book (pages 160 and 232), acknowledging, "brands represent more than the use of symbols, fonts, color combinations, and navigation bars. Think of a Web site as part of a larger branding strategy in a broader theater of communications, where competing brands contend for mind—and market—share."[6]

The transition from branding to Web design must be a well-supported bridge, ready for heavy traffic. It is a pity when a well-articulated brand fails to be leveraged effectively on the Web, perhaps the most compelling opportunity for brand visibility in the history of business. It is equally sad to see a great business idea poorly executed because it lacks the strong brand framework necessary for attracting and keeping a faithful audience.

Planning the Tactical Marketing Components: Web Site Brand Partners

The framework stage provides an opportunity for the executive and marketing teams to plan the marketing components needed to complement the Web site. Before Web sites became marketing centerpieces, collateral supports such as trade show booths and magazine ads had to be just as complementary and represent the brand just as consistently. Logos and colors had to match, messaging needed consistency, and updates had to be highly coordinated. In that sense, nothing has changed. However, in many cases the Web site has become the driving force behind the brand, or at least must be intimately tied with any other marketing efforts. At a high level, the executive team has strong ideas about what marketing materials it will need in addition to the Web site, such as annual reports and presentations.

For companies with significant bricks-and-mortar infrastructures, the challenge for marketing is to ensure that any ad campaigns, pricing changes, promotions, and new products, services, and designs appear on the Web site (or at least are taken into considerations) as soon as they are released. Back-to-school campaigns, major trade shows, news releases, and contests must all be coordinated. These, of course, are tactical considerations and have little relevance to brand framework other than that the framework stage is the time for the executive and marketing teams to set the standards into place to ensure the Web is fully integrated into the company and not just an effort taking place in a vacuum. Difficult as it may be for some bricks-and-mortar executives to believe, the incidence of people locating the company and getting information about it and them on the Web increases exponentially every day.

nPassage, a company providing Web-based services for the transportation industry (e.g., container shipping, freight forwarding, etc.), which was named and branded by the Garrigan Lyman Group in 1999, initially found resistance in the transportation industry to being Web-enabled. For an industry several centuries old, the methods of tracking freight—even with basic PC technology—had not involved the level of marketing and corporate communication and *community* the Web stood ready to provide. In fact, one connotation of "nPassage" is "rite of passage"—and indeed the freight industry is passing through an interim stage as part of its adaptation to the New Economy. In the period of a single year businesses in this industry saw a radical and highly noticeable change, the increase in Web access availability on the shipping-room floor signaling a transition from executive skepticism and doubt as to the need for Web access, to it being a corporate requirement.

This change is partially because a few pioneers in the industry "jumped the fence," after which other companies realized they'd better follow suit quickly. Still, the Web sites of many traditional bricks-and-mortar industries reflect the vertical nature of the industries. The equestrian business, for example, with hundreds of companies producing saddles and tack, selling horses, and providing transportation services and equipment, both in business-to-business and business-to-consumer models, has only recently awakened to the fact that its target audiences are not only geographically diverse and in high income brackets, but very Web-connected as well. The market still has not progressed much beyond providing news online, with a few equestrian ecommerce sites that are, for the most part, unsophisticated and poorly designed.

Both of these very different but very established industries—transportation and horses—have in the past relied on or still do rely heavily on physical marketing materials: ads, collateral materials, signage, and so on. As the Web becomes more prominent and begins to permeate every aspect of day-to-day business, the ability to coordinate the transition of established brands onto the Web requires executive direcion and edict in order to move effectively beyond simple brochureware.

Target Stores has mounted one of the most extensive efforts to coordinate marketing online and offline. Its Web site features new products; some of them are available only in Target stores, and others can be purchased online. The store is constantly scrutinizing pricing against competitors such as Kmart and Wal-Mart, and it frequently sponsors contests, promotions, and events (such as the Target Grand Prix car races). Its marketing coordination ranges from ensuring that the drivers of racing cars with the Target logo have their names spelled correctly on the Web to making sure that any changes in APR on the Target credit card terms also appear on the Web site.

Every instance of marketing coordination is an opportunity for the brand to be extended or contracted. During the framework stage, it is incumbent upon the executive team and marketing management, at the very least, to set the standards to ensure that the desired result takes place. The effort requires extensive checks and balances, but it's the only way to ensure that the brand is fully leveraged.

Addressing Markets: Vertical, Horizontal, and Geographic

The framework stage requires branding efforts that build more than just the functional structure of the brand. Branding serves as a bridge between company, product, and market, so the permutations and combinations of relationships are huge. Building a virtual campus and its components requires more than just setting up a company online—it also means building a network of services responsive to the needs of a diverse community or set of communities. In general, for the purposes of brand mapping, understanding which portions of a brand are vertical, horizontal, and geographical impacts the development of the brand structure.

Some portions of large, horizontal brands—such as Amazon.com, for example, are "virtual verticals": mechanisms tracking the interests of members provide focused information based on a person's behavior. If a chiropractor goes online at Amazon.com to purchase books on alternative healing, that is tracked and the next time he or she goes online there are recommendations for books in this area. Amazon.com has, through its software infrastructure and Internet mechanisms such as cookies, established a vertical market for that person.

More frequently, and as they become more sophisticated, horizontal brands will allow online vertical "communities" to form, with discussion groups, chat areas, and various types of information and product exchange. The software that identifies which other products a client might like can also be used to suggest that person join a number of other people who might have the same interests. By sponsoring and catering to vertical markets, large horizontal brands appear less monolithic and increase their ability to make clients feel they are being personally attended to.

Geographically diverse markets are a specialization of some sites. The site www.LocalBusiness.com, for example, is a regional portal for business information. Users entering the site see a list of major U.S. cities. Clicking on a particular city causes regional business information about the city to appear, including press releases from local companies, local business news and financial information, and the like. Differentiating itself from local companies that may have distributed information nationally or internationally, the Local-Business.com portal is a brand attempting to build local recognition by providing regional business information. Unlike www.yahoo.com or www.msn.com, which compete with national and large regional newspapers and their Web sites, www.LocalBusiness.com competes with local papers and radio to provide information about a given area. Another company with a regional, geographic branding model, www.CitySearch.com, provides all types of information—for example, entertainment, such as restaurants, theater listings, and concert events—for a wide variety of communities.

Another twist on regional branding is the localization of a Web brand for an international community. For example, one of the first things some sites provide as an option for the surfer is to enter the country in which they are located, as on the Yahoo! main screen. Clicking on a country localizes the site, moving the surfer to information specific to the country and in the language of that country.

Each type of regional branding—local U.S. cities or countries around the world—poses specific problems that must be addressed in depth during the framework branding stage. For companies that intend to target individual markets or regions as a specific part of their business model—for example, www.CitySearch.com and www.LocalBusiness.com—the need to incorporate regional brand considerations into the framework stage is obvious, as well as the need to build in important accompanying attributes, such as an online infrastructure offering local advertising, news stories, and current listings like weather and stocks.

However, for the nonregional business model, vertical markets and various regions pose an interesting problem. What level of regional focus should a company have? How much is too much? How much allows the brand to seem more locally alive and personal? To what extent should a large, horizontal brand allow vertical markets to grow within its online realm? How much internationalization is necessary to reach target markets in various parts of the world, or audiences who speak different languages?

For example, www.att.com has to reach many people speaking many languages in the United States, and has gone to great lengths to localize information at www.att.com/global. As discussed in Chapter 2, after users choose a given language, they see information localized to them. For example, photographs taken from advertisements featured on television or in print in U.S. Korean communities and in Korea itself appear in the section localized to the Korean language; the site also lists rates for calling Korea.

AT&T has extensively mapped localized cultures and languages on its site—incurring substantial infrastructure-development costs but greatly benefiting from the availability of that localized information. Making the decision to build this type of site and its various components—and understanding that it is really all about building a Web brand, not just about increasing the number of minutes it's selling—takes place in the brand framework phase. This sets the stage so that the various more tactical elements of branding, such as naming, design, and tag-line development, can take place significantly more easily. This often means putting into place a phased approach, so companies can prioritize where they want to build localized brands over time. For instance, Germany is typically the non-U.S. market of most interest to U.S.-based business-to-business Internet brands, and therefore German is often the first language into which sites are localized.

Following are some of the considerations for vertical, horizontal, and regional issues that come up during the framework stage:

- Will the Web brand be horizontal, vertical, or regional?
- If horizontal, will it need to appeal to regional or vertical markets? Which ones?
- How can this placement be used as an advantage in terms of competitive differentiation?
- If vertical, what are the specific attributes of the vertical market?
- Are there legal issues in that market (for example, licensing issues, as with as pilots) which may have brand impact?
- As a vertical market, is it a business-to-business or business-to-consumer brand?
- How open will the site be to nonmembers of the vertical community?
- What horizontal and vertical Web and non-Web brands already target this market?
- What are the implications for building a site map and virtual campus? How large will it be? Can it be served by common facilities— for example, will any single set of ecommerce capabilities provide solutions for every region involved?
- What attributes of the market need to be expressed in the Web

brand—for example, any logos of organizations, designs/colors specific to that market, etc.?

- For international Web brands, what are the language, cultural, and infrastructure issues:
  - Will the site be localized into various languages? Which ones? In what time frame? What criteria are being used to prioritize the markets?
  - What cultural factors exist to be considered? For example, are particular colors and designs appropriate or inappropriate? Will certain images be a problem? What might be offensive to the target culture? Are there any political issues to be considered?
  - Will the tag line remain in English, or be translated?
  - What will the site be like in terms of infrastructure? Will the site be managed in various international regions by local Web masters and Web designers? What will need to be put into place to ensure they understand and extend the core brand messaging and strategy?
  - What business-to-business and business-to-consumer issues need to be taken into account? What about currencies? What about different stocks? How will those be represented?
  - Will people from other regions be able to use the site? For example, will a resident of Singapore be able to order clothing from the German site of a U.S.-based retail operation?

4

The Verbal Articulation Stage

Words to Live By

Who hath not own'd, with rapture smitten frame,
The power of grace, the magic of a name?
—Thomas Campbell, "The Pleasures of Hope," 1799[1]

The words describing a brand build upon its structure, sculpting its identity and defining its tone, personality, and character. Verbal articulation, whether content in a Web site or annual report, the name or tag line, or messaging in an ad or press release, often represents the first impression a brand makes. Of the five stages of developing brands both on and off the Web, verbal articulation is the linchpin connecting the structure and strategy of discovery and framework with the creativity and tactics of words, images, and execution.

Naming theories abound in brand-related texts and articles, frequently describing the phenomenon without mentioning the other structural, tactical, and creative stages of branding. This is analogous to describing the process of photography by explaining how to find a good image to shoot, but leaving out how to operate the camera, the basics of photography like lighting and exposure, the choice of equipment, and how to develop and process the film. Without planning what it will take to capture a picture and what to do with it after it is taken, a good photographic subject is nothing more than an idea.

Creatively finding the right subject is essential to good photography *and* good branding—but, with both, it's only one part of the process. The verbal articulation stage involves much more than naming, although naming is what most people think of when they hear the term "branding." Verbal elements of branding involve integrating the core message, brand strategy, personality traits, character attributes, brand hierarchy, and audience-specific messaging with names and tag lines.

Making Sense of Naming

Naming is both a hot news topic and a highly popular online pastime. *USA Today,* in its July 3–4, 2000 issue, featured as the top front-page story "What's in a Name? The Fading of Dot-Com." Services such as www.domaindiscover.com, www.register.com, www.spot.cc, www.registrars.com, www.ccnames.com, www.great domains.com, and other companies daily provide tens of thousands of name seekers access to domain names to register or buy.

It's been said that virtually every common word in the English language has been registered by someone, as well as thousands of phrases, foreign words, hybrid words (combinations of real words), and neologisms (made-up words, like "Acura") as a .com, .net, .cc, .org, or any of several other registration options. Stories abound about people missing million-dollar domains by a matter of hours, the legal world struggling to interpret new challenges to ownership, and Pacific-island nations basing future government revenue on name registrations using their countries' abbreviation as a suffix.

All the brand books emerging on the market today discuss naming at length, the New Economy periodicals such as Business 2.0 and eCompany write articles about it, and the topic has produced a gaggle of experts and consultants armed with a link to www.register.com and little else. Yet, while naming is certainly part of branding, branding doesn't equate to naming. Names help identify and characterize a brand, but a name is no more a brand than a person's name is that entire person—people have a personality, a set of behaviors, family relationships, and so on. Likewise, a brand name identifies the brand and serves as a way to direct a person to a company's product(s) or service(s) or to an organization's mission or initiative.

The right name can do a brand a great service, and the wrong name can do irreparable damage. For both existing and for new companies, being able to find the company or product quickly on the Web is an absolute requirement. Take "delta." The URL www.delta.com has been a real problem for many companies, and, for some, remains an issue. Until late in the summer of 2000, companies with "delta" in their names, a common-usage word for a primary name, struggled because entering www.delta.com into a search engine didn't yield Delta Airlines, Delta Faucets, or Delta Financial; instead it provided a redirect for several "Delta" companies, including those three. Which company had the clearest legal claim to the name? In fact, multiple companies with the same name can legally trademark the name as long as they are in distinctly different areas of business. According to records available in www.register.com, on July 20, 2000, Delta Airlines finally did purchase www.delta.com, which it now uses as its primary URL—at the expense of Delta Faucets, Delta Financial, and any other "delta" out there seeking to be found on the Web. A quick check of U.S. federal trademarks shows there are over 1200 actual, pending, or abandoned uses of the word "delta" in company names, products, and services. How can this be resolved so average Web surfers can find the "delta" they are looking for?

Trademarks *do*, as it turns out, count, and may be the legal tie-breakers for many corporations. In the September 5, 2000 issue of the *International Herald Tribune*, the story "Who Owns a Site Name? Round One Goes to Trademark Holders" appeared and stated "In the continuing battles between owners of trademarks and individuals with Internet domain addresses identical to them or nearly so, the trademark owners appear to be far ahead. Of 1000 cases that have gone before four approved arbitration boards including the World Intellectual Property Organization, three-quarters have been won by trademark owners."

This area is still incredibly immature in a legal sense, especially when it comes to arbitrating international issues, and it appears that international trademarking is a key factor in favor of the owner. Given the many various extensions both within countries and among them—the .com and .org in the United States, for example, versus the .co.uk in the United Kingdom and the .de in Germany, and so on—the more legal steps a company takes in the trademarking effort, the better. Unfortunately, international trademarking is an expensive proposition, and start-ups without the funds for trademarking in various countries around the world may find themselves embroiled in legal battles as they grow and extend their brands abroad. And the more generic the name, the bigger the problem. Common English words are *very* popular in site naming around the globe.

It's not simply a matter of one culture against another; the global naming legal problem has many angles. For example, Brian Livingston, famed author of the *Windows Secrets* series and columnist with CNET and *InfoWorld*, has written extensively about the various legal aspects of naming URLs, including the heated initiatives of ICANN (the Internet Corporation for Assigned Names and Numbers). In a July 2000 column Livingston wrote about this very topical issue and how some feel the "little guy" is being KO'd by big corporate interests in the name-acquisition arena. In his article, he states, "A new coalition says legitimate mom and pop businesses are losing their domain names to larger companies at an alarming rate." A watchdog for the naming business, Livingston has dedicated many columns and much personal effort to ensure that people are treated equally and fairly in naming issues on the Web (go to www.brianlivingston.com to reach many of his articles on the topic). For Web naming, however, it doesn't matter that companies with the same names are in different business areas: There can only be one www.delta.com, which means additional context must be added to aid surfers in finding the company they really want. To some extent, search engines provide this ability; they list the major organizations (such as Delta Airlines or Delta Faucets), but may not list lesser-known companies named Delta. That means the person looking for a "delta" company has to figure out how the name is used in the URL, because there is no common standard. Frequently the name is combined with a generic company product line; for example, the URL for Delta Faucets—www.deltafaucets.com. Delta Airlines can also be reached by typing any of the following:

www.delta-air.com
www.delta-airlines.com
www.deltaairlines.com

The official URL for the Delta Airlines site was, until recently, www.delta-air.com. But the airline could not, and still cannot, be reached at www.deltaair.com, which is a redirect to a site named www.sunfinder.com. Fortunately, that site provides a link to Delta Airlines. Delta Airlines, however, has virtually no legal means to take ownership of the www.deltaair.com site.

Clearly, it can be difficult and frustrating, even for firmly established global brands, to build identity if no consistency or standards exist for stating the brand. The only companies truly safe are those whose brands are names not in common usage which they have trademarked. Even these, however, are not protected from companies who buy URLs with slight spelling differences. For example, as of this writing, www.micro-soft.com is owned by three different people on two continents, and although Sunkist Growers, the orange company, owns www.sunkist.com, www.sunkist.org, and www.sunkist. net, any version of www.sun-kist was available for purchase. Conflicts like these create "brand noise" clutter, hindering prime clients and contacts from finding the products and services they are looking for, just as a slow Internet connection or interrupted cell connection would.

The value of a brand name's URL has become wildly inflated, with companies such as GreatDomains.com even listing a formula for calculating how much can be expected for selling a brand, likening it to the purchase of a diamond using the diamond-store method of rating the "four Cs: color, cut, clarity, and caret." GreatDomains.com evaluates a name on the basis of three Cs, instead of four—"characters (number of characters), commerce (appropriateness to the market), and .com" (does it have a .com extension?). There is even a valuation chart, ranging from nothing to millions of dollars. For more information, see www.greatdomains.com/domains/valuation. asp.

GreatDomains.com also offers an additional domain name appraisal service to help individuals or companies determine the value of a brand name (for a fee, of course—see the "Domain Name Appraisal" option on the GreatDomains.com home page). Services such as these continue to swell the ranks of "cybersquatters"—the thousands of hopeful and greedy name seekers lured by stories of multimillion-dollar name sales, grabbing up obscure words as fast as they can register them—affecting the Web like the 1849 Gold Rush affected California (and often with equal disappointment).

With all real-word names taken—either by cybersquatters or by those actually using or intending to use their name(s) in real Web sites—it becomes even more essential to have a logical, methodical process of brand development. Should the name be descriptive? Should it be a radical hybrid? (The change of www.computerliteracy. com to www.fatbrain.com was one of the most notable and radical early name changes in Web history; it succeeded in taking the online bookseller to new levels of visibility and success, but also led a virtual stream of "wanna-be" companies to come up with meaningless word combinations.)

The process of naming involves much more than simply finding an available URL or blowing a lot of cash (sometimes huge quantities of cash) to acquire one. Just because the naming of www.phone.com (now openwave.com since the merger with Software.com) turned out to be a highly successful telecommunications business play doesn't mean that every company should come up with a completely descriptive name, nor does it guarantee that the right clients will find the right vendor online. There is no magic formula for ensuring that the right name will be found in a single step. Some books and articles suggest that a completely descriptive name is a death knell; others, that it is a boon. Both generalizations are false. There is no substitute for engaging an organization's executive and marketing teams in an analytical and methodical naming process. Any naming theory is just that—a theory—and could be used to argue for or against any given name.

No aspect of building a brand, including naming, is simple. Nobody writes a business plan haphazardly, without planning, and nobody develops products or services that way, either. If companies treated online transactions the way they often come up with the names to describe the services offered, not a soul on Earth would trust his or her credit card number to them. Brand development is not a game, and it can't be relegated to a creative team kept at arm's length or beyond. It is a mission-critical task which can never be too high level and which has a fundamental bearing on a company's success or failure.

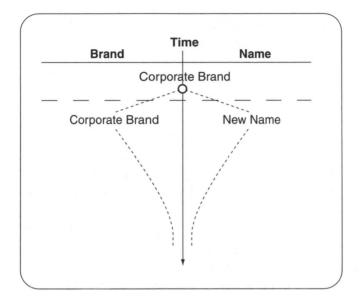

FIGURE 4.1. When a new name is introduced, it takes time for the brand and the name to once again become "one." At first, the name has little real integration with the brand; with proper branding methodology, the two begin to converge and, hopefully, become seamlessly connected.

Even after a well-managed process, new names are often uncomfortable, and launching them may require deep-seated acts of faith. Therefore, the verbal articulation stage deserves the methodical, undivided attention of the best thinkers in the organization, for the direct benefit of the target audiences. It takes time after a new corporate name is introduced for the brand identity and the name to become one again (see Figure 4.1).

General Name Development Tenets

Are there any "key truths" in name development, especially in a New Economy context? Ponder these brand development notions:

- As important as knowing what will work is understanding what *won't* work.

- Both "me-too" and individuality can be right—the key is under-standing the difference and what's best for individual circum-stances.
- Borrowing equity characteristics from already established brands can be highly opportunistic.
- The comparative process is vital: Shop around for various naming options in order to better understand the *ultimate* option.
- On occasion, being different involves being more of the same, and sometimes being more of the same is the best opportunity.
- Simple is sometimes diverse; diverse is sometimes simplistic.

Naming a product, service, or company is likely to yield mediocre results if the process becomes too bureaucratic and fails to allow creativity to shine through. More than one brand has missed a great name because a kind-hearted, benevolent CEO, with the best of in-tentions, involved too many people in the naming and branding ef-forts, resulting in "management by committee" results. While crea-tivity is of course necessary, overly creative and less tangible efforts lacking business acumen and methodology produce a wide, volu-minous, and often unmanageable range of opinions, which can delay and obstruct a qualified branding process.

As it is, new names and brand definitions are emotionally charged issues for employees. When existing company names are about to be changed, its not uncommon for there to be threats of resignation, angry letters and comments to management, and disruptions to the work environment. Board members, in particular, can be tremen-dously vocal in their opinions about naming; even if they are not qualified to judge and there is no real justification for their opinions, their opposition can nonetheless have potentially devastating effects on the emergence of a promising new brand identity.

It takes a strong CEO to stand behind a brand decision in front of board members, clients, partners, shareholders, and employees, and it is especially difficult if a name or other visible part of the brand (a logo, for instance) has been developed without a defensible process. Equipped with the tools and structure of a strong method, however, the CEO can offer reason and logic combined with crea-tivity to present a compelling brand story and conclusion. Presen-tation of a brand strategy and its results, just like the presentation of a sales, financial, or product strategy, is best received when it's clear the strategy was developed thoughtfully and thoroughly.

Elements of Verbal Articulation

Words in many forms express the brand. Articulating the brand in verbal form requires a high degree of consistent communication across many styles of writing, appearing in many venues. It is here that the efforts in discovery and framework stages begin to take form and bear fruit in content and creativity.

The many forms of writing must encapsulate the core messaging of the company and the brand, as well as the targeted messaging for the specific audience and venue each form is addressing. A primary challenge for brand management, marketing, and corporate communication is to ensure consistency—across all communications, in all languages, in all possible iterations. Each of these, however, presents its own challenge.

Web Content

The Web content often poses the greatest challenge, simply because it will have the largest quantity of text, and in the broadest variety of forms, in one place. Press releases, ad copy, white papers, sales materials, presentations, and corporate history will all be within one or two clicks of the other. Blatant disparities and differences are frequently much more obvious on the Web than they are anywhere else.

Advertising Copy

Ads are frequently short on information and long on message and branding; as a result, attention must be paid to tone and to first impressions. People reading ads in magazines, drivers looking at billboards on the road, and Net surfers seeing ad banners on Web sites don't linger for long on the message, so it is essential to portray the brand quickly and accurately. Today, directing people to the Web site where more substantive information is available is often the primary purpose of an ad.

Collateral Materials

Much information is available on the Web today, and it can be changed daily. Printed materials, however, stay in print; they are "out there" as long as anyone keeps them. As a result, the information in printed collateral materials—whether a brochure or a company pro-file—has to be able to withstand the test of time and so must be more generic. These materials should lead readers to the Web site for information that is changed frequently—for example, pricing, product updates, individuals' names, etc.

Naming of Products, Services, and the Company Itself

Coming up with a name for anything in the company with significant exposure must be in tune with the core brand strategy, personality, and characteristics.

The Tag Line

Tag lines serve as a segue between the name and the message, and provide a way for anyone encountering the brand to more easily understand the company and its components. It must lead people closer to the message and to the essence of the brand.

Press Releases

Communications to the media must provide more than topical news and information. They are an opportunity to position the company and reemphasize the brand strategy and core messaging. Both press and nonpress often turn to the company boilerplate at the end of a press release as a primary source of information about a company, and press releases are often a quick, concise, and (usually) clear way to give media and industry analysts (such as Gartner, Forrester, Zona Research, and IDC) basic but high-level information about the company.

White Papers

Whether they're written for marketing or technical audiences, white papers provide detailed, in-depth information about the company and its offerings. However, white papers that do not express brand positioning that is in line with the core brand steer readers away from what the company really does. Each white paper is a fresh opportunity to educate highly interested and intelligent readers about the brand, competitive differentiation, and company strategy.

Annual Reports

Annual reports are frequently the most comprehensive source of information about a company, going beyond the legal requirements to give customers, investors, employees, media, and analysts a tangible, physical manifestation of the brand. As such, it is crucial that they be closely synchronized with the Web site, verbally as well as visually.

Direct Mail

Direct-mail promotional literature has declined with the advent of the New Economy and Internet capabilities to communicate quickly and easily. However, for many industries, direct mail still stands as a viable form of communication—especially for customers who are, perhaps, not strongly connected to the Web or who may need prompting to look at the Web site for information.

Presentations

It isn't uncommon for presentations to be left out of the library of literature and information managed and scrutinized by marketing and branding professionals, if for no other reason than the fact that presentations are often prepared in the last few days before they are given. However, ongoing sales, marketing, and corporate presentations can benefit greatly if standardized branding guidelines, including primary brand points essential to incorporate corporate messaging, and the proper and improper ways to express the brand(s), are provided to presenters ahead of time.

Naming: Branding's Outspoken Offspring

Naming is a significant part of the verbal articulation stage, a highly noticeable and emotionally charged part of the brand process. As a result, it often gets the most attention and the highest amount of discussion and debate. Changing names is often a *really* big issue, and it's rare when a company knows for certain that it needs a new name. It takes a *truly* bad name (and even those are debatable), or, more frequently, a threatening lawsuit from another company with a similar name (for example, two technology companies battling over use of the name "Platinum") for an organization to unilaterally acknowledge the need for name change.

Frequently, companies with mature parent brands face the question, "Should we change or alter our existing corporate name or our dominant subbrand since we've changed courses in either philosophy or product/service offerings?" While each situation is case-specific, often one of several very predictable categories of corporate reasoning drives the issue:

1. A new management leader or team doesn't appreciate the brand history and thinks it's dated or nonapplicable to current aggressive growth objectives.

2. "Brand noise" is becoming a corporate distraction, with audiences taking a brand for granted and failing to appreciate real new claims to glory, for example, technical advances made through R&D.
3. The brand message is becoming overshadowed by a dominant competitor or even another subbrand within the corporate stable of brands.

Handling these types of situations requires a clear understanding of the existing brand's *believability factors*. Will audiences be likely to trust a specific extension claim made from the brand, and what ancillary communication methods could be used to enhance that trust? Depending on the circumstances, the decision may be made to stick with the name-changing course or (and this is often more prudent) to stay with the current naming course and utilize complementary messaging as reinforcement of a growing corporate or dominant brand.

In the case of Software 2000, which became Infinium, and Traveling Software, which became LapLink, the dominant subbrands were promoted to corporate status. Other situations may call for an entirely fresh, unique naming convention, as in the case of Platinum Software, which became Epicor Software.

Platinum Software, based in Irvine, California, faced a unique situation. It had registered the trademark Platinum with the U.S. Patent Office, but it did not own the URL; that was owned by Platinum Technology in Chicago, which had simply been quicker to the draw in claiming the domain. As with "delta," a common word had been used in several arenas. Platinum Software decided to change names, but only after conducting detailed market research among its audiences to garner competitive perceptions of leadership, quality of product and service, and specific preference rankings across many intent-to-purchase criteria.

What did it find? There was indeed an opportunity to introduce a new, invigorated promise, one that clearly proclaimed leadership and centralized service, in the crowded midmarket enterprise resource planning space. This was the beginning of the transformation to the Epicor name and the simultaneous solution to the domain issue with Platinum Technology.

Name Changes at the Customers' Expense

A name change can be expensive—not only in terms of the cost of the branding effort and the accompanying "collateral" costs to marketing and business materials, signage, trucks, Web sites, and so on—but also in terms of the confusion it can cause customers, leading to a loss of credibility. Perhaps the most uncontrollable type of name change, and the one that entails the greatest risk of lost business, is that resulting from a corporate merger. Here are but a few of the reasons customers may hightail it when a merger takes place:

- They had a bad experience with one of the companies, so don't want to deal with the new combined one.
- They are confused by the new name or don't like it.
- They don't like larger corporations, assuming (often correctly) that service and support will diminish in quality.
- The emotional appeal of the previous organization is diluted or lost.
- The new organization does a bad job of transitioning customers.
- The new company ineffectively educates employees about the name change: why it (or the merger) occurred, how to articulate the new name and change.
- The brand team fails to follow through on a method and process beyond simply delivering a new name.
- The new company fails to communicate clearly why "bigger is now better," linking the larger size with bigger benefits.
- The new brand is not integrated cohesively with popular sub-brands, which remain after the merger.

Shackled by Its Legacy

When Price Waterhouse and Coopers & Lybrand merged in July 1998 into PricewaterhouseCoopers, not only was the resulting name long and clunky, but lack of agreement in the branding "process" failed to yield a consistent identity between verbal and visual elements. The www.PricewaterhouseCoopers.com site contains a logo, which, unfortunately, is difficult to read on a conventional screen (perhaps by design!). However, the difference between the logo and the name is significant, because the companies could not agree on which name came first. Consequently, the logo lettering is "PCW" when the verbally stated name is in a different order. Petty? Absolutely. Confusing? Possibly. The impression left with customers who notice it? "I hope they aren't treating my business with as much confusion, disagreement, and lack of process."

To compound the problem, the primary URL for the company is www.pwcglobal.com, although www.pricewaterhouse.com and www.pricewaterhousecoopers.com both also pull the home page. However, www.coopers.com yields a simple and plain redirect to www.pwcglobal.com, but, curiously, not the home page (if they have the URL, why not make it a prime redirect?). The site www.waterhouse.com belongs to an entirely different company, a brokerage house called TD Waterhouse; www.pcw.com is an inactive site owned by an individual; and www.pwc.com is the Navy Public Works Center in Norfolk, Virginia. The existence of these other Web sites, combined with the PCW/PWC snarl, adds up to real confusion, especially for the person trying to remember the URL.

In cases such as these, often the best solution is to create a new name to serve as a parent or umbrella brand, and to at least consider using the legacy names as subbrands. Instead, the new company seems to have figured that PriceWaterhouse and Coopers & Lybrand were two such well-established, old, and recognized brands that the new name had to incorporate at least 75 percent of the original four. For the new organization to come up with a unique, short, and memorable brand name, one that fitted within parameters established during a strong branding process, would have been initially painful, but ultimately such a name would have been much more useful and accessible. Of course, the new name would have been validated in the discovery and framework stages as part of a broader branding process. In the PriceWaterhouse/Coopers & Lybrand case, it seems unlikely that a real branding process took place, because the resulting name is so awkward and difficult to use, especially for a company attempting to build a strong business-to-business Internet brand and be a leadership business model in the New Economy. The press release announcing the new company in 1998 only stated the new name, saying nothing about its meaning or where "Lybrand" went, and not making any reference to branding. In an FAQ released that same day, the following statement appeared:

> Our external advisors confirmed our belief that it was critically important to preserve the substantial equity and value associated with the names Price Waterhouse and Coopers & Lybrand. In choosing a name, we sought to harness the vast reservoir of reputation and trust that both organizations had established over more than a century of client service. At the same time, we wanted to signal that we are creating something new and exciting out of that great heritage. Our new name and its visual presentation communicate the combination of an enormously successful past and a breakaway future.[2]

The name does preserve the equity of the Price, Waterhouse, and Coopers names, but "Waterhouse," without even the distinction of beginning with a capital letter, is buried in the middle and Lybrand has disappeared altogether. Further, this too-long and awkward name offers nothing new, breakaway, or exciting. It simply sounds like lawyers got hold of it and wouldn't let go.

Companies often begin the brand development process because they want a name, but a naming issue may only be indicative of a deeper branding problem in the company. It's like a couple going to see a marriage counselor because their frequency of intimacy is waning, when really more significant problems lie beneath.

Sometimes a new marketing VP or other executive will decide that the "name has to be changed," as in the case of Computerliteracy.com. The new marketing VP was convinced the name wasn't right for the third-largest online bookseller. The president felt the name was good but conceded after market research yielded strong, painful, and unilateral data showing that the name was, indeed, not the best: not only did it not mean "books for sale online," it wasn't memorable, either. After an extensive naming process, the name Fatbrain.com was chosen for the company, and market research later showed that "fatbrain" was more memorable than almost any other name researchers had encountered before. The name subsequently had to withstand a hailstorm of controversy, primarily internal; however, when the name launched, the company enjoyed huge, instant growth in its ability to reach customers (Fatbrain has since been purchased by Barnes & Noble).

Blue with Envy?

When does a once-creative name begin to be overused? Blue, for example, has become a very popular word in the names of companies, products, and technologies:

Blue Martini Software	Customer interaction software
Blue Pumpkin Software	Workforce management software
Bluetooth	Wireless connectivity technology
Bluestone	Enterprise interaction/management tools
Blue Mountain	Electronic greeting cards
Blue Monkey Enterprises	Web site hosting and maintenance
Bluestream	Database software
Bluebox	Convergence software
Blue Moon Software	Forms processing software
Bluetrain	Communication and collaboration applications
Bluestreak	Interactive marketing technology and services
Blue Nile	Online diamond retailer

With such a proliferation of "blue" names, the question arises whether using a generic color as a competitive point of brand differentiation really works.

Sometimes names have been created for companies as placeholders or for convenience until marketing becomes a viable business issue. The CEO, the executive team, and the entire company know the company name will be changed and really cannot wait for it to happen. Other companies create a name as a placeholder and it sticks. Scale Eight is just such a company. The San Francisco–based Internet company, which provides petabytes and terabytes of data access and storage for large files such as film, video, and music, began as the vision of founder Josh Coates to "provide the first Internet storage infrastructure service that is massively scalable, allowing companies that create, manage, and deliver rich media to focus on their core competencies."[3] The company went through a branding exercise at the behest of a new marketing VP, Wendi Norris, who was just as ready to validate the existing name as to look for a new one.

After mounting an extensive companywide effort, spearheaded by the executive team, to establish the characteristics and personality traits of the corporate brand, talking with customers, press, and analysts, and going through extensive branding sessions with creative and branding agencies, Scale Eight decided to keep its original name. It meant scalability, it meant eight bits to the byte, it meant the number 8's relationship to the infinity symbol. It was, overall, a memorable, unique name. Further, after going through the brand validation process, the company knew—not just guessed—that the name worked as a strong reflection of the core brand.

The Naming Method

The topic of name development can easily fill a book, and a simple section of a chapter hardly does it justice. So many issues surround naming. Should a name be descriptive? When should it be changed? What is the right name for a given brand? How can anyone intelligently and methodically sift through the thousands of available names to come up with a manageable selection from which to choose the right one?

The New Economy, especially, catapulted the naming issue into mainstream awareness; perhaps it should have been called the "Naming Economy." Often wacky and seemingly nonsensical dotcom names had the Internet community abuzz about naming and what it meant. Web surfers went home at night, logged in to www.register. com, and invented every possible letter combination they could imagine in hopes of finding the name that would make them rich. Today, companies perplexed about what their name should be both offline and online hire branding experts to help them make the right decision. New implications about international naming and trademarking provide new opportunities for attorneys to build their businesses. It seems that every existing name is being called into question, and that virtually any pronounceable combination of words is fair game. The days of the acronym have passed suddenly, with only the most stalwart acronym brands remaining: IBM, NEC, NBC, and BBC. In fact, the most common consumer acronyms, radio and TV station call letters, are also falling by the wayside, with stations and syndicates giving themselves names such as "The Wave," "The Buzz," and "Fox."

"Veronica," for example, is still the name of a popular radio station in the Netherlands, which began in the 1960s as a "pirate" station, located on a ship outside the country's legal limits in the North Sea. At that time it was illegal to broadcast rock-and-roll music from within the country, so the ship stayed out at sea but close enough that a line-of-sight FM frequency could still reach major metropolitan areas.

Since the ship wasn't held accountable to the government, it could choose any frequency it liked and call itself anything—hence the name "Veronica." It also solicited advertisers within the country and distributed its play lists and flyers in the on-shore record shops. Today, years after Veronica was allowed to move into the country, the name has not changed. As a result, the station is far ahead of its radio competitors in brand attachment and identity, and far more memorable for those looking for the station online. In fact, the radio station is now a mere portion of a popular entertainment portal, www.veronica.nl, which offers everything from music and film to sports and shopping, and is also a major television station.

Thoughts on New and Extended Web Names

The Web uniquely provides primary and positive audience factors of personalization and directness, which play well alongside quickly recognizable brands such as business.com. The Web also provides a good opportunity to use generic names, since these can't be trademarked without the dotcom—at least for now—in the offline world.

What's the future for generic Web names, as opposed to individualized and stylish names like Kozmo.com, Gomez.com, and Beenz.com? A transition from dotcom dependency will ultimately need to occur (for many brands, it already has), but the established equity and audience acceptance in the oh-so-noisy Web make the choice of a generic name a good, if not completely strong, branding strategy. Those echoing the legacy line that generic names have no place in Web branding are displaying a lack of depth in understanding the ability of Web marketing to speak directly to individual audience members and encourage a consistent relationship with them. Generic names actually do this well, and with the dotcom suffixes, they can be associated with progressive deliverability. Eventually, generic names will no longer seem progressive, and companies with brand foresight will deploy a transitional plan to take them beyond the dotcom.

As important an issue as naming is today, however, it remains an elusive creature to everyone from executives to New Economy pundits and journalists. In spite of the frequent appearance of articles with titles like "Net Economy Branding," "The Making of a Dotcom," "The Dotcom Crash," and "Bricks-and-Mortar versus the New Economy," the information available is remarkably unhelpful when it comes to real understanding and information about brand development and naming. Most of the articles and even books consist primarily of case studies and offer little or no interpretation.[4] A significant reason for this knowledge gap is the lack of solid understanding of what a brand is and how it is created, and how naming fits into the branding process. In fact, although naming is part of the overall brand development process, effective naming is a process in and of itself. It draws directly on the information provided from the previous framework and discovery stages, and feeds directly into the visual articulation and execution stages.

It is positioned in this order for two simple reasons:

1. A name cannot be created effectively until a framework and structure exist, based on intelligent market and situation analysis.
2. Design, launch, and content cannot be developed until the new name—or a validated existing one—is established.

For product names, the process isn't quite as elaborate or involved, if for no other reason than that the legal issues are less complex (e.g., multiple products in noncompeting industries can have the same product names, but corporate names need to be differentiated). Also, sometimes, but not always, owning a unique URL is not essential. (Obviously, for house-of-brands companies like Kimberly-Clark, having URLs for the products is a much bigger issue.)

Without a subprocess for naming, clients may not even come to the realization that they need a name when, in fact, it could be the best thing for them. Further, without a process yielding checklists of attributes and personality factors, winnowing the myriad name possibilities gets to be like choosing a perfume: After a while they all begin to smell the same.

Widevine Technologies

iDirectMedia was the prelaunch, stealth-mode name of a Seattle-based provider of "streaming security" technology—infrastructure optimized for providing easily encrypted and de-encrypted broadband data transfer. The company worked with the Garrigan Lyman Group to create a messaging platform and communication strategy prior to the launch of its first product, after which the firm was able to apply verbal and visual articulation methodology to create a new corporate name and logo. The name chosen was Widevine Technologies. In addition to being much more memorable and interesting than iDirectMedia, the new name allowed the company to realign its brand with its technology and business plans, especially in the context of the emerging and highly dynamic broadband market. Furthermore, it resulted in streamlined messaging: The first new product was called the Widevine Cypher. The parallel introduction of a new company with a revolutionary product greatly benefited both, and the connection between them was crystal-clear. Finally, the new tag line for Widevine Technologies—"Technology Solutions for Streaming Media—provided a descriptive segue to the message in company communications.

Typically, the verbal articulation process, which follows the framework stage, involves multiple sessions of naming tasks. It can take several weeks to several months, depending upon the availability of the critical decision makers, the complexity of the task, and the availability of the names. If, for example, the company decides it wants to purchase a URL from another company or a cybersquatter, the process can be held up while the name goes into escrow and the legal exchanges take place. (For 360.com, for example, purchasing the URL from a company in Korea added several weeks to the final naming process.)

Naming is more a process of selection than a process of elimination, an essential point of competitive differentiation, and a process resulting specifically from having built a strong framework and strategic foundation. Simply eliminating names from a list without structure or reason focuses on what names are not liked rather than what names are liked, and the attributes of the discarded names (which may be very useful) often get thrown out as well. Method-driven naming, conversely, focuses on choosing words and word parts which meet carefully predefined criteria, creating a virtual "reduction" (in culinary terms) of words, all of which work well with an already well-defined brand.

A surprising beginning to the brand process for many "names" is that the first naming list presented by the brand team contains few or no names that could become the actual final name, nor does it list available URLs. Like a minidiscovery session, the list is meant to ascertain the group's level of interest in various name and name parts and to ensure that the group is in line with the brand character attributes and personality traits established in the framework stage and outlined in the brand-mapping exercise. Often a CEO or other executive will dislike a name at first sight, but will warm up to it when he or she realizes it absolutely fits the preestablished criteria. Similarly, visually enhancing a name in various ways—font treatments, for example—can radically affect the way a name is perceived.

Naming can be divided into two broad categories: naming corporations or organizations and naming products or services. While there are similarities between the two, there are also points of divergence. Further, from a bricks-to-clicks standpoint—building brands on the Web—the two processes have different roles to play. The process of naming companies and organizations is the most complex, permanent, and noticeable.

The Naming Process

Following the framework sessions, and assuming that a strong brand map, personality traits, and character attributes have been clearly identified, the naming process begins in earnest. The process takes place with the primary name—often the corporate name or a primary product—before any subbrands are addressed. A number of issues must be considered at the outset:

- *Is there an existing company name?* The difference between starting from scratch and working with an existing name is substantive.
- *What is the time line?* This can have a direct effect on how many names can be reviewed, as well as how frequently a team must convene.
- *Is there broad acknowledgment that a new name is necessary?* Reservations within a company about the need for a new name should be identified early in the process and dealt with directly, so subsequent efforts won't be undermined by a "benchmark name" factor.
- *What obstacles exist in naming?* For example, is there an emotional attachment to the existing name? If the old name was created by a family member of the CEO, or, perhaps, *is* the CEO's name, and if the CEO has not agreed completely that a new name is warranted, trying to find a new name can be an uphill battle.
- *Is the company willing to spend any money on purchasing a name?* What is the most it will spend?
- *What historical name issues/factors need to be taken into consideration?* The process of creating a new name, while moving the company forward, must yield results that effectively acknowledge the past and communicate existing brand equity when the name change occurs. Often this is accomplished through tag lines (see below), but sometimes through the new name itself. For example, in Cobos Group, the new name for HR Resources, Cobos is the name of the founder, which is highly meaningful for those who know the company. In contrast, names such as PricewaterhouseCoopers result from a driving need to leverage the past at the expense of the future and of users' ease of access.

- *Is the existing name already an owned URL?* How good is the URL, and what is its equity? New names will need to have the old URL as a redirect, at least, to ensure seamless migration to the new name.

The First Naming Session

The issues listed above are addressed and firmly established both prior to and during the first naming session. It is imperative to get the team on the same wavelength in the first naming meeting, especially if the team involved is different from the team that participated in the framework and discovery stages. Once established, the team is presented with a preliminary list of 50 to 100 names. As mentioned earlier in the chapter, this list usually doesn't include readily available URLs or trademarks. Many of the names meet the criteria established in the framework stage, but are meant to get the team to express areas of interest, disinterest, like, and dislike. A session like this typically shouldn't go more than two hours; after that, effectiveness begins to decline. However, at the end of the session, the people driving the session need to have a reasonably good idea as to the styles of names to include in the next session.

There are virtually limitless points to consider in the first session, but several are notable. Discuss each name, one by one, probing various issues:

What parts of the name are good or bad? For example, "dungaree" could be construed negatively if the word part "dung" is reminiscent of "manure"—although the overall word might sound acceptable.
- Is there a particular prefix that sounds good, such as "ara" or "max" or "cent"?
- Likewise, is there a particular suffix that sounds good such as "ent," "ar," or "ava"?
- What about the "infix"—the center part of the word—for example, "iza" or "era"?
- Are there specific letters to avoid, such as X, Q, or Z?

- What about single-letter prefixes—highly popular and over-used in Web naming—such as "e" or "i" (in names like e-biz or i-solution) to be considered or are they taboo?

Will the name of the company be a dotcom—not just as a URL but as the offline name as well? The trend is definitely to move *away* from having a dotcom company name because such names have fundamental limitations for long-range business and brand identity. This has a strong effect on how the name of the company will sound.

How long can the name be? Typically, shorter is better unless the word is highly memorable and happens to be long, like www.singaporeair.com or www.mercedesbenz.com. A limit can be set at the beginning of the naming session, such as the name cannot be longer than seven characters, or, even better, five. This has value especially for more abstract, neologistic names that will need to be easily remembered and spelled.

Does the name evoke certain good or bad meanings?
- For example, does it sound too foreign, or not international enough?
- Does it sound like another word that may or may not have desirable associations? Sometimes a word may sound too much like a car or a drug, or like something from witchcraft. Conversely, it may sound like a beautiful flower or plant, or it may simply sound positive and upbeat.

Is one style—for example, Latinate words or names that sound like a constellation—more interesting than another? Is it important to have words that mean something, such as business or genetics, as part of the name?

What issues may have been missed in the discovery and framework stages? For example, does one of the names sound like that of a competitor's product line?

During the first session, then, the emphasis is not on coming up with the perfect name. Sometimes the name will be there, but at the end of the meeting it won't be obvious. If the brand team's objective has been properly executed and met, the result will be a keen sense of how the first list of actually available names will look. "Actually available" means the URL is clear, the name adheres to the standards established, the trademark is legally available—or at least seems to be (lawyers will get involved later)—and the name isn't stepping on any competitive toes.

Some branding firms rely on name-generation software that spews out literally thousands of words and names that may or may not be available. Having numerous options for a name is great, but sorting through thousands of options—without a clear process of refinement readily available—is a huge task. What's the right number? No more than the group can reasonably analyze or at least categorize in a two-hour session—usually no more than 100, at the most.

Paradoxically, the best names are still "homemade," created by a savvy and experienced brand team and not generated randomly by a software application. Sometimes branding teams will use software to generate ideas and to augment creativity, but relying solely on software to do the job—at least at this stage in the development of intelligent software applications—is akin to trusting language translation software to catch the subtle nuances of a personal letter.

An interesting Web site to use as part of the naming exercise, and one that also helps illustrate the inherent difficulties in using only software *sans* process, is www.naming.net, owned by WriteExpress Corporation (www.writeexpress.com). The company was started by a programmer from WordPerfect Corporation (WordPerfect is now owned by Corel Corporation in Canada), Robert Stevens, and a professor from Brigham Young University named Melvin Luthy. The site, which is definitely worth a look, lets users enter a few choices about a desired type of name, word parts with which to combine it (various prefixes and suffixes, rhyming parts, Latin and Greek word parts, etc.), and syllables. The site even offers the ability to add a .com, .net, or other Internet extension to see how the words will look.

Naming.net also offers free naming advice, including "Ten Questions to Keep in Mind When Naming"[5] along with detailed explanations for each. The list is a worthy synopsis of naming considerations:

• Who are my consumers?
• What am I naming?

- What type of a name do I want?
- How long should the name be?
- Do the sounds in the name have the right appeal?
- What associations should the name evoke?
- What are the foreign language implications of the name?
- How should I test the name?
- How will the name appear in directories?
- Can I trademark the name?

The Second Naming Session: Real Possibilities

Anywhere from a few days to a week should elapse between the first session and the second; this gives the team a chance to process all the information from the first session and to generate an appropriate first list of "real" names. Prior to the session, the team assembles the list of new names to be presented and discusses each at length: what the name may imply, how it will be interpreted, how it will be pronounced, how it sounds with other brand and product names, how it sounds as a partner name, how it might look as a design (although that is *very* premature at this stage), and how it might look on a press release or a Web site. The naming team must be able to rationalize each choice for the executive team. Consider the analysis of a word like "enzata" as part of a branding session; an analysis like the following would have been prepared by the brand team before getting the executive team together:

The name "enzata" has a Latin-sounding quality; it could be reminiscent of an Italian city or a Mexican resort; it also is a frequently used French connective. The "en" suffix is used in many positive-sounding or strong words or phrases, such as "ensemble," "energize," and "en masse." The "Z" is an unusual letter and will stand out as memorable; however, to have this name as a corporate brand name, it would be important to also own "ensata," if possible, to help anyone who misspells it to be redirected to the site. It might be good to also own "inzata" and "insata," if possible. The word also has the advantage of being short and memorable, and really it isn't too difficult to spell. As a URL it is unique, and it has a big-company sound: "We just partnered with Enzata" sounds good. It's somewhat of a progressive name on the conservative-to-progressive continuum, but not too progressive; it's actually closer to midrange between the two. It is, however, abstract, rather than descriptive, and has no specific meaning. As a result, it will be important to use a descriptive tag line—at least until it becomes an established brand name and recognized in the market—to enable customers and others to quickly identify it.

This type of descriptive analysis is done for each word that, presumably, fits the criteria established in the framework stage and is thus a viable candidate.

In the second session, the group is presented with a list of names, all of which are available URLs and strong trademark candidates (or potentially available for purchase or, in some cases, acquisition). The list, typically around 50 to 75 words, is presented with about 10 words to a page, leaving lots of room for making notes and comments.

For several hours, the team rolls up its sleeves and goes through the words one by one, identifying keepers and throwaways. Be warned, however. Sometimes a gem that ultimately becomes the final choice is tossed out at this session. Why? Often the best name is moderately to highly uncomfortable for the team, if for no other reason than it's human nature to look for something safe, and a name that is similar to an existing name may seem safe while an unfamiliar name may not. When companies have an existing name—even if the name is acknowledged to be a placeholder and the team knows it needs something more abstract or progressive—it often takes an emotional effort to warm up to a different name. From a name like "Smith Developers," a team would be much more likely—at least at first—to jump on a name like "panalogics" than it would "enzata."

According to Sir Isaac Newton, stationary objects tend to remain stationary until moved by a significant force. And make no mistake: It takes a significant force to get a company to a new level of brand identity and awareness. Further, change is uncomfortable, even painful. The brand team has to be able to push the team past the level of comfort and appeal to a sense of process and logic. Even though the brand must ultimately generate emotion, at this stage the team must go beyond emotion.

Take "panalogics" versus "enzata." (This example is adapted from a real case. "Smith Development" and "enzata" are not the actual names, but "panalogics" *was* the alternative with which the board and executives at first felt significantly more comfortable.) "Panalogics" is a much safer-sounding technology name, with a twentieth-century-corporate sound to it. But it has no pizzazz; it is not memorable (there are numerous "pana" and "logics" names, many of which sound similar), and there's nothing New Economy about it. The name simply doesn't stand out. Furthermore, being able to surround the name with available URLs would be nothing short of impossible.

It's not hard to see, however, how a team might find it difficult to get from "Smith Development" to "enzata" right away, especially during the analysis of the first list of available names. Enzata is a huge leap from the existing name, and while it might completely fit the logically established criteria, when a team actually sees name candidates, emotions kick in and the proverbial turtle recedes into its shell. It is at points like this that the brand team can succeed or fail. More than one branding project has completely fallen apart because it inappropriately pushed too progressive a name at this juncture, or simply went along with the inclination of the group to "stay safe" and keep a less-than-interesting new name. In the case of the too-progressive name, the executive team may feel it's being railroaded into accepting a new name which it really doesn't want. With the "safe" name, the executive team may conclude that the boring candidate isn't much, if any, better than the previous name—so why go to the trouble?

The brand team needs to stay calm and move through the list, not making any recommendations at this point—simply facilitating and aiding analysis. It may very well have developed some strong ideas about good name candidates, but at this point it's better to keep quiet and let the process work.

Nothing spectacular happens at the second naming session, and the executive team is told that at least one, and preferably two, more lists of completely available and new words will be presented. Yet it's critical to go through these stages because it's the only way the team can develop a sufficiently strong perspective on the types and range of words that might ultimately become the new brand name.

Sessions Three and Four: More of the Same

At the third and fourth naming sessions, while subsequent name lists are increasingly fine-tuned based on what's been learned in previous sessions, the procedure is similar to what takes place in the first and second meetings. It is sometimes helpful during these meetings, as the team becomes craftier and more adept at the naming process, to have a live Internet connection in the room with www.register.com online to explore name possibilities that may be related to the words being explored. Names that are found online may or may not be available, and the consideration of whether it is feasible to purchase a potentially good name can be investigated by the team between sessions.

During these sessions the team will find itself increasingly pressured to choose a name, but it's up to the brand team to keep moving forward. It will become readily apparent which names hold interest and which do not. It's very important to have a person dedicated to keeping track of the name choices and remarks in one central list. It is virtually impossible to go back and mark the names by memory.

The names in the third- and fourth-session lists need to integrate information from each previous list, but the names will increasingly reflect the types and styles of names that the earlier sessions have identified. If, for example, the team has indicated a preference for "zata"-type names, there should be numerous names on the list with "zata" as a suffix, prefix, and infix. It may be that while going over subsequent lists, one or more of the combinations will be immediately liked—or disliked.

At the end of each session, anywhere from 5 to 10 names should be tagged and carried forward to a more final list, which will appear in a fifth session. The fourth session tends to become quite tedious, and participants may even become restless and wish the process would move forward more quickly. This is normal, and indicates that the sessions have actually been very productive. When a team feels it has exhausted numerous angles and word types, the results are ultimately a great aid to the executive team, because its members can stand behind a chosen name with the confidence that all possibilities have been fully explored.

The Fifth Naming Session: Refining the List of Finalists

At this point, the team is usually highly charged because it's looking at the cream of the crop: the names it has chosen from the various lists as the strongest candidates. It also may feel that there isn't a single name on the entire list that could work. This is a normal re-action after winnowing through so many names; in a way, the team has been desensitized, like the cook who isn't very interested in eat-ing the meal he's prepared for a group of people even though the food is delicious. *If the team has really dedicated a good, solid effort to the naming process and if it was diligent in the discovery and framework stages, then there is every chance in the world that a great name exists on the list.*

The list of finalists will include from 20 to 30 names, and while the list has been pared down to a group that broadly fits the team's standards and parameters, it is nonetheless relatively wide-ranging. It will include names that are by far too stodgy or too edgy, even though they fit all the criteria. The challenge for the team is to de-termine which these are!

In the fifth session, the names are explored in depth. For branding groups with a link to an online trademark/patent database, such as www.trademark.com, it can be highly useful to look beyond URL availability to legal ownership at the trademark level. This will give indications of abandoned marks, ownership of active ones, the same name in a variety of federal classifications, the use of the name in various trademarked phrases (such as product names or tag lines), corporate ownership, and international usage.

When making final choices, a trademark database is not a substi-tute for the services a trademark attorney provides. In fact, beware of any branding consulting firm that tells the company it will provide final legal guidance for a name unless the company has a licensed trademark attorney on staff (which is unusual). Corporate legal counsel is obligated to research, file, and execute a trademark for a corporate name, so any branding firm offering this as a service is merely charging a client for something it will have to do, anyway. Once a few names are chosen, typically a primary and secondary name, it is time to have corporate counsel look into name availability.

International laws are now beginning to play a significant role in URL selection. Companies and individuals alike may purchase a URL in one country that is a legitimate trademark in another. If that URL were to be marketed and distributed in the country in which it was already trademarked, the distributing company would run into legal difficulties. As the international side of Internet branding becomes increasingly important over the coming years—and it will, there's no doubt—filing for legal URL and trademark ownership country by country will become an increasingly active field of legal endeavor, just as it has been with corporate trademark names.

The fifth-session goal is to reduce the list of names to no more than five, any one of which could be used as a final corporate name because all of them so closely fit the established framework, personality, and character of the company.

At the end of the first hour of the meeting, after discussing the list overall and having the group discard names ruthlessly, the name list should be down to about ten names. This is where the fun begins: If there was ever a time for healthy corporate debate, this is it. The team needs to intelligently and thoughtfully explore the final 10 names in great depth and gauge the level of consensus for each. A useful tool for this is the "name analysis scoreboard," a tool for the entire group to use to vote on the various names in light of their various attributes and personality factors. The 10 finalists are listed at the top of an 11-column table, and the various characteristics against which the name is being scored are listed in the leftmost column of the table.

For each name and corresponding attribute, the team is asked to vote out loud, one by one, as to whether the name scores a negative one (-1) on the attribute, a zero (0), or a positive 1 ($+1$). A quick summation by a note taker with a calculator gives a combined sum and subsequent average for the group. For example, if in a group of five people, three people voted a positive 1, one person voted a 0, and another voted a negative 1, the total would be a 0.4, or $\{[1+1+1+0+(-1)]/5\}=0.4$.

Once a name has an averaged compound score for each attribute, an averaged score for all the attributes for that name is calculated and entered at the bottom of the column. In this manner, the names and attributes are analyzed in a reasonably methodical manner. Furthermore, individual aspects of each name can be reviewed and examined. Often group review reveals that some attributes are considered more important than others.

This exercise, which can be gamelike in effect, is often highly spirited, a refreshing break for the group after the long naming sessions. It also quickly reveals which names are losers and which are winners, and it can even yield some other-side-of-the-brain ideas and new names—which should not be dismissed, by any means.

It's important to note that it really doesn't matter where creative insight comes from, or from whom. A branding session is really no place for egos to battle. While it's exhilarating to create a new name, and especially a new name that ultimately is adopted, the process by which the name was created is really the star of the show. It is what lays the foundation for solid creativity to take place, and for ideas based upon reason and logic to build into enduring brands.

What words or phrases should be listed in the attribute boxes?

- Various personality traits identified in the framework stage
- Various character attributes identified in the framework stage
- Sounds corporate or bigger than life
- Is unique
- Doesn't require lots of explanation
- Is easy to pronounce
- Is easy to spell
- Is short and memorable
- And so forth

Depending on the company and team, the attributes listed can vary widely and cover a lot of territory. However, they should not be frivolous; they must be real characteristics by which the names will be judged.

As stated previously, at the end of the fifth naming session, a core list of no more than five names will be carried forward to what will be the final naming decision point. It may be that at the end of this meeting, the team is comfortable enough to reduce the list to two or three names, which is acceptable. However, it is unwise to avoid making a *final* naming decision because there are still a few name housecleaning chores to be accomplished before the party begins.

The Final Steps

Very often the staff of a company carrying out the naming process is highly curious, and it is seldom they don't know what's going on. There may be undercurrents of controversy, or there may be anxious anticipation. Many company employees wonder why they aren't involved more deeply in the process of creating a name, or perhaps why there hasn't been a naming contest or similar activity. The answer is first that the naming process isn't really a democracy. People can't be allowed to vote on the "most popular name," certainly not without a significant degree of analysis. It's virtually impossible to proceed through the process with a group larger than five or seven members, much less an entire company. It is, however, essential to communicate to the staff that the process is taking place, so they understand how it works. That said, it's also important to involve the staff on some level. This can be done, for example, by holding a company meeting and inviting the brand team to discuss the brand process and to answer questions about branding, naming, how it works, and why it's important. It may also be important for the executive team to point out the results of any research or feedback about the existing name, and to show support for the coming name change.

Often employees will be quite vocal—even to the point of anger or strong emotion. The brand team needs to be quiet, methodical, responsive, and smart about how this is handled. Branding is an inherently emotional area of business, and strong feelings and the expression of those feelings is to be encouraged (within reason, of course). It's also quite reasonable for employees to be invited to submit their own name ideas, which will be considered along with any criteria they choose to submit. No promises are necessary on the part of management to put the names in any final lists or do anything beyond consideration. At this stage, the "friends and family" test can be helpful as yet another data point. The list of the final names can be distributed to groups of employees, friends, professional acquaintances, members of the press or analyst consultants, or even key customers, with a request for feedback on the names.

Significant consideration can be given at this stage to doing market research on the name among potential audiences. While extensive focus-group testing is overkill for all but the biggest brand efforts (and quite time-consuming and expensive), a simple telephone query to 25 or more potential or actual clients and industry contacts can be highly revealing. Journalists, industry analysts, financial analysts, and industry pundits love to give their opinions, and will often gladly comment over the phone or in email in a naming project. It's important to realize that such research is merely another data point, and the results are unlikely to be the driving factor that will determine the choice of the final name. As part of the overall process, market research needs to be factored in with the significant amount of logic, process, reason, and "gut feel" the team has already invested. In fact, however, a very important reason for making sure that the brand team is allowed to keep the project on track and as tangible as possible is to avoid being swayed by the opinions of a simple straw poll, which might otherwise have devastating effects!

Between the penultimate and final naming sessions, the brand team needs to closely scrutinize the final few names in a variety of areas. First, every possible similar URL needs to be examined and any similar-sounding URL needs to be purchased. Negative URLs should also be purchased to ward off any malicious cyber-warrior or competitor inclined to create a site that could target the site of the brand being developed. Choosing a good URL often means finding numerous similar URLs to serve as "brand buffers" for redirects and protected sites. For some companies, this is a real concern and must be taken into account when finalizing the name. The name "Entricom," for example, was chosen as the new corporate brand for Digital Counterpart, Inc., a business-to-business telecommunications services firm, because the "entri" prefix offered more than 160 variations that could be paired with descriptive terminology to create a broadly "buffered" brand name system. The "entri" word part was also a continual reminder of the point-of-entry technology developed for the telecommunications industry.

Brand names that are translated into other languages can also produce unpleasant surprises:

- When Toyota launched the MR2 car in France, it hadn't realized that the name, pronounced in French, sounds remarkably like "merde," which means "shit."
- GM's attempt at marketing the Chevy Nova in Latin America fell short because the company hadn't realized that "no va" in Spanish means "doesn't go."
- The marketing efforts of the Japanese manufacturer of the popular Japanese sports drink Pokari Sweat were doomed because nobody in America really wanted to drink sweat.

Depending upon the business and where it is to be primarily built, the brand team needs to look at meanings of the word and word parts in major languages, or languages of any specific countries in which the company could find itself doing business. Using native speakers as part of the exercise is always preferable. Branding firms with international offices and/or contacts will provide services for name review as well, and software translation packages can help give general direction.

Choosing and Getting behind the Name

In the final naming session, the team chooses a name. This can be a long, drawn-out discussion with much debate, or it can be completed in 10 minutes. Even after a final name is chosen, a slew of variations with multiple implications has yet to be explored:

- Will there be an extension to the name such as "corporation," "partners," or "group"?
- What does the specific name mean?
- How is it potentially mispronounced?

- What will the "telephone test" sound like (e.g., saying "Good morning, XXX Corporation, may I help you?")?
- What are the product-naming issues, such as how the name will be pronounced in conjunction with other subbrands?

A useful exercise for this session involves filling out a "brand analysis scorecard" that is very similar to the attribute/naming matrix filled out in the previous session, with a slight twist. Again, names and attributes are listed on a white board, but the attributes are even more focused, and only names in the final running appear (all variations, for example, "partners" versus "group") should also be listed. At this stage, *all* of the final names are positive choices, so no minus scores will be entered.

Each person, once again, raises his or her hand with one, two, or three fingers for each attribute for each name and name variation. The *total* number of points (each finger is one point) is then entered on the chart. Adding the scores for each name and the variations of that name and then dividing by the number of variations yields the final score. Suppose, for example, that name 1 has a total of 99 points, name 2 a total of 107, and name 3 a total of 90. Name 2 is 7.5 percent stronger overall than name 1, and name 2 is 16 percent stronger than name 3, both statistically significant deltas. Note that it may be desirable to carry out this exercise with more than one group, such as the executive versus the branding team, if further discussion is necessary.

Market Validation of Potential Names

If time permits, testing audience perceptions of a new name(s) is desirable. Soliciting responses from members of the target audience and asking specific criteria questions about each finalist may reveal factors about the potential success and possible downsides that were not considered in the boardroom. For example, does Brand X sound like a company that produces superior technology? Does Brand Y sound like a brand a customer would trust to deliver quality service? Purchase preferences and favorite choices can be recorded so that the valued-audience perspective can be weighed. It is important, however, to remember that market validation is merely one part of the overall equation and not necessarily the answer. It is difficult to measure the effect a name has on future extendability, subbrand continuums, global consistency, and even simple "gut feel" solely from audience research, yet these are crucial factors in making the ultimate decision.

Information obtained from audience research, whether achieved through a simple poll of "friends and family" or through a commissioned, statistically significant study, can push the group in a given direction, especially when various name variations are under consideration. The name "partners," for example, might have a very different connotation for a potential audience than the name "group." In the case of the Cobos Group naming project (see Chapter 2), an informal review of clients and partners revealed that the group was ready to partner both with the HR professionals the company was placing in various companies as well as with the company's clients. For a tightly knit, collegial organization, "group" sounded very natural.

At this point, the branding group will be in high spirits if it has successfully chosen a name. But there may also be a curmudgeon or two in the room who still isn't convinced the name is right, or opposition from a significant board member or other key individual. For that reason, it is essential for the brand team to agree *firmly* on a name, and for any debate about it to be left in the conference room. During the naming sessions, virtually anything goes. However, any divisive behavior outside the conference room will immediately serve to undermine the brand and short-circuit its ability to begin to converge with the corporate brand. If gating factors or any other notable issues arise concerning the name that may not have been considered in the naming sessions, the team should immediately reconvene and discuss them behind closed doors.

Letting the Name Out of the Conference Room

Announcing a new name, especially after so much analysis and build-up, is really exciting, and the company staff is usually waiting with bated breath to hear it. For that reason the team, before it opens the conference room doors, needs to have an action plan as to how the name will be announced internally. This occurs far ahead of any considerations for launches, press releases, or other external events; rather, it is meant to bring the staff into the decision. For smaller organizations, the internal announcement is relatively straightforward. The staff can be assembled, and the new name can be announced with the caveat that it is internal information only at that point and that the logo and design have yet to be developed, the launch plans finalized, and key customers, analysts, and others informed.

For larger organizations, and especially for public companies, *much* more caution must be exercised. A new name in the wrong hands (e.g., an uncontrolled leak forcing a public announcement) can be damaging to the brand, and dribbling the name and then the logo and the tag line changes to a large staff is a sloppy way to communicate a new brand.

The Elevator Speech

The phrase "company elevator speech" refers to the recital a person gives in a minute or two—typically the amount of time it takes to ride an elevator—upon being asked "What does your company do?" by a fellow vertical traveler. For most executives, telling someone what the company does in a couple of minutes is a tough challenge—on an elevator or anywhere else. Furthermore, the variation between elevator speeches, even among the members of a closely knit management team, can be surprisingly wide.

A new name often provides a good opportunity not only to give the elevator speech many times to many people, but also to train management and staff in how to tell the world what the company does in a concise, *consistent* manner. For technology companies, especially, being concise is often difficult because the person giving the elevator speech feels compelled to dive too deep, too soon into what the company technology is all about and why it's important. The speech, consequently, lacks context. However, when different people are asked to shorten the elevator speech, the results frequently suffer from a lack of consistency because each person has a different set of priorities that he or she thinks is important to convey. With enough time to go into detail, most managers, at least, will touch on most of the major points of the company.

Just as with any of the other components of branding, a logical method can provide invaluable assistance in developing and deploying a consistent, accurate elevator speech. The elevator speech incorporates the core messaging of the company and puts it into a marketing, branding, and business context that can be communicated quickly.

The best way to educate staff members of a company in an elevator speech is to organize it into a set of three or four primary points that can be used in any situation, from the conference room to a backyard. These points can then be adapted for whoever is listening to ensure that the audience members receive a message customized for their optimal comprehension and benefit.

What's important to convey? Consider the following factors:

- The market the company is in
- Competitive differentiation
- How big the company is, whether it's public or not, how many employees it has
- The problem(s) the company solves
- Where it is located/headquartered
- Its notable customers and partners
- Parent/sister organizations
- Notable subbrands, product brands
- Company mission and vision
- Relevant corporate history
- How the company sells its products
- Interesting or notable facts that will help people remember the company

Launching the New Brand

In the conference room the brand team must contain its excitement and focus on how the name will be announced and what the implications of getting a new name out might be.

- When will the board be informed?
- How will employees be informed?
- Who is responsible for training employees on the new elevator speech and how it is delivered?
- Will it be necessary to wait until the tag line and logo are developed, and even, perhaps a new Web site is designed, before the company at large is briefed?
- What will happen if the new name is leaked to the press or analysts?
- How long will the existing company name remain visible, such as on the home page of the Web site, or in press releases?
- Who will be the key spokesperson about the name change?
- How will the new name be articulated?
- What is the time line for launching the new name to the outside world of customers, partners, media, and analysts?

Verizon: Using the Web the Right Way for a New Name

The merger of Bell Atlantic and GTE, one of the most significant corporate mergers to directly affect the American and international public, achieved a relatively smooth and well-accepted brand transition, in large part because of the power of the Web. The change, which affected 95 million access lines and 25 million wireless customers, had to be carefully and methodically orchestrated and announced. The branding team couldn't just run out the doors and yell, "We've got a new name! It's 'Verizon'" to anyone within earshot, and they couldn't just fire out a press release the same day.

It took a significant effort involving teams from all aspects of the company, and especially from marketing, who had to change everything carrying the logo—from phone bills to signs on buildings—all within a relatively short period after the announcement. The central point of coordination for the effort was the new Verizon Web site, to which any of the preexisting GTE, Bell Atlantic, AirTouch, or other corporate brand Web sites had to now redirect.

One of the biggest questions on the minds of everyone from the press to customers was "Why Verizon? What does that mean?" When the launch occurred, a statement appeared about the new name and logo in the "about Verizon/merger information/name &

logo" section on the Web site, just a click away from the home page:

> Verizon (pronounced "Vurr-EYE-zon") comes from the Latin word "veritas," which means truth, and also connotes certainty and reliability and "horizon," which signifies the endless possibilities ahead. Verizon represents a new breadth of capabilities for a telecommunications company—a unique mix of local and long distance, national and international assets, voice, wireless, data, Internet, and more.
>
> The new logo is a bold red, black, and white rendition of the name with a graphic emphasis on the "V" and "Z." You should be seeing it on buildings, pay phones, vehicles, bills, and other materials soon!

Before the advent of the New Economy, communicating this type of information would have been by direct mail, communicating through the press (which is unreliable in terms of providing this level of detail), or advertising. Enter the Web, and all it takes is a single page of carefully worded explanation.

GTE and Bell Atlantic were *huge* corporate brand names. They were bigger, in fact, by a larger margin than PriceWaterhouse and Coopers & Lybrand, yet the latter didn't do a good job of communicating its merger online or anywhere else, and it failed to come up with a strong corporate name that would carry the company into the twenty-first century. The name Verizon serves to clearly pull the many corporate brand entities under one strong umbrella name, and the Web was the unifying element allowing that to happen.

Who Gets to Hear the New Name First?

For most companies, there needs to be some planning about how to announce the name; this, however, is covered more specifically during the execution stage in terms of actually launching the name and the newly defined brand.

As the naming effort comes to completion, the next stage, visual articulation, is essentially ready to begin. Designers for the Web site as well as the logo and other graphic elements can be involved in the last stage of the naming exercise, as they often provide invaluable input to the choice of names and how they will be graphically cast. Web designers can already be thinking about how the name will appear on the new Web site, and other creative specialists, such as advertising creative staff, can be giving thought to how a new name will affect advertising display.

Those in charge of content for the Web site and collateral materials are also first on the list of those who need to know about a new name, because the process of writing compelling copy is time-consuming and intensive. They are also the ones who inevitably must write the interpretation and explanation of the new brand and how it is to be communicated to the world, as in the Verizon Web site example.

There are many variations and possibilities as to how the name of a new company is announced. Suffice it to say, for the purposes of this chapter and book, that the Web is a core part of the way any brand today is launched and communicated to the world at large. Furthermore, it's always easy to let the proverbial cat out of the bag when launching a name, but once out, it can't be retracted. As a result, even given tight deadlines, impending commitments, and "running on Internet time," remember the adage "Brand in haste, repent at leisure!"

Using Tag Lines

A tag line is an invaluable tool for the brand. It gives the company name some meaning and flavor, making it more memorable, providing a tone to the brand, and, in some cases, telling what the company does. At a functional level, it provides a segue between the company name and the company message, a communication bridge between the two. It accelerates the process of convergence between the brand name and the corporate brand, helping the two become one entity— simply "the brand."

Typically an inverse ratio exists between a corporate brand name's level of descriptiveness and level of abstraction. And, for names which don't mean anything obvious, having a tag line that leads peo-

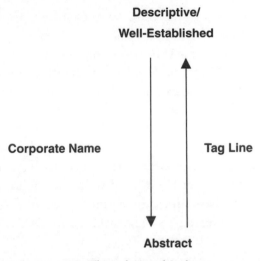

FIGURE 4.2.   The relationship between
the corporate brand name's level of descriptiveness and level of abstraction.

ple closer to what the company does is important (see Figure 4.2).
For descriptive names, that's less important. For example, it's
reasonably obvious what markets www.phones.com, www.
screensavers.com, and www.mailboxes.com are targeting. It may not
be obvious, however, that www.business.com is a business-to-
business company. For this company, even a slightly descriptive tag
line can help people looking to buy phones online for their houses
to quickly realize this isn't the spot for them—whether they see the
name in an ad, on the Web, or on a billboard. In this case, the name
is closer to the descriptive end of the descriptive-abstract axis than
to the abstract end, but not at the extreme end: there is still an abstract element to the name, because what the company does, specifically, is not conveyed by the name.

Well-established brands can use abstract tag lines to increase the
emotional appeal of the brand. In fact, some professional branding
consultants who have spent most of their efforts with small companies and projects don't understand that a well-established, significant brand has creative leeway in some areas, and can even benefit
from being intentionally curious or enigmatic.

Such tag lines, for example, can offer original, creative, and inspiring statements that are the envy of many lesser-known companies, which often try out the same types of tag lines way *before* their brand can support this kind of abstraction. Many of the world's most accomplished and well-known brands—business to business or business to consumer—also have some of the best and most sophisticated and creative tag lines, rich with double-meanings, emotional appeal, and brand tone:

Company	Tag Line	URL
Philips	Let's Make Things Better	www.philips.com
Microsoft	Where Do You Want to Go Today?	www.microsoft.com
Sun	We're the Dot in Dot .com	www.sun.com
Coca-Cola	Enjoy	www.cocacola.com
Siemens	Be Inspired	www.siemens.com
The Economist	The Only Thing Dry Is the Ink	www.economist.com
Hewlett-Packard	Invent	www.hp.com
Oracle	Software Powers the Internet	www.oracle.com
Toyota	People Drive Us	www.toyota.com
John Deere	Nothing Runs Like a Deere	www.deere.com
Canon	Know How	www.canon.com

However, some relatively large companies stumble when they attempt to follow the lead of these major, world-class names by using equally abstract tag lines when their names aren't as well known in consumer or business circles. In spite of being catchy, many "slogan" tag lines are not right for companies trying to build a brand and become better known, and are most often more closely tied with a message in an ad than in helping people to understand the overall purpose of the corporate brand. In this age of information overflow, being cryptic or simply trying to be catchy is often counterproductive, irritating those who bother to read on to the message, thinking erroneously that they might be interested. Or, even worse, potential customers may simply skip over the ad or Web site—meaning the tag line has failed in its duty.

Many of the companies most guilty of this are the emerging

ebusiness consulting companies, which are commonly poorly differentiated and lack a solid brand foundation. Are these companies widely known? Do their name and tag-line combinations inspire interest and curiosity, or define what they do, beyond those who might already know them? Do all the tag lines begin to sound alike, or do they actually provide unique, definitive meaning? What *do* these companies do, anyway? How many people have heard of them? Are the tag lines helping to expand knowledge, or do they simply confuse readers and Web surfers? How naturally do the tag lines, names, and URLs work together? Many of the tag lines below border on the silly or absurd; they might work as headlines, but really have no place as corporate tag lines. It's a busy world, and most people don't have the time, interest, or inclination to surf to a Web site simply because its name or tag line sounds cool:[6]

Company	Tag Line	URL
Acxiom	Creating the Future without Fear	www.acxiom.com
TIAA-CREF	Ensuring the Future for Those Who Shape It	www.tiaa-cref.org
Walker	We Mean e-Business	www.walker.com
Aventis	Our Challenge Is Life	www.aventis.com
Eon	New Energy	www.eon.com
MarchFirst	A New World. A New Way	www.marchfirst.com
Copernus	What Revolves around You	www.copernus.com
Cadence	How Big Can You Dream?	www.cadence.com

In contrast, the tag lines in the group shown below, which were created by companies representing lesser-known or new corporate brands (such as Agilent, a spin-off of HP that handles its medical, scientific, chemical, test/measurement, and semiconductor component business) are often both descriptive and memorable. They quite specifically help the reader or Web surfer to better understand the corporate brand immediately; they speak to the mission of the company and thus provide a much smoother segue into a message.

These companies have acknowledged (to themselves) that there are members of the target audience who may not have heard of them or are not able to come up with what they do simply upon seeing the name; they have chosen tag lines that are effective and appropriate. The cost of choosing tag lines like these is that the brand name and the tag line may seem redundant. If this is too obvious, it can be intellectually offensive, but in most cases the tag lines do serve to reinforce the definition of the company. Occasionally, companies will use double tag lines where a company descriptor is combined with a creative phrase. This method, while not the cleanest or most creative, "gets the job done" in helping the audience understand the company or a specific division of a large company.

Sometimes, the URL by itself helps define the company, as in the case of USF Worldwide, which is a division of USFreightways. The company can afford to have a relatively abstract name *and* tag line, since the URL is highly descriptive. The result is that a more targeted, appropriate audience is driven to its Web site, and people can use its marketing materials to quickly understand what the company does and determine if it's what they're looking for. Once the company gets to cruising altitude with its brand, it can tweak the tag line to reflect its increased prominence.

Company	Tag Line	URL
Agilent Technologies	Innovating the HP Way	www.agilent.com
Selectica	The Internet Selling Systems Company	www.selectical.com
Aether	Wireless Solutions for a Portable Planet	www.aeithersystems.com
USF Worldwide	You'll Think the World of Us	www.usfreightways.com
LapLink	Powerful Software Solutions for a Mobile World	www.LapLink.com
Ariba	Making the Net Work for B2B	www.ariba.com
Commerce One	Many Markets. One Source	www.commerceone.com

Company	Tag Line	URL
Niku	Transforming the Service Economy	www.niku.com
PrimeStreet	Changing the Way Small Business Gets Financed	www.primestreet.com
Register.com	The *First* Step on the Web	www.register.com
Widevine Technologies	Technology Solutions for Streaming Media	www.widevine.com

Many tag lines don't tell the reader what the company does; this may be because a company is so large there's no way the name could do the business justice or because the company is so well known it's unnecessary. Further, the great tag lines filter out the unwanted and attract the target audience, but they don't give away the farm, inspiring the reader to look further. A good tag line gives the brand name an even stronger connection to the brand consumer, making consumers feel closer to the company and more interested and intrigued by the brand.

For new companies about to launch with an abstract brand name, a descriptive tag line is an essential tool. However, the tag line must be more than just descriptive: it must still provide color, tone, and memorability.

Entricom, the Web-based telecommunications service provider referenced earlier, launched in 2000 after being renamed from DCI Communications. Because the company provides, among other things, sophisticated order-entry capabilities to the complex and often chaotic and highly technical world of telecommunications, it needed a name that didn't specifically say "order entry" (which would have been limiting) and that offered a comfort zone amid the complexity and chaos.

Following the corporate naming process, the company underwent a tag-line naming effort consisting of the following steps:

- An initial session to identify the types of tag lines that would work for the company
- Two or three sessions of tag-line development beginning with a list of potential tag lines, paring down the list to a much smaller group of preferred choices
- A review all of the preferred tag lines together, to determine the final choices
- A final session to complete the process by picking the official new tag line

At the end of the tag line sessions, Entricom came up with this final choice: *Bringing Order to Telecommunications.*

The tag line communicates order entry without using the specific words. "Bringing order" is slightly edgy, even moderately arrogant, perhaps, but reflects the personality of the executive team, people who are strong-willed, smart, and opinionated, but eager to provide a very powerful and useful service. The reader, however, clearly understands the company is in telecommunications, and can probably guess it's a business-to-business operation that provides the industry with some type of technical service.

The tag line gets people closer to the message and the brand, but it doesn't need to tell them everything. At some level, the tag line needs to be a bit tantalizing, teasing the reader into wanting to explore further—which also enhances memorability. For companies with descriptive names, the tag lines are often more abstract, or they can communicate other messages (such as transition, in the case of a name change).

How are tag lines used online? On the Web, a major advantage is that the tag line can be placed nearly anywhere on the home page that it seems to be useful and where it can help the reader. It doesn't necessarily need to be immediately underneath the name, as it typically would be in print or television advertising, or uttered aloud, as on a radio spot. The primary, driving purpose is to use the tag line to help the reader understand and become closer to the brand (not just the brand *name*), as quickly and effortlessly as possible.

Tag lines are transitional; after they have been used for a period, they can be changed. In this, they differ significantly from corporate names, and can be an extremely useful tool in building and launching a new brand. It is clear to many executive teams of new companies that their first tag line is designed to get them over the "brand hump" to the point where they are recognized, at least in their own industry. At that point, the tag line can be changed, if necessary.

When the Transamerica headquarters in San Francisco (the distinctive white pyramid structure) was built, there was significant controversy over it "destroying the skyline." Yet the building has come to be one of the city's most memorable features. And so it needs to be with a corporate tag line. Every company wants a tag line with staying power, one that conveys a vision and is a memorable and distinctive part of the corporate brand. Microsoft's "Where do you want to go today?" was controversial at first, simply because it didn't say anything specific about what the company did, and it was unique in that it posed a question instead of making a statement. But, over time, the tag line has proven highly memorable and has paralleled the company's growth into a variety of markets and technologies both for consumers and business. In fact, what tag line could be more appropriate as the company begins to address the automotive market, providing operating environments to connect the various personal entertainment, information, and educational capabilities of in-dash online devices (such as Clarion's AutoPC, for example)? Yet it took Microsoft many years—and many other tag lines (which, for the most part, are long forgotten)—to migrate to its current tag line, which has now been in place longer than any of the others. Microsoft's current tag line is timely, appropriate, and visionary.

Writing Headlines

For many journalists, headline writing is the most creative part of their jobs, where they get to express a serious news story in a manner meant to attract the reader. In fact, in many news organizations, the art department often gets to write the headlines, if for no other reason than they must fit within a predetermined space. On the Web, headlines are also a highly creative portion of the home page and strongly tied to the brand. In the same manner that a tag line ties the brand name to the core message and corporate brand, the headline ties the corporate brand with the product or service being featured or highlighted.

There are several notable types of headlines:

- Typical conventional news-type headlines found on www.msn.com or AOL
- Business-to-consumer product- and sales-oriented headlines on sites such as www.amazon.com or www.bluelight.com, meant to drive sales and tell about new products or lines of products
- Business-to-business corporate headlines meant to attract investors, clients, and the press to read more about products and services, and to generate interest in the company overall, such as on www.ariba.com or www.cisco.com
- Business-to-consumer and business-to-business headlines for major corporations that are touting information of interest to a broad range of people, such as on www.att.com, www.microsoft.com, or www.intel.com.

In all headlines there is a strong element of creativity; unlike tag lines, which are strategic in nature, headlines are tactical. Thus the tag line and the headline work in concert to form an important brand image and forge an identity between the name and the ultimate message.

Words to Live By

"The good brands are able to build consistency and a set of expectations, even in their name alone," said Michael Miller, editor-in-chief of *PC Magazine* and executive vice president and editorial director for Ziff Davis Media. "Branding is obviously important for attracting customers, and you want your brand to stand for something. You go to Microsoft, you know what you'll get. If you go to 'Joe's Software,' who knows what you'll get?"

"Many times I think URLs are far more complicated than they need to be. You want people to find you, and not confuse you with someone who *sounds* like you. People get upset if they type www.whitehouse.com and they get a porn site. . . . [A]s a customer of the federal government, that's not what I expect!"

The topic of verbal articulation of a Web brand is a broad one, with subtopics ranging from the name of a company to how it is described at the end of a press release. The content by far exceeds the space available for discussion in this chapter. It is clear, however, that verbal articulation does not exist as a vacuum. Naming cannot happen in the absence of process and the other areas of creating a brand, deploying a Web site, and building a business. Nor can companies allow their brands to be randomly talked or written about by untrained members of the organization.

"If you have a name like BN.com [Barnes & Noble] and you didn't use it, it would be foolish," said Miller. "Brand momentum can carry you farther than people imagine—for example, Amazon.com has a strong brand name combined with a powerful brand and it's worked wonders for them. Building an unclear brand with cryptic messaging or naming just because it seems cool simply doesn't work in terms of drawing traffic. However it's done—through the name, tag line, message, ads, or whatever—it has to be crystal-clear as to what the company does in order to attract business. I've heard some people say we start every day with zero traffic and have to build it. A great marketing campaign may get people to try your site, but what do you do to get them to stay?"

Verbal brand articulation is, perhaps, the most essential form of expressing a brand framework and structure. For many, it is the most memorable part of the brand, and, in today's Internet world, the way in which people find a company. Designs, business models, and revenues are all important, but when push comes to shove, people find companies by typing their names into a search engine or a browser. The way in which the company brand is reflected in the name, and the strength of the brand in its verbal form, are essential to the ability of the company to succeed on the Web—which, in many cases, is mission-critical to the organization's ability to succeed.

5

The Visual, Physical, and Sensory Articulation Stages

I'll Believe It When I See It

The age demanded an image
Of its accelerated grimace,
Something for the modern stage,
Not, at any rate, an Attic grace.
        —Ezra Pound, 1920[1]

It took television many years to get beyond the notion that it was primarily a verbal medium with images, basically just radio with pictures. The tendency is to view new technology in a known context: people think of DVD players as a combination of CDs and VCRs; cell phones as a wide-ranging cordless home phone; digital cameras as conventional film cameras that let you skip having to scan an image. *New technology is only new to those for whom the introduction of it occurred after they were old enough to be aware of it.* For anyone born after the 1920s, telephones don't seem like new technology, but when they were introduced, they were every bit as whizbang as a new Rio MP3 player or new Palm is today. For those born in the 1980s and 1990s, PCs aren't anything new, nor are CD players or cell phones. The Internet, for anyone who's a child in 2000, isn't new technology, either: it's simply a normal part of life.

In a sense, the Internet isn't technology, really, at all: It's merely a venue for technology. In fact, most companies building anything for broad consumer or business markets today don't want technology to be the main association people have with their brands; rather, they want to transcend technology because doing so makes anything seem more complex and less approachable. People want to know that great technology went into the building of their automobiles, but they really aren't too interested in hearing about it except on a superficial level. The programming and development communities are slowly being pushed farther and farther into the nether regions of industry; they've been replaced with "information officers" and "Web masters." Kids in school today aren't learning Basic programming, rather; they're learning how to build a Web site. There are programming elements inherent in understanding how to do that, but programming skills are no longer the primary objective.

This has laid the foundation for form—rather than function—to become a considerably higher-level need in building a brand on the Internet. The audience is virtually limitless and global, the competition is stiff, and even venture capitalists care more about branding than about technology. For branding to appeal at a truly personal level, both expressing the personality of the company and playing to the personal interests of the target audience, a company must integrate visual, sensory, and design elements into its brand.

For the Internet, these elements are distinct:

- Strong logo design both offline and online
- Colors that work offline and online
- Navigational and design elements that make sense at a functional level and don't just look good
- Accommodating the access needs of a prioritized set of key audiences (for example, an online broker needs to provide immediate access for stock purchases)
- Industrial design for physical devices to match the Internet and the new online world
- A natural, believable brand that is neither too stodgy nor too ostentatious
- A strong and thoughtful combination of text and graphics
- Animation, graphic elements, and film clips used appropriately for the given audience and culture
- Seeking out the newest technologies available that can make a big under-the-hood difference in building the online brand
- Special consideration to nonvisual sensory issues—such as sound—

with regard to market viability and opportunity versus difficulty and barriers to integration

As with verbal articulation, visual articulation builds directly on the information, method, and process created in the discovery and framework phases. Without that information, combined with what has been created and written in the verbal stage, design will take place in a vacuum and, as a result, will have limited genuine benefit and will consequently limit the life of the brand.

The objective of the fourth stage of building brands on the Web is to integrate all information and content into an effective Web design and implementation capable of generating immediate interest for site visitors, and driving repeated return and "viral marketability" for the site. "Viral marketing" is a fancy term for word of mouth on the Web, where individuals motivated to talk about what they've seen and done invite others electronically to join and participate, and generally spread the word both online and offline.

The Nuances of Design

"Design communicates in a much more nuanced way than words. So what should you consider before designing your Web site? I recently interviewed a man who had some insightful thoughts on this question: Rolf Fehlbaum, President and owner of Vitra, a renowned furniture company in Birsfelden, Switzerland. Fehlbaum has worked with many famous designers and architects, from Frank Gehry and Bruce Mau to Charles and Ray Eames, Jasper Morrison, and Philippe Starck. Here's what Fehlbaum had to say about design:

"Design isn't an abstraction. It's a direct manifestation of your philosophy and your attitude. That's why, when people are thinking about joining a company, they want to see the Web page and look around the office. They may not be able to articulate exactly what they learned by doing so, but they learn it nonetheless. And they think, 'I fit here,' or, 'I don't.' Design speaks volumes about a company's culture. It tells you if a company is egalitarian or hierarchical, if it's easygoing or uptight.

"So how an organization chooses to translate its value system into design is enormously important. Now, design can certainly lie; you can always hire a professional liar—a designer to choose your image. But that doesn't work in the long run, because ultimately the lie will be discovered. You'll be unmasked by the reality of who you are professionally and personally. People will say, 'Ah, the company tried to give a certain impression, but obviously that's not what they're really about.' So the role of a designer is to offer tools to express the true values of an organization." (*Jill Rosenfeld, former Senior Writer at* Fast Company *magazine—www.fastcompany.com*)

The Importance of Structure and Words in the Design of Web Brands

Too often design and creation of the visual elements of a brand—the Web design, the logo, and other design elements—are conducted in the absence of a brand framework or verbal articulation of the brand. At the core of the natural branding concept lies the belief that no part of the branding development stages is an island. For a brand to be truly credible and durable, all stages of development must be highly dependent upon one another. It is essential that those involved in the efforts to complete and conduct the various stages share information, hold transitional meetings, and generally be as communicative as possible at each level of handoff. This is true whether one or many agencies or consultants are involved or no outside agencies have been consulted. However, the more different agencies and outside sources involved, the more complex the effort it takes to keep everyone informed and sharp on brand points. *The more intangible the information, the harder it is to ensure clean handoffs!*

The reason this point is being emphasized is that it is common for a branding project to lose its luster right about the time the word people give the project to the designers. Often these teams are in separate areas, and even separate companies, and if the handoff isn't done properly, the comprehensive brand information will be diluted.

The words and structures created in the two previous stages are essential to the designer in understanding the creative and visual parameters in everything from development of Flash programming elements in the Web site's opening sequences to the types of fonts and basic colors used. The brand map, with its continuums of descriptive versus abstract and conservative to progressive, is considered along with various points of research—for example, a cultural breakdown of the target audience or an analysis of the types of consumer traffic on the site. All this serves as a guideline for the designer who is sensitive to brand identity.

It is helpful to have the Web designers and logo designers participate in the final stages of verbal articulation so they can begin their efforts with a current and lucid understanding of the brand objectives. These people may also contribute significantly to the verbal stage by offering very constructive "right-brain" considerations and alternatives. Likewise, people who were involved in the verbal articulation stages—naming, Web content, and other areas—should stay in touch with the visual designers to lend guidance and perspective.

At the risk of sounding trite, it's highly important that everyone involved in building a brand work together and share what they know. That's a basic concept, but far too often it doesn't happen. Naming specialists move on to the next naming project. Designers don't like having their shoulders looked over. The verbal synopsis is skimpy and really doesn't reflect the true brand structure. The designers have a preconceived notion of what the site or logo should be like. There are endless reasons why marketing communications components end up being siloed like corn, wheat, and oats. But brands resulting from efforts involving siloed areas of discipline will be disjointed and lack cohesion and continuity, and will struggle as a result. All areas of marketing and business development must ultimately be in the same voice, key, and timbre to achieve the union of image and identity that characterizes truly natural branding.

Great Visual Branding on the Web: A Multiplicity of Disciplines

Designing, building, and deploying a Web site, and keeping it in line with brand objectives, involve much more than a copy of Microsoft

FrontPage and someone with a keen eye. Web sites that truly express a brand require scrutiny at all levels of the process; the site must be designed from the ground up. Companies such as Verio (www.verio. com), a large Web hosting firm, provide basic Web design services for clients at extremely aggressive rates (see home.verio.com/custom/ pricing.html). However, the sites are frequently simple and are developed "off the shelf," with some custom design work. This limits the amount of real branding clients will be able to get from the site unless they come to the project armed with prêt-à-porter brand information (see "The Cost of Building a Web Brand," later in this chapter).

But this is the age of running on Internet time, and people are an eleventh-hour rush to get their Web sites running. So why not at least get *something* live? Isn't it better to have at least a "business-card site" with corporate contact information? The answer is no, simply because launching a Web site without any serious consideration to branding and brand process is corporate suicide in the New Economy. However, most companies are so frenetically obsessed with getting their sites up that they're willing to cut corners in any area they can—including the branding process. After all, branding is a "fuzzy" science, and who knows what it could mean in terms of delays in turning the site switch on or, even worse, what it could mean if the process revealed something more significant about the company which might need to be fixed? This type of corporate paranoia has short-circuited some of the best "almost famous" brands that never made it big. Again, first impressions count, and skimping on a rollout sends a message to potential clients, customers, investors, partners, and analysts that the company might skimp in other areas, as well.

What does it mean, in terms of time? Of course, this all depends on the parameters of the brand challenge, whether it's an existing brand being deployed to the Web, a new company with a new site, a big company, a small company, integrating an ecommerce site with a corporate site, and on and on. But whatever the challenge, the issues need to be worked out before the business goes live on the Internet. The Internet isn't going away, and the long-range value to be gained from putting proper branding principles and method into play *by far* outweighs the short-term gains made by putting just any old site up. Remember, "Brand in haste, repent at leisure."

Visual articulation integrates brand savvy with key creative areas: software development, typography, graphic design, photography, animation, and user-interface design. Each of these areas represents a distinct discipline, but each must yield to the brand as a point of common reference. Checklists created in the framework stage must be constantly referred to by the entire team.

Matt Harper, senior designer for The Garrigan Lyman Group, points out that to instill a real brand into a Web site, the effort must go beyond mere parts and pieces: "Take BMW—its brand on the Web (www.bmw.com) is an interactive process that is actually *not* intuitive—it's not an interface you've ever used before but it gives you a sense of mystery and excitement . . . what's behind this button, this image, and so on. Likewise, the 'bug' commercials for Volkswagen on television as well as its Web site (www.vw.com or www.volkswagen.com) are more about giving it personality than describing a car—it doesn't matter if it works, that's not what they're talking about. For consumer sites, especially, building that type of emotional appeal into a site is what makes them memorable. We always suggest forming and expressing a personality: the original hit is critical, and the person at the site for BMW or VW should want to fall in love with the car."

So what, then, makes a brand shine in a Web site design? Is it colors? Fonts? Images? Navigation? The answer is a resounding "yes" to all the questions collectively, but "no" to any one individually, because each of these elements is effective when developed in concert with the others. The reason some off-the-shelf Web sites, such as those provided by Verio, look good is that Verio has cast all the design elements ahead of time, and what the company provides is much like a desktop publishing template. From that standpoint, Verio-assisted sites are balanced graphically. However, although arranging the elements according to a company's taste, and adding content and images according to its preference, gets closer to casting a unique brand identity, the site will still lack the subtle, nearly subliminal factors which separate a marginally acceptable brand from a great one.

But it costs more to build a custom site, right? Once again, a company may decide not to run the branding obstacle course in favor of going live quickly. The prices listed in the Verio site are *awfully* appealing, especially to a company with unplanned Web costs, or a start-up still on the prowl for venture capital. But the real question is not so much what the Web site will cost, but, rather, *what will it cost to go live with a Web site lacking a brand? What will that do to business and opportunities after the launch?* It's like the difference between a prefabricated house and one built from the ground up: The differences are sometimes subtle, but they are also substantive.

Function or Form?

One of the first questions posed by the Web design team in terms of brand is what is more important to the target audience who will be using the site: form or function? Will the site be like a chair that is beautiful to look at, made with beautifully crafted wood and upholstery and unique in its memorability, or will it be one that is simply incredibly comfortable—comfort being its most memorable feature? This consideration applies to both business-to-business and business-to-consumer sites, although, in general, business-to-business sites are typically more functional, while business-to-consumer sites leverage form. For anyone doing business on the Net—whether a consumer buying a CD or a law firm looking for a new partner in China—having to machete one's way through confusing screens, long-loading graphics, and poor writing immediately overrides any considerations of beautiful design. The most elegant font or the most vibrant, Web-optimized color scheme won't make a shred of difference if the transaction doesn't take place or if the information seeker doesn't find the data. Dead links, outdated information, and typographical errors (such as in email address links!) all amount to a bad brand experience.

The objective is to the make the chair both good to look at *and* comfortable to sit in. The site must meet the needs of each potential audience as quickly as possible, and look good at the same time—which is part of the allure of a prefab site. As a branding watchdog, the executive in charge of a company's Web site and brand must be adamant that the site design be a strong mix of form *and* function.

While the BMW site is mysterious and nonstandard, finding information is still tremendously easy. And while NetRadio's site is highly functional, it still provides an attractive interface and unique personality.

The same is true of www.ibm.com and www.compaq.com—both of which need to appeal to a wide, highly diverse set of Web travelers (investors, IT managers, analysts, large businesses, government, executives, consumers, journalists, job seekers, etc.) and get them to their destination of choice quickly. But the sites must also be unique, with elements of originality and design that make them memorable. The IBM page emphasizes form more than the Compaq site, but retains a high degree of functionality. The Compaq site appears much more consumer-oriented and functional—it's easy to find anything, but the site is not especially attractive—but it still emphasizes high degrees of brand recognition through color, feeling ("Power for Life"), and excitement. The Compaq site feels like the products are ready to order today; the IBM site feels like a sales rep probably needs to call in order for a user to get anything.

Merely throwing links on the page to corresponding information pages won't cut it for a business that has built its entire reputation on marketing and branding. However, there's just not enough room on an 800 × 600-pixel page (the standard, default resolution for Web pages) for all of the information required by a major, complex business brand. Therefore, building a home page that meets both the functional needs of a broad audience and the form needs of building brand appeal and memorability are a real challenge for the visual articulation team. And, again, it's why the executive team *must* be involved and not allow the Web site to be built in a vacuum!

The Black Hole of Web Design

A black hole is broadly understood by astronomers and astrophysicists to be a collapsed star, a place where a tremendous amount of matter has been compressed into a small volume, creating huge gravitational forces—so much so, in fact, that it pulls light into it, thus creating a blank darkness in space. Building a Web site is not unlike creating a black hole. It's as if all possible ads, trade show booths, press releases, customer visits, investor presentations, store windows, and company billboards or signs have to be compressed into the space of a 17-inch screen, creating every bit as much "pull," and even more, than all of the parts and pieces collectively. And, like a black hole, a poorly designed Web site can be completely invisible to everything around it. But it doesn't have to be—to stretch the metaphor, it can also be something that attracts everything around it.

This is why Web site design decisions are so hard to make, and why complex companies face incredibly tough choices. IBM and Compaq have both made distinct choices as to site design, based upon extensive brand discovery, framework, and content analysis. Their home pages, like the home pages of many thousands of other organizations, are the ultimate image gateways: single screens through which any possible company contact must pass to get information or to do business.

Without going through the framework stage, many Web designers could come up with good links to information, packaged in an attractive design, but would the design meet the needs of the company in correspondence with how the target audiences are prioritized? The remainder of the chapter on visual articulation focuses on issues surrounding the process of instilling a brand into a Web site, as well as analyzing the differences between several popular portals to understand what they are doing from a visual perspective. Just as this book is not intended to teach basic branding, neither is it intended to comprehensively describe the design process; rather, it's meant to emphasize the process and method of branding, how that's applied to building a Web site, and what that means in terms of visual articulation and design.

Logo Development and the Web Site

The visual articulation stage frequently begins with the development of a logo, or a minidiscovery process to understand how the logo will be treated on the Web site. For new companies, designing the logo is the perfect bridge from the naming and verbal articulation process because the logo uses the name just created or positioned.

"Beginning with a logo often leads to interesting design opportunities for the Web site and other materials," says Matt Harper. "You can use the logo as the beginning of a graphic standard, and if you need to push it one way or the other, you can do it. It's exceedingly helpful to have a logo that expresses the personality of the brand, and if you don't, you can change it at this stage. If you have already designed or are designing the Web site or collateral material, for example, you don't have the luxury of being able to make minor changes with big impact. Furthermore, you end up with a 'regression to the mean' and sometimes taking the least common denominator approach, resulting in a plain-vanilla look and feel."

As stated in Chapter 4, the logo designers should have been at the final naming and tag-line meetings, so they will be up to speed on what the brand parameters of the logo should be. The brand map and four-quadrant matrix showing conservative/progressive and descriptive/abstract brand identity will be extremely helpful, both to the logo team and to the Web designers, giving them a clear sense of overall direction.

The first session for developing the logo should include as many high-level team members as possible, even the CEO and president. While they need not be present at all the intermediary logo and design meetings, having their initial input is often a godsend—especially if there are any personal factors that affect an existing logo, or which must be taken into account when designing the new one.

Executives often find it difficult to think visually, and may not be able to articulate what they want in a logo. For that reason, it's helpful to review existing logos from other companies as a guide. One of the best collections of a broad diversity of logos can be found on Ariba's Web site, by clicking on the "partners" button at www.ariba.com. This collection of logos ranges from the simple but distinctive logos of Microsoft, FedEx, SAP, and Visa, to the highly decorative and, some might say, overdesigned logos of Saqqara or Wipro.

Keep track of the following factors when analyzing the various logos:

1. What are the primary colors being used?
2. What are the font styles like?
3. Which logos represent the name of the company itself versus names with a separate graphic element?
4. Which logos seem like they work well online, and which don't?
5. Are any of them used with a tag line? How is it used?
6. Is there any pattern common to the better-known brands?
7. Is there any pattern common to smaller firms? Larger firms?
8. Is there any pattern with different types of business? For example, does it appear that more conservative companies have more conservative logos? (Remember, not all of the companies have undergone extensive branding efforts!)

Identify the logos everyone likes and why, and analyze them. Just because an executive or even a designer likes a logo doesn't mean that style is consistent with the company's brand framework. These points of analysis will provide a foundation for logo development, in congruence with the key branding points already created. Consider the following example guidelines:

1. It must use a serif font. A serif font is one with decorative elements, or "trim," that start at the upper and lower ends of the strokes of the letters (sans serif fonts are devoid of trim). Times Roman and Garamond are serif fonts; Arial and Helvetica are sans serif fonts.
2. The logo must not be highly stylized, although italics might be acceptable.
3. Colors such as blue or green are good, but red or yellow are not. These must match the corporate colors and have specific PMS references. (PMS stands for Pantone Matching System, a trademarked index of colors used by designers and printers.)
4. The logo will not include any separate graphic elements.
5. The logo cannot be multiple colors, but there can be different shading or values of the same color.

While the logo is being designed, the site mapping can take place, or at least the existing information can be analyzed and reviewed by designers so that they can come up to speed. Navigation, which is really more of a framework and structure activity, nonetheless is a critical part of building a Web site and has strong visual implications. Where people see the areas to which they need to go, what standards of navigation are in place or are to be put in place, and how are visual cues coordinated in site mapping?

The Logo: A Brand Doorman

Rebecca Lyman, cofounder of The Garrigan Lyman Group, drives the firm's logo services with various branding clients. Her background in marketing at Pepsi, as well as experience with a broad range of clients—from start-ups to the *Fortune 500*—provide her with a unique insight to how a logo is created and what happens during the process. Here she provides a few strategic thoughts about logo development:

"Looking at other people's logos is an important part of the process, mostly because the opinions of the key management team help identify how they believe characteristics are expressed visually. For people who don't normally think visually, their reactions offer very good insight into their thoughts—what looks "hip" to them, what looks appealing, what sorts of shapes effectively express the company and the company's business. It is extremely important for the logo to accurately express and reflect the various brand character and attributes; however, the logo can't be ALL of them, else it results in a cacophony of messages saying ultimately nothing. . . .

"During the process of logo development, the various characteristics and attributes become prioritized and the logo, ideally, yields a result reflecting the 'essence'—the key ingredient—of the brand. Color, then, is a key to supporting that essence and adding to it, with additional characteristics and attributes supported and developed by the supporting color palette, messaging, imagery, and other complementary elements. In particular, this is why the Web site is such a critical component of the brand: It is where all the characteristics, attributes, and messages come together. . . .

"The logo process is often fascinating to the uninitiated, and frequently unlike what anyone's expectations were initially. While the guidelines are helpful in the process to establish likes and dislikes, it is not uncommon in the process for them to evolve or, in some cases, actually be discarded. The logo and all visual articulations of the brand must always support the company mission, strategy, and vision, as opposed to what might be a more tactical and 'burning' concern at the moment of development. Comfort levels are pushed and stretched, and, subsequently, the final logo can turn out to be a surprise to everyone. . . .

"For new companies, or companies with a new name, the way in which the logo is spelled has a significant effect on what is being communicated. For the last generation, and as common-usage names have become increasingly difficult to obtain or own, there has been a huge growth in hybrid names (frequently with mid-word capitalization, such as 'PeopleSoft'), as well as the use of international word parts and names or seemingly random letter combinations. As a result, spelling and capitalization have become some of the most significant variables, along with color, that need to be attended to in the visual articulation stage of branding."

Logos are a brand's doorman, serving dutifully as one of the best introductions to, and first impressions of, a company. They can also be a significant liability if they create an immediately negative impression of the organization and brand, or if they are merely bland. Building a strong brand with depth, strength, and endurance requires paying close attention to the logo's development and deployment and a commitment to ensuring that it will play a powerful role in creating a memorable, positive, and emotional attachment to the brand.

Coloring the Brand

Logo development continues through several iterations of designs, and, much like the naming process, involves a systematic fine-tuning of the appealing creations that meet the branding criteria. While color often plays a key role in how a logo is remembered (for example, the red in Compaq's logo or the blue and red in Air France), the choice of color is often the last factor involved in logo development, chosen long after fonts, designs, and graphic elements are presented.

"We don't like to show color to clients at first," said Lyman. "It tends to bias their abilities to objectively review the logo designs. They may have a favorite color, or one they don't like, and color has such emotional impact that it gets in the way of really scrutinizing a fundamental set of design elements. Color acts as a filter, directly affecting the psychological response to whatever it is shading. When logos appear in a monochromatic presentation, we've optimized the brand team's ability to make decisions logically and with a mind to branding factors—which really helps a group decision to take place effectively."

Once a final logo is chosen, the color selection process takes place, which involves looking at the logo in a series of color combinations, shades, and selections. However, actually choosing a color can be a tremendously difficult decision, influenced by myriad factors—both conscious and, in some cases, subconscious. Over the years, numerous psychological studies have that shown that color can have significant impact on a person's interpretation of an environment, object, or design. How does this affect the brand, either in terms of the logo or the colors used on the Web site? There are many choices to make, ranging from the color of the logo to the overall dominant colors of the site. Does the fact that blue seems to be highly dominant (looking at the Ariba partner site clearly illustrates that) hark back to the blue screens which dominated DOS applications? Probably not. Blue is easy to look at, it is calming, and it looks good on either LCD screens or tube-based screens. "Primary and secondary, bright, intense colors, like blue, green yellow, and red, work on the Web, because everyone's monitor is calibrated differently," says Matt Harper. "A light gray can look gray on one monitor, but bluish or yellowish on another. Bright colors, however, speak more directly— even with minor variation. This can be seen looking at a monitor— especially a flat-screen LCD screen—from the side.

"The acid test is if I'm driving down the road in front of lots of billboards, and all I see is color, what colors would I recognize? I wouldn't recognize taupe, raisin, or cream. Instead, the average person sees orange, red, and green. Those are the memorable colors, and those are the ones to stick to, for brand reasons. The red in Coca-Cola, for example, is highly recognizable even in absence of the logo or product, and people can pick it out among a sea of reds. That's what we look for when choosing color for a new brand—especially on the Web."

So coloring the brand involves understanding something about human responses to colors, not just choosing a color that simply "looks cool." And, at a broad level (although this is not an absolute), for certain types of industries some colors will be more or less appropriate.

The selection of color can make a big difference in how a brand is perceived. Through testing color success in the discovery branding phases, for example, by asking focus groups or people in a telephone survey what they like or dislike about various brands and logos, as well as testing the new brand once it is deployed, color can be discerned as a factor in brand attachment as well as in a Web site's "stickiness." Even for some otherwise wonderful sites, something as simple as an inappropriate color, one that makes fonts difficult to read on various pages or creates the wrong effect, is enough to prevent visitors from returning to the site. A good example of simple but effective color usage is the familiar "flying Windows" opening screen for Microsoft Windows: red, green, blue, yellow—all basic, easy-to-view colors highlighted against a pastel blue-and-white cloud background.

There are various utilities allowing printers to calibrate color with on-screen images, and there are even devices and utilities for professional designers and graphic artists to use to calibrate screen colors to a very precise level. However, the variations among monitors used by the average person, even people with high-end monitors and expensive graphics cards, is still so significant that, unfortunately, a least-common-denominator factor exists. Colors in magazines and billboards are much truer than colors seen on monitors because printers are able to reproduce, on paper, precisely the colors specified. All it takes is a trip to a neighborhood electronics store with a wall of televisions to see that even TVs haven't been able to come up with a way to standardize colors and quality—they're all different, even those from the same manufacturer.

In the end, three basic rules drive color usage on the Web site, and in the logo as well:

1. Use strong, basic colors and color combinations.
2. Be sure there is good contrast and/or "agreement" between fonts and color backgrounds.
3. Color usage must be appropriate for the market and audience.

There's one final test. Take away the logo, the headlines, and the images: Is it still a uniquely identifiable Web site?

Typography: From Ransom Notes to Readability

At the end of the 1980s, around the time desktop publishing came into vogue, the use of fonts on the personal computer represented a major leap in "personal brandability." The availability of these fonts, and PC-based design software, allowed a virtually limitless variety of designs and styles to adorn personal and corporate newsletters, signs, business cards, and stationery. No longer did individuals or businesses have to rely on graphic designers and expensive printing services to magically produce typography.

Unfortunately, the *abuse* of fonts was soon rampant, and many newsletters and other productions looked more like ransom notes than professional documents, with more fonts than subjects. People went wild, spending lots of money on exotic fonts and using wild combinations of serif and sans-serif faces—potpourris of type that were barely legible, much less recognizable brand elements.

Regrettably, amateur Web sites today really aren't much different from some of the documents produced during the early days of desktop publishing, featuring odd-looking fonts on sites that should look anything but odd. The choice of fonts in desktop publishing and in Web development, to be successful, still needs a trained artistic eye if a high-quality look and feel is to be achieved, and the design needs to be customized to provide a unique brand identity. Many of the fonts in major logos, for example, are designed from scratch; they're not existing commercial fonts, but rather digital alterations of existing fonts.

Fonts can have the same effect as color: certain dominant brands create a recognition factor for a particular font, even when the font is cast in a different color or used for a different brand. What makes a type treatment special may be the decorative element of the font, or the basic style, or the use of capital versus lowercase letters, or a combination of factors.

"Apple has Apple Garamond, which is a modified version," says Harper. "Is there a standard among the sea of serifs, san serifs, decoratives, and moderns? Virtually all books are typeset in serif fonts because a serif, like Times Roman, is more readable on paper. While most body text in paper form is cast in serif fonts, and is consequently more readable, headlines are most often cast in sans serif. However, on screen, sans serifs are easier to read because the resolution is lower than paper—a considerable difference meaning the decorative, serif elements are harder to read online.

"Typography is about working to transcend the font type to emphasize readability. Fonts are like colors, in that there are times when you can, for example, see an uppercase A in Apple Garamond, and know it's Apple. Modified type for logos frequently lets a real customized and recognizable identity be built for a company. Franklin Gothic, in many forms, is very common, which is what Microsoft's logo is—so it looks recognizable to almost everyone online. It's actually a great font, and Microsoft has claimed lots of brand ownership with it. The result? Any site anyone sees with this font at least subliminally makes them think 'Microsoft.'"

An interesting Web site to visit is an online museum of typography: http://members.tripod.com/abc-typography/. It features interesting discussions and examples of many font styles, providing a wealth of background and data about fonts for anyone interested in pursuing font education a little further.

In general, there are several key factors to keep in mind when working with fonts in building the Web brand, and especially when casting readable type for the Web site that will be usable in other formats:

1. Use font sizes large enough to be read comfortably, typically about 10 or 11 points.
2. Use a sans serif for online body text, and a serif font for offline body text.
3. Avoid the "ransom note" effect—limit the number of font styles to one for body text and another for headlines. Provide good contrast between headline fonts and body text, either by using very different typefaces, serif or sans serif, or using a serif face for one and a sans serif face for the other.
4. Avoid excessive use of italics, as too many italicized sections lower readability. Save the italics for single words or short phrases needing emphasis.
5. Avoid large sections of boldfaced, "heavy," or "wide" text. While useful for occasional emphasis or headlines, in body text they tend to tire readers quickly.
6. Separate paragraphs with spaces, not just indented first lines. Here, what works well in a book or magazine will not work as well online—a little white space goes a long way in keeping readers attentive. Indentation is unnecessary if space appears between paragraphs.
7. Be cautious about "reversing" font and background—for example, putting a light font against a dark background; this can be asking for readability trouble. As a general rule of thumb, the more paper-white the background, the more readable the font against it. (Incidentally, this is why print on paper, at least for the time being, is still easier to read than type on a computer screen.)
8. Make body-text paragraphs short, and not too wide—very much like a newspaper. Web sites featuring long sections of unbroken text are counterintuitive to the channel-surfing mentality that dominates Web activity today, and will simply not be read. By the same token, don't make the sections too short—an entire page of single-sentence paragraphs looks very odd.
9. For the most part, left-justified text works best. Justified text does not work as well in very narrow columns, although it can

look nice in medium-sized text blocks and in certain designs. Don't mix and match the styles, however!

10. Watch font colors—they can dramatically affect how legible a font may be against a certain background. Further, while they might look perfect on a well-calibrated monitor, they might be barely visible on another. Further, test how the Web site looks when it is printed on both black-and-white and color inkjet and laser printers—sometimes what looks great on screen looks ghastly when printed.

11. It's important, from a brand perspective, to play to the audience, but without being patronizing: Don't assume that a children's Web site should be cast in a crayonlike "kid's" font; that a site for seniors has to have giant fonts; or that a site for Asians has to have fonts that look like sticks of bamboo. On the other hand, much can be done with fonts to give brand character and identity, as long as it's tasteful. The Web site for the American Association of Retired People (www.aarp.org), for example, very tastefully addresses seniors in a respectful manner. The Asian American Network, an organization dedicated to communication among Asian Americans (www.aan.net), is a very well done, culturally sensitive site overall, and it provides good use of typography—especially considering the challenges of casting non-Western fonts on a Western Web site.

12. Foreign font styles, letters, word lengths, and keyboards differ widely. To read some Asian Web sites, for example, readers must download specific fonts. While most character sets will cover various accented lettering—such as those found in Portuguese, French, Spanish, and others—languages with a different alphabet (Cyrillic, Japanese, etc.) are another problem altogether and must be given serious consideration. A good example of how to properly cast a wide selection of languages and fonts is the AT&T global site (www.att.com/global). When providing a form-based entry in a Web site, remember to provide enough room for various words that may be longer in length when translated into a foreign language. (See Chapter 8 for more information on this and other language-related topics.)

Web Implications of Grammar, Style, and Punctuation

Maybe grammar doesn't belong in a chapter on the visual elements of branding. Then again, it's often the Web masters and designers who are responsible for the most glaring grammatical errors. Most Web site content is created and edited by writers and editors, and is usually at least close to being grammatically correct. But the headlines, promos, and other highly prominent text elements in a Web site are frequently written by nonwriters.

A style guide needs to be specified for any Web site, but it is not sufficient to simply say a Web site should, for example, "follow AP style."[2] Requiring designers to read a reference work, understand it, and then use it is expecting too much. How can the average Web designer be expected to know every last rule? The answer, once again, lies in process, method, and teamwork. Just because the Web brand is in the visual articulation stage doesn't mean the verbal people should hightail it for new projects. They must retain a commitment to ensuring that the verbal aspects of the site follow the highest standards and that any errors are promptly reported and fixed.

Stylistic consistency in writing is very important. For example, if the Web site uses commas in a series of three or more items in one place and not in another (e.g., "We have offices in the Americas, Europe, and Asia" versus "We have offices in the Americas, Europe and Asia"), the site will look sloppy. It also looks bad if in one area listed points are preceded by bullet points and in another they are simply listed in paragraph format, or if the site features colorful, descriptive text in one area and a highly technical style of writing in another. What this really means is that every Web site needs an editor, in the true, copy-editing sense of the word, who is responsible for watchdogging every word and phrase in the site. If nobody internally or at an agency can do it, then it needs to be outsourced to a specialist who can continue to edit the site.

Another factor to consider is which nationalities will use the site, because this may makes a difference in grammar and punctuation. While for non-English-speaking areas the site might be localized into another language (see Chapter 8), and grammar and punctuation will be different when the content is translated, for the English-speaking world the site will need to be consistent in grammar, punctuation, spelling, and style. Most of the English-speaking world follows what is known as the British English style (for example, commas and periods are placed outside of quotation marks; "centre" instead of "center"; etc.). But the majority of Web sites and Web traffic involves U.S. business and consumers. So what's the answer? The answer is to be as consistent as possible, and to take into consideration the point of origin of the Web site. Anyone used to British English who is reading a book written in "American" style can turn to the copyright page and see where it was published (probably in the United States); conversely, an American reading a book written with British English styles can check to see the place of publication (probably the United Kingdom or Canada). Similarly, knowing where a company is headquartered helps the Web site visitor understand certain aspects of the writing style.

Of course, that can still leave the impression that the site is from somewhere else, which can have negative implications internationally. For growing organizations with high amounts of Web traffic and the ability to colocate a Web site in various parts of the world (not just having servers in one location), it might even make sense not only to localize the foreign languages, but also to have both a British English site and an American English site. This may be a hassle, but it's been common practice in collateral productions for many years. Failing that, a decision may be made to "translate" certain things, such as paper sizes (the U.S. 8.5- by 11-inch letter paper versus the European/Asian A4) and units of measure (the metric centimetres versus the U.S. inches), etc.

The bottom line is, the grammar, style, punctuation, and spelling on a site have to be clean and well managed in a site, or they can be a big distraction for the reader and detract from the brand image overall.

Graphic and Design Elements in the Web Site

Every Web site needs graphic elements and a fundamental, consistent design that enhances "viewability" and builds the brand. However, just as with fonts, words, and colors, the graphic elements in a site can work for it or against it. Too many graphics, which prevent the site from loading quickly or which make it difficult to find information, weaken the brand. A design that overwhelms the rest of the site, leaving navigational and readability elements behind, also erodes the brand. But a site with almost nothing but text also has detrimental effects on the brand, making for poor memorability and a "flat" image.

The key lies in balance and a good sense for matching the overall design to the audience. Obviously, for a company like Corbis (www.corbis.com), the largest repository of online, original photography in the world, having images up front is a must—although they must be chosen extremely carefully given the sheer quantity and diversity of images the site contains and the markets it is targeting. Conversely, for a site such as that of Kidder Mathews & Segner Inc., a Pacific Northwest commercial real estate firm with a global business (www.kmsoncor.com), the home page needs lots of space for information, so having large amounts of graphic images on that page would be difficult. The company solved the problem by opening with a splash page, followed by a strictly text-oriented but nicely styled home page with limited graphics. The effect of the site is to give some brand personality via the splash page, but to have enough space in the home page so that it doesn't feel cramped.

Some splash pages, however, especially ones that are very demanding (they can't be interrupted) or that prevent quick access to a frequently used site, have been criticized because they just "get in the way." It's easy to see why, when everyone is running on Internet time and nobody really wants to sit and wait for a site to load, even if it is displaying a beautiful image.

It's time the world faced up to one important fact in the business-to-business Web world: Clip art has very limited value and does very little, if anything, to enhance a brand. Building a Web site is not like giving a PowerPoint presentation (where clip art is only of limited value, as well, but slightly more tolerable), and anything cartoonish simply looks silly (unless it's on a site like www.nickelodeon.com, although that doesn't contain any clip art, either . . .). Clip art on a Web site looks unprofessional. Why? Simply because it makes any branding seem frivolous and amateurish, as if the site wasn't intended to be taken seriously. On occasion, a piece of highly original art, placed *very* carefully, can be acceptable, but it's a rare occurrence—especially in business-to-business sites. Sites such as www.clipart.com provide a wealth of original clip art images where a choice, one-off morsel can be located, but *proceed with caution!*

There's a big difference between custom-designed cartoonlike graphics, such as the cute airplane on www.expedia.com, and overused and tired clip art, looking like it was cut and pasted from the Microsoft PowerPoint default samples. Generic clip art simply looks terrible, and it's important that any custom-designed graphics on a Web site don't *look* like clip art.

While clip *photos* don't look quite as bad as clip art, they can also be amateurish and detract from the brand. The tired old photos of an airplane taking off or a group of happy businesspeople—all ethnically correct, of course—in a conference room have been way overused (note the photos on www.shippingfinder.com, which is guilty of this). For businesses that are highly people-oriented, such as public relations, for example—it makes sense to show people, but with *original* photography of the *actual* people at the company. Look at the Web site, for example of A&R Partners, one of the strongest and brightest PR agencies in the high-tech world, at www. arpartners.com: All of the photos on the site are of actual employees; the feeling is decidedly non-clip-photo, and very personal.

To be certain that the site design is appropriate for the audience, it's necessary to conduct basic market research with targeted groups of people. It may seem time-consuming, but it's better to do at least a quick research project before the site launches than to find out afterward that there are some fundamental problems.

As soon as the Web was born, search engines became popular in consumers' eyes. Many of these engines had unique techniques for searching through millions of Web pages, which formed brand loyalty. "I like the kind of results this search engine pulls up" people would come to say, which meant that WebCrawler, AltaVista, Yahoo!, or whichever was the brand for them. Today most search engines have transformed themselves into portals (Google being a notable exception) and, in an effort to build brand loyalty, offer news, shopping, email, chat, games, and more. But as soon as any one of them offers a new, innovative service, you can be sure that the rest are not far from offering their own versions. It's hard for one company to garner loyalty when all of the competitors are doing the same thing.

Brand loyalty, then, is the only real way portals will make money: the more users they have, the more they can charge for ad, link placement, and search result placement. So the race is on to create loyalty through brand personality. Like magazines and newspapers, the look and feel of the various portals is beginning to speak to their potential audiences. People are starting to be attracted by editorial factors, ease of use, and coherent organization, and, later, by what cool utilities and services they offer.

According to Matt Harper, "Portal designers have to think about combining the functionality and user interface of an application used every day with the personality and ease of use of a newspaper. Yahoo! has made a brand out of being minimalist, and it uses very few optimized graphics so even a slow connection can get to the information quickly. This gives Yahoo! speed as a brand attribute, and also makes its look very distinct.

"MSN (www.msn.com) has a new, very adult brand that instills a confidence reminiscent of the NBC peacock. Its overall layout is very distinctive, serving to counteract the color-change problem. Notice the forty-five degree angle to the right of the logo, a seemingly small element which actually effectively acts as differentiation from other portal pages, the idea being the more times it is recognized, the more the user will be attracted to it."

Beyond View: Nonvisual Sensory Articulation

In the 1960s, people didn't have to be sitting on the couch to know when the television was switched to NBC; they could be anywhere in the house. NBC's three-chime sound was so distinctive the average 10-year-old could sing it on key. Over the years, other sounds have come to represent brands, as well: the AT&T "sparkle" sound, Intel's "da-da-da-da" jingle, the Microsoft Windows start-up sound, as well as a host of songs and melodies identifying various TV shows (the *Cheers* song, for example, or the *M*A*S*H* theme song), radio and TV stations, and so on.

For the most part, sensory brand articulation, at this point in time, means auditory brand articulation. While various capabilities are in embryonic stages on the Web, such as tactile feedback (used in games) with motion-producing joysticks and other devices, and PCs with the ability to "smell" their surroundings (used, for example, in industrial settings to detect carbon monoxide, etc.), the Web is still a long way from being able to provide touch, taste, and smell. There are some early efforts underway to develop devices that emit odors synchronized with various Web-initiated activities (such as the smell of roses accompanying an online greeting card), but these, too, are still a long way from broad-based consumer reality.

Sounds identifying companies and products are pure branding, however, and are readily available to anyone wishing to develop them. They create emotional attachment, memorability, and identification in a unique manner. How can this be leveraged on the Web? It already has been, and it has even been the subject of a movie: *You've Got Mail* has entered into the culture of the Web, and, just as with the NBC chimes, identifies AOL to anyone whether he or she is in the room or not—as long as the person is within earshot. This brilliant move by AOL has been single-handedly responsible for tremendous emotional attachment and immediate identification of the brand, as well as a strong, positive connotation: Who doesn't like getting mail?

With the exception of AOL, few Internet businesses have, to date, taken advantage of this type of brand opportunity online. Most people have speakers and a sound card on their computers, and multimedia systems are big business for home and business alike. A few of the online radio stations, such as www.kksf.com (a San Francisco-based light jazz station), play a sound when the site is launched, but many people behind online brands feel that playing an unsolicited sound upon entering a URL is too obtrusive. Is it? Certainly, AOL disagrees, because it both begins and ends an online session with a sound (OK, the "you've got mail" sound doesn't occur when there's no mail). In truth, those not wishing their system to emit a sound can simply turn off the sound. There are plenty of situations where sounds aren't welcome or appropriate, and the off switch is the answer, not the absence of sound altogether.

The more sound that is integrated into various Web capabilities, ranging from online video clips and videoconferencing to Web phones, TV, and radio, the more auditory branding will become not only common, but necessary. This requires companies building brands and Web sites to identify up front that auditory branding is an opportunity for them and to develop it along with the other elements of their brands.

However, for most business-to-business brands—with the exception of multimedia, film, design, or other firms using sound as a specific part of the business—auditory branding probably doesn't have any immediate value. Realistically, sound has the most opportunity in the business-to-consumer brands appealing to broad consumer audiences—such as that of AOL.

Most branding firms, however, will return a blank stare when presented with the idea of auditory branding, and won't know where to turn to create a jingle or a chime. If this is important, find a company adept in building multimedia or video production to aid in this effort. The low-end options in this case are *clearly* unacceptable, such as using a cheesy MIDI file song on the site; that will only cause brand damage. Auditory branding is somewhat similar to the use of Flash at the beginning of a site session: there are clear opportunities to use it effectively, and there are times when to use it would be a mistake.

Done right, it can be powerful. Here's how to do it right:

- Be original: Create a sound or a spoken phrase that is unique and memorable.
- Ensure that it's not intrusive or obnoxious and that it fits in with the site's purpose and general use.

- Keep it short.
- Leverage it in other ways: in corporate videos, demos, CD-ROMs, trade shows, etc.
- Use real, recorded sound, not digitally produced computer sounds—in other words, don't use MIDI files.

Remember that sound is very powerful, and can work against a brand as much as for it.

Physical Branding: The Shape of the Internet

Physical shapes long predate the Internet in brand identity. The shape of everything from silverware to airplanes embodies branding: Absolut Vodka and its highly memorable bottle shape, the dashboard of a BMW, the style of a Stetson hat, the shape of a Fender Stratocaster guitar, the Gillette Sensor razor, and even works of architecture such as the Eiffel Tower or Corcovado (the statue of Christ soaring above Rio de Janeiro). Three-dimensional objects help define brands in a three-dimensional world, but how do they define them in the two-dimensional world of the Web?

Certainly, the Web is surrounded by three-dimensional objects of access: PCs, monitors, printers, digital cameras, mice, keyboards, desks, scanners, modems, hubs, and on and on. These devices all carry with them the concept of branding in a physical sense, and support the experience occurring on the Web. Many of the accoutrements of the Web, such as hand-held PCs, are three-dimensional devices that almost let users "touch" the Web. Phones that provide Internet access, such as the AT&T PocketNet, are physical devices almost completely integrated with a Web experience.

To an increasing degree, companies producing hardware devices also must consider the software and Web implications of these products. People speak of the not-so-distant future when the world will be a set of connected and communicating devices, an intelligent mix of embedded systems and Internet access, all controlled by and aware of virtual "alpha" humans with their own identifying devices. Whether a refrigerator, a PC, a car communications and entertainment system, or a printer, they will all be connected. And they will all have a physical character and brand identity that will need to be integrated into the Web design.

Companies that build devices with an electrical engineering architecture and layout, and simply cram them into off-the-shelf, generic boxes, are missing the opportunity to connect their physical, three-dimensional brands to their two-dimensional brands on the Internet. That involves more than just plastering a logo onto a device: It means applying brand attributes, personality, and (here it is again) *process* to the design.

Physical branding is industrial design plus brand development, and it's the difference between the value of a pair of Nike sneakers ($200 or more in Japan) and the value of a generic pair from a cheap shoe outlet. It's what made the Gillette Sensor—driven by the design genius of Dieter Rams at Braun (owned by Gillette)—such an immediate sensation. Why else would just another razor become so immediately and dramatically popular? (Clue: It wasn't the extra blade.)

This all boils down to the following concept that applies to any company building a physical device or product: integrate it closely into the branding process taking place for the Web and other parts of the company. It is yet another opportunity to build higher levels of brand consistency, emotional attachment, and return business.

Web Design with Branding in Mind

Designing Web sites is big business today. It stands as one of the top 20 businesses *on* the Web, and the kinds of Web sites being designed range from those created by 13-year-olds with a copy of Microsoft FrontPage building a relatively simple site for their schools to vastly intricate, transaction-based commerce sites with hundreds of page views and extensive use of Flash programming.

Portals such as Yahoo!, Lycos, and AltaVista essentially provide many of the same services: news, search engines, entertainment, weather, shopping, auctions, and email. Yet they differ considerably in how they present themselves from a design and brand standpoint.

The process of project management, particularly management of software development, traditionally involves a step called "require-ments gathering," which is derived from standard software devel-opment methodology. Web development in the New Economy de-mands a committed marriage of traditional requirements-gathering methodology with the most progressive marketing savvy.

Great Web project managers inspire great Web development by transcending traditional requirements: they also combine customized components for Web site development with brand matter resulting from brand framework and articulation. These serve as valuable tools in both the creative and technical aspects of Web site development. The resulting Web site development strategy is a product of the brand process combined with the requirements for competing in the New Economy. Because this strategy stems directly from the brand-ing process, constructing Web development and strategy requires key milestones:

• Clearly defined brand strategy
• Clearly defined business objectives
• Clearly defined site objectives
• Identifying and understanding the Web site's target audience(s)
• Competitive analysis from the perspective of the Web

Why care about these milestones? Brand strategy answers the ques-tion, "Who are we?" The answer helps define the consistent identity being created in the market. Clearly defined business objectives an-swer the question, "What do we want out of the Web site?" Site objectives define the purpose of the site; they are the "call to action," traditionally a key factor in any advertisement and equally important in creating an engaging Web site. The site objectives are a carefully selected subset of the broader business objectives achievable via the Web. Understanding the target audience answers the question, "Who are we communicating with?" as well as "What motivates them? What are they looking for on the Web? What are their online be-haviors?" Finally, competitive analysis allows the developer and/or designer to understand who else is in the space, and helps drive de-velopment of a site that is more effective than the competition.

The Web strategy is the cohesion of all these elements and is what drives the creative and functional design of the site. Everything in a Web site needs to reflect the brand: every page, every paragraph, every image, every font, and every headline. It's essential to be as diligent as possible, and to educate everyone involved in building and designing a site as to what the brand expectations are and what the essential branding criteria require.

The Cost of Building a Web Brand

How much should it cost to build a Web brand, including a name, a tag line, a Web site and its design, and the infrastructure to support it? The question is a difficult one to answer, simply because so many variables affect the answer, many of which extend beyond the bounds of basic design:

- What are the expected revenues of the company?
- How much financing does the company have?
- Is the financing venture capital-based, "angel"-based,[3] or personal?
- Is the Web site meant to be a primary point of business or merely a way to direct business to other locations?
- Will the Web site conduct ecommerce, such as selling products or exchanging money?
- How localized will the Web site need to be in terms of international language factors, currency exchange, etc.?
- Does the company already have established brand parameters that can be extended to the Web site, or are they being created from scratch?
- How much traffic will the site need to support?
- Will the company need to hire additional staff to run the Web site? How many? In what areas?
- How does the company expect the Web site to affect revenue stream in the coming year(s)? Will it drive new business to the company, or will it be simply in support of an existing revenue stream and not expected to build new business?
- Will the site need to have an intranet capability for internal use,

or an extranet capability, capable of providing private, secure access for partners and vendors?
• What level of security will the site require?

Clearly, many issues affect building a Web site beyond the design. A simple corporate Web site without any ecommerce and without much thought given to building a brand might be obtained off the shelf for $5000 to $20,000—which can be provided by companies like Verio. The "I know somebody who knows someone whose brother can build a great Web site" factor may also play a role, and many companies have trotted down the road to Web site ruin (and brand ruin, as well) by listening to the siren call of frugality.

That's not to say a Web site and brand development have to be overpriced, either—although the two areas are awash with stories of astronomical pricing. Because there are so many variables, and because the market is so absolutely new, design and development costs vary wildly. It's not uncommon for a company to issue an RFP (request for proposal) to three or four different creative service firms for the design of a new, relatively modest Web site, including detailed articulation of the branding, development, design, and infrastructure requirements, and for the proposals to be returned with price estimates ranging from $10,000 to $200,000. How can an executive evaluate such a range? On the one hand, the low price is attractive and will get the company going quickly. On the other hand, if another firm's estimate is so high, it must be offering something that isn't in the cheaper ones, right?

The answer is a resounding "maybe." Frequently the lower-priced professional Web sites are produced by companies that limit the costs of development by leveraging one basic design into many (like the Verio model). For some companies this is adequate, especially if they already have a good sense of their brand and feel it can be effectively shoehorned into a prefab Web design. Often the high-cost Web sites are produced by name-brand design houses, which may or may not be worth much. For many start-ups, having Web sites built by huge, overly bureaucratic design and branding conglomerates may get them nothing more than a flurry of young account execs anxious to earn their junior-branding merit badges, even at the cost of a client or two.

Perhaps that's too cynical: The name-brand firms, like Landor, Interbrand, and others, provide phenomenal services and build world-class brands that literally define the market. But they're not for everyone.

For a relatively well-funded new company, or one that is looking to redefine itself and relaunch, probably the solution is to look for the best of both worlds: a consulting firm that pays good attention to it, provides good services, has good references from both small and large companies, understands branding, and knows technology and the New Economy—and won't charge a fortune. Even for the Fortune 500 firm looking to create a new image, in today's world the answer isn't necessarily to look to a behemoth design firm for the right solution.

Look for process. Demand process. Don't pay for a design or a Web site; *pay for a process.* Insist that the company articulate what it does in clear terms. If a process seems overly complicated, ask for it to be explained. A process is worthless if it can't be adapted to fit the situation, so ensure that it can be. Off-the-shelf Web site designs will require the company to fit within a rigid process, and the big-money designs may offer a process so complicated that even an engineer would have trouble deciphering it. Either of these can be a warning signal, and it is worth having face-to-face meetings with the design firms to understand better how the process will be applied.

Building a brand and a Web site isn't a simple process. It's not a cheap process, either. It's important to match the right solution to the company so that every possible dollar is properly leveraged and comes back with a high return—both in actual revenue and perceived value. Analyze the variables, be as specific as possible in the RFP, check references, and conduct in-depth questioning of the various potential teams as to their processes and their abilities to thoroughly understand a brand and its implications. Then, and only then, cut a check.

The results of the visual and sensory stages of building a Web brand often make the difference between attracting and deterring business. The right design is a tremendous asset to a brand, while a poor design causes immediate erosion. Failure to integrate this stage with the framework and verbal articulation stages is the single most important cause of a an ineffective handoff from the initial branding effort to the more tactical side of marketing, yet, integrating these stages seamlessly ensures a powerful, enduring brand.

For companies extending brands to the Web, it is essential to look at design and visual—and even sensory—articulation as issues of considerable interest and concern at the highest levels of the company. Coca-Cola's greatest brand exposure, in terms of sheer numbers of consumers, may still be its soda cans, but for investors, partners, financial and service providers, and other high-value contacts, with interests far beyond a simple product, the Web site may be the primary introduction to the company as well as an ongoing place of contact.

While "pure" Internet companies take Web brands seriously, many bricks-and-mortar firms still view the Web as an electronic brochure. It's clear the entire business world is in a state of flux, evaluating and attempting to understand the impact of integrating the Web into normal business life. It is also clear that business-to-business brands have *particular* opportunities to extend business on the Web. The consumer brands, such as Coke, will always sell soft drinks, no matter what their Web presence is. But many businesses, such as industrial transportation, industrial service providers (such as garment manufacturers, for example), and telecommunications service providers, may find their businesses chipped away by companies who have established a powerful presence on the Web.

For those responsible for building and maintaining a brand, this type of competition and change in industry means the visual articulation of the brand has to be closely synchronized with all other aspects of the brand, and that the brand's visual identity both offline and online needs to be carefully monitored. For many firms, the right visual articulation can provide a tremendous opportunity to leapfrog the competition and advance market position.

Visual articulation can be the most emotional and "sticky" element of building a Web brand. If the Web site is the window to the brand, then by all means make the window beautiful, clear, and bright and frame it well, creating a medium that illuminates both the people looking through the window and the company that developed it.

6

The Execution Stage

Launching, Pruning, and Rediscovery

Three things are to be looked at in a building; that it stand on the right spot, that it be securely founded; that it be successfully executed.
—Johann Wolfgang von Goethe; *Elective Affinities,* 1808[1]

A brand, and a brand on the Web in particular, once developed must be given the proper environment, cultivation, and nurturing in order to grow and flourish. And, like any other spirit, it needs the proper amount of attention and guidance in order to mature and attain its full potential.

Products and organizations alike, freshly branded, require a purposeful launch and a golf-swing attitude toward followthrough in maintaining a brand freshness far beyond the labors of naming, framework, and design. The execution stage of Web branding takes the new brand through launch and life cycle, ultimately returning the five-stage cycle to rediscovery—in essence, coming full circle. This does not mean that every product and company has to *recreate* itself; on the contrary, an enduring brand—such as IBM, Nestlé, and Mitsubishi—can live for astonishingly long periods. But every enduring brand has cycled through the stages of discovery, framework, verbal and visual articulation, and execution numerous times in different ways as the markets and competition have changed, as new business opportunities have come about, as consumer trends have migrated and mutated, as technology has evolved, and as brand awareness has grown.

The execution stage of Web branding comprises activities that normally take place when a company or a product launches and extends itself into a business cycle. What differentiates the execution stage of branding is that the life of the organization or product is considered a *part* of the branding process, instead of simply the *result* of it. A brand isn't simply a baton being handed off to the next runner in a relay—it's the entire spirit of the team. The execution stage is broken into three distinct stages:

1. *Launch.* Ensuring the new Web brand is appropriately and successfully introduced
2. *Pruning and maintenance.* Keeping the Web brand alive and healthy, responsive to and thriving in a variety of market conditions
3. *Rediscovery.* Reevaluating the brand, understanding how effective it has been, and determining future direction

As with so many other areas of this book, such as the discussions on design, research, and name development, entire texts could be written on any one area of execution. This chapter is intended to provide a broad-brushstroke view that emphasizes the need for continuity and process and analyzes how a brand is redefined in the context of the Web. Many of the operative principles don't represent profoundly new thinking in and of themselves; however, the Web has made it necessary to take a fresh look at how the principles are leveraged and managed. For any type of organization—from nonprofit to legacy to pure technology—the Web has become the common denominator that exposes all of them to Internet-connected humanity. As such, branding itself must move up a notch to the next level of performance and service—in essence, to a stage of rediscovery. The New Economy allows branding to build upon the significant awareness it has enjoyed over the last 50 years and to apply it to the biggest opportunity for success it has yet encountered: the Web.

Launching the New Web Brand

Chances are, having completed its due diligence in the discovery, framework, and articulation stages of branding, a team of eager executives anxious to begin a stream of revenue will do just about anything to launch its new Web brand. In fact, the team may have the brand up and running well before it is launched in a marketing sense. "Stealth" launches, before a new brand goes public, are intended to test the site and to begin to serve a quiet group of key clients or partners. This is not unlike what community business and retail shops have been doing for decades, opening their doors for preferred customers well before the local chamber of commerce dignitaries come equipped with giant scissors to perform the ritual ribbon cutting in celebration of the grand opening.

As noted in earlier chapters, there are many types of Web brands: those which are replacing a previous Web site, pure technology brands where the Web site is directly responsible for generation of revenue, showplace sites for consumer product brands, and sites designed simply to generate leads for doing business. Whatever the purpose, launching a Web brand requires that a number of key questions be answered before the proverbial grand opening can take place:

- For what audience is the Web site being launched: consumers at-large, a vertical business community, a special-interest group (e.g., environmentalists)?
- What cultures, languages, or countries is the site intended for?
- What will the impact be on the market?
- Will the launch be relatively quiet, or a big splash?
- What competitive issues will need to be considered?
- Which venues of marketing communications (e.g., advertising, PR, events, etc.) will be the most effective and economically sensible to use for the launch?
- How will the success of the launch be measured? What factors need to be in place at the outset in order to gauge outcome?
- Outside the company, who needs to be informed of the launch prior to it taking place: partners, analysts, investors, key clients, press?
- What are the possible negative implications of the launch, if any: release of company information to competitors, criticism from outside groups, negative press?
- Is the company prepared for business to begin in earnest? What if

the launch is so successful that it begins a stream of business inquiries or orders that cannot be handled?
• Is there any specific event or other industry occurrence to take
  into consideration that may impact the launch or provide an opportunity for higher levels of visibility?

Before the tactical elements of marketing can begin to roll, a realistic launch date must be set. Typically, this is less of an issue for
the company that already is doing business and has a Web site, and
is simply launching a rebranded site and image. For new companies,
however, or for new products or services being launched, the launch
date is a serious consideration.

Why not just put the site up and begin marketing? Launching a
brand on the Web usually means letting people know about it *off*
the Web, through various marketing communications tools. The
irony of the Web is that it is really a very poor venue for splashy
launches, with broad simultaneous visibility to large groups of people. The Web is much more effective as a one-to-one tool for ful-
filling a brand promise made through other vehicles of publicity and
marketing. And because these require planning and timing to coordinate, picking the right date is important.

One of the foremost tasks that must be accomplished before the
launch team can begin its job is to ensure that everyone on the team
has been fully briefed about the brand: its attributes, how it is articulated, the reason behind its name, and what it intends to achieve.
Once informed, the team can begin to identify appropriate venues
and tactical tools for launching the brand that will ensure that the
brand becomes as established as possible, as quickly as possible. Just
as the verbal articulation team needs to ensure that the design and
visual articulation team is fully informed about the brand, so must
the group that has created the brand do everything possible to give
complete information to those launching it.

Light the Fuse and Run . . .

"Okay, so you've built your brand identity. You've read all the books
. . . invested in the focus groups . . . done some online research . . .

whatever it took. The result? People now recognize your brand and associate it with your value statement.

"But wait. Before you go any further, give some thought to how that brand will be transmitted in the electronic age. More than ever before, the appearance of your brand identity is affected by a number a factors. In the past, you made sure that your logo was reproduced with the specified Pantone colors. You worked diligently to ensure that the copyright (©) or trademark symbol (™) was attached and displayed properly. But the bottom line was, you had control over how it was presented.

"In the electronic world, you give up some of that control. You can make sure that the graphic file you use on your Web site was created using the right colors. But you have no control over how that logo is being viewed. The user's monitor may need adjusting. Or the user may be viewing your content on a screen with limited viewing options, such as a handheld computing device or a Web-telephone device. The bottom line now is, you've got to focus more on the value of the brand name and less on its appearance.

"Another issue facing today's brand managers is how to deliver the company's images over an increasingly congested Internet. When customers hit your Web site, the last thing you want is for your image to take forever (read: more than 2 seconds) to load. But depending upon how wildly successful you are in your endeavors, you may have millions of people hitting your page at once. The solution? Divide the load. Don't rely on one system to serve up your whole site. Look into load-balancing systems that can serve up various portions of content quickly. This also provides a backup system if one machine (or segment of the Internet) goes down. Service providers exist today that can spread your content over numerous machines located in disparate regions of the world.

"Finally, there is an insidious danger lurking in the world of electronic branding—brand hijacking. All too common are tales of users typing a trusted, well-known Web address into their browsers, only to find a much different message than expected. You don't want customers visiting www.yourcompany.com to be greeted by a personal message from Olga the Porn Queen. If you're going to let your trusted brand out into the Internet world, make sure you've made the investment in the security measures needed to protect this valuable asset." (*Allen Biehl, director of national consulting practices for CompuCom, a Dallas-based IT/ebusiness consulting firm*)

At this point the launch team should have a comprehensive document discussing the brand, what it means, and the justification for its creation. Everyone on the team needs to have a copy of this, and to read it carefully. At the very least, and as part of the launch process in any event, there needs to be a kickoff meeting of the launch team where the brand team makes a presentation on the brand and is available to answer any questions or concerns. The brand team may also want to present specific ideas about how the brand should be launched, and may have information about the advisability of particular marketing communications ploys.

Sometimes, especially in the case of small, start-up companies, the brand team and the launch team may be made up of the same group of people. In most cases, they will have been assisted in developing the brand by an outside firm, but may be using other services to launch it, such as an advertising agency, PR firm, or events company. It is absolutely essential that representatives and *active* members of the team or teams get together at the outset of the launch and discuss how everything will work together to ensure that the launch is successful and *consistent*. The success of a brand launch, on the Web in particular, is directly dependent upon how effective the team has been in determining the right venue, mapping to the articulated business plan and brand, spending money wisely, and coordinating its efforts.

Guidelines for Analyzing Marketing Communications Opportunities

There are pros and cons to the many marketing communications opportunities that are available to Web brands today, and impulse isn't the best guide in determining how to spend a hard-earned (or laboriously located) launch budget. At this stage of executing a Web brand, it is useful to examine the pros and cons of the various types of marketing activities to determine what venues are best for maximizing the visibility of the new brand in the target markets, taking into account the type of product or service, the business model (e.g., business to business or business to consumer), and marketing budget.

A preliminary comparison of the various combinations, where each is evaluated against all the others, can be surprisingly effective. It's amazing how various ideas which seemed so good—or even so bad—can change colors when compared with other opportunities. There are always specific considerations for a brand that will be listed either as pros or as cons, depending on the company: budget issues, how easy the brand name is to remember (which has a direct bearing on whether or not to advertise on billboards or the radio), the timing of certain opportunities and events, the level of visibility of certain board members or company leaders, and so on.

In general terms, every type of marketing activity needs to be considered as a potential launch tool. Each, however, offers specific opportunities as well as drawbacks, especially when considered in the context of the Web as an integrated part of the brand and launch. Discussed below are the major available launch tools, with high-level pros and cons and specific issues relating to the Web listed for each. It's important to keep in mind that no two situations are exactly alike, and what is a boon for one company may be a disaster for another, so these are *general* guidelines. The intent is to paint a broad picture of the communications tool set and describe how each tool is affected by the New Economy.

PR with Purpose

Long the marketing bastion of credibility, especially for technology companies, public relations has taken a beating over the last few years, primarily because of the explosive proliferation of Web companies. While 30 years ago the term "public relations" meant a wide variety of nonadvertising promotions, with media and analyst relations being merely one component, today PR in the United States is, by and large, only relations with the press and analysts. Big nontechnology companies still turn to PR methodology to generate interest, such as community campaigns or philanthropic sponsorships, but people doing business on the Internet are likely to think of one thing when they think of PR: getting ink (digital or conventional). They also think about whatever they can do to charm the analyst community (industry analysts, like Gartner, IDC, Forrester, Meta Group, Giga, Dell'Oro Group, etc., as opposed to financial analysts, which are a different lot). Bear in mind the need to generate meaningful visibility and brand recognition, not simply increased exposure.

THE PR AGENCY PROBLEM

Public relations agencies today turn down business routinely (many agencies even have full-time staff whose job it is to politely reject new business opportunities), but executives of start-ups still expect that agencies will jump to be able to represent their hot new Internet play. While this is changing somewhat as the economy softens and fewer start-ups roam the streets, the complaint that start-ups can't get agencies to return their calls is still all too common. When they do obtain a meeting with an agency, the agency's attitude is "don't call us, we'll call you"—hardly what the average CEO wants to hear from a service provider. According to an August 2000 article in the *San Jose Mercury News,* "Alexander Ogilvy PR, one of the largest firms, had 1600 unsolicited incoming new-business inquiries, and signed only 15 new clients in 1999."[2] The agencies today that are taking the lead are the ones that maintained more of an open, approachable policy during the dotcom boom years, and are known to have the best new-client attitudes in today's growing "Customer Economy."

THE PRESS PROBLEM

But agencies aren't the only issue. As recently as 1996, lining up a press tour for a little-known, perhaps even completely unknown, company was quite easy. Setting up a two-week fishing expedition could yield meetings with two-dozen technology and business journalists in Boston, New York, Washington, D.C., and San Francisco. The expected outcomes were several key articles (assuming the pitch was good and the company and its technology were sound and newsworthy), the beginnings of good relationships, and a CEO excited about the prospects of media coverage and newly educated in its mostly positive realities. Today's journalist is a different animal, more cynical than ever (or else entirely junior), and, unfortunately, lacking the time to build the relationships that gave PR a good name eons ago.

"We were expected, as soon as the publication went online, to write two-for-one stories," confidentially confessed a senior writer from a major high-tech weekly publication. "All of a sudden, the monthlies and weeklies were competing for daily coverage on the net, our workload doubled, and all the while the magazine told us 'It's really not any more work.' It was. And it is. I don't have time to do research like I used to, and PR flaks hound me every hour of the day thinking they have the greatest story since Watergate and the best product since the Palm."

Further compounding these media problems has been the gradual decline of the broad-based appeal of technology publications such as *InfoWorld, Information Week,* and *eWeek* (formerly *PC Week*), which have retreated to "techie" reader bases as New Economy publications like *Business 2.0, The Industry Standard,* and *Red Herring* have taken hold of advertisers and readers who don't need to be technocrats to understand what they're reading. As a result of the shift in interest to these publications, agencies and PR professionals have had to build entirely new sets of media targets, and new contacts as well.

So what's the good "news," so to speak? For one thing, the importance of self-publishing has grown. Every Web site is its own online publication, and companies that keep the information on their sites fresh keep interested readers coming back. Vertical information sources, such as industry-specific portals, have also become increasingly important. Often vertical industries use news from these portals as daily or weekly "feeds" to their sites to make sure their own customers will keep coming back. While in the past companies might have considered vertical publications and news sources only as secondary targets, today they are primary targets if for no other reason than a savvy PR person has given the company a realistic picture of today's broader business and technology press.

For the big companies, no matter what the market, PR has always been and always will be a strong and necessary part of the communications mix, and the Web has simply become a way to disseminate information more broadly and effectively. And, especially for the lesser-known firms, high-quality PR techniques are more important than ever, and PR people must have a consuming passion for heeding the requirements and interests of the press. The quickest way to be blacklisted is for a company to pitch the wrong story or to ignore protocol with an editor who's already running out of time when he or she picks up the phone.

Realistic Releases

"Sometimes a press release can overreach what a product does—for me, as a reporter, that undercuts the company's credibility. It's not uncommon that when a company is new they come out with a whole spate of customers they've had—which is hard to believe. Also, when it's hard to figure out what they do, I lose interest quickly. If they can't tell me in a paragraph what they do, how can I have a grasp of it? A product with a relatively simple name combined with a well-articulated message and description is important to help me understand what it is. For example, "nomad" is a great name for a wireless email service. But I see that being *too* descriptive, as well, can be a problem and can limit a company or a product as they expand.

"The bottom line? Tell me what you do, don't make false or unbelievable claims, explain it quickly and articulately, and make it memorable. Then you've got my attention." (*Jeanne Lang Jones, Senior Correspondent, LocalBusiness.com*)

For the vast majority of firms today, company-generated PR turns out not to be an option, even for a small start-up firm in a vertical market. Why? Because once the URL goes up, the public sees the company. The media become interested and they call. At this point, for companies with no PR planning, the situation becomes instantly reactive. Remember, "media" is the plural of "medium"—and the press is a medium through which a brand reaches an audience, not an end in and of itself. Understanding and managing the media is what PR firms are paid to do. This isn't to say that every company needs a top-10 PR agency and has to spend a quarter of a million dollars annually on PR. It, should, however, have a savvy marketing communications person or department that knows how to handle the press and to write press releases. It also means the CEO needs to understand what PR is and what to expect from it. Here are some tips for thinking about PR:

- Try to publish press releases on a regular basis, at least one per month, and have a "press room" as part of the Web site. Sporadic activity, once every couple of months or even less often, makes the company appear inactive and unsuccessful.
- When PR is a commitment of the company at the president/CEO level, it has the highest opportunity for success. Companies that put the PR effort on the back burner rarely succeed in building a strong public image.
- Look for speaking engagements within an industry, market, or region: They reinforce the company's public image, and the press often looks to speakers for quotes and stories.
- If finding a big agency is a problem, consider using a new type of agency and service, known as "prelaunch PR" or "start-up PR." This service is designed to get a company up and running, introduced to the press, launched with first press releases and maybe even a press tour, and educated on media relationships. Once the company is up to cruising altitude, the start-up firm can introduce it to big PR firms (with whom the service may have established relationships). Be sure, however, that the PR firm—start-up or not—really has a good grasp of corporate communication and what it means, and isn't just serving as a "press release machine."
- Unless the executive team has strong experience with the press, go through media training. There are "do's and taboos" with the press, and tried-and-true methods of communications that can be learned only through training and practice. Most agencies will provide media training services, which can range from a few hours spent reviewing technique to all-day sessions complete with videotaping and interviewing using live journalists. One note of caution, however: Check out the service with the agency carefully. Some agencies are gaining reputations for charging outlandish fees for

media training, often with outsourced facilitators who could care less about the client's brand.

- Make the most of partner press opportunities, and, for every major sales success or other agreement, work with the customer on issuing a press release.
- Companies with business outside the United States should engage firms that have a strong understanding of global PR and that have partners or a presence elsewhere. Make sure consistency is strong, and be aware that PR differs from country to country.
- Be responsive to the press—make them the highest priority if and when they call. A senior PR staff member at Intel said that Andy Grove has stated that "he can be interrupted in *any* meeting—with the exception of a board meeting—by a PR person who has someone from the press who needs him. Furthermore, he *expects* to be interrupted."
- Build strong relationships with industry analysts. The press goes to them for analysis and market detail, and in turn alerts them to new players in the market. Meeting with analysts is often the first thing to do before launching a company or product, well before the press is informed. This means, however, that a budget needs to be established for analysts because the only real way to get their ears is to be a paying client (unlike the press!). Analyst firms range from small, one-person shops to giant behemoths such as Gartner or IDC, and fees vary accordingly. But strong analyst programs can make an *immense* difference in the success of an emerging brand, and industry analysts can help significantly by playing Devil's advocate and advising on business plans, corporate presentations, and market research. When establishing a PR program, put the analyst issue at the top of the list.
- *PR pros.* Public relations efforts are highly credible and relatively affordable, especially when compared with advertising although PR agency retainers have climbed considerably, and often begin at retainer levels of $30,000 or more for top agencies and $20,000 for midrange firms. They present qualitative information, which is helpful in explaining a new, complex business. PR is an excellent extension of the branding process and a strong and compelling

method of increasing customers and building confidence among partners, vendors, and investors.

- *PR cons.* There are no guarantees. No amount of advertising will convince an editor to meet with a company (in the United States, at least, a common misconception among young companies is that the press will give priority to advertisers, which could not be further from the truth, and a surefire way to get blacklisted). The PR process is long and arduous; unlike advertising, it can take months to gain visibility, and there is no predictable outcome; once the campaign is launched, it can be dramatically difficult to get recognition or create "newsworthy" events.

- *Web implications.* Public relations is truly different today than in the pre-Internet days. It is no longer a good-old-boy network, although, over time, editors can become trusted allies and relationships can be built. There are many new venues of PR activities as a result of the Web, such as vertical portals, the Web site itself, and the ability to post press releases on partner sites.

It All "Ads" Up

It's nearly impossible *not* to see Web brand advertising today. Internet brands are everywhere, from massively expensive TV ads during the Super Bowl to taxis in Singapore, and even candy bars and laundry detergent have URLs listed on the package. Ironically, in fact, the least viable place to advertise a URL is *on* the Web. For most companies (with a few exceptions), Web-based banner advertising has been a failure. Instead, most companies have turned to ads in newspapers, radio, magazines, TV, packaging, billboards, biplane-dragged sky banners, store receipts, direct mail offerings, and restaurant menus to encourage traffic to the Web site.

"We dumped literally *hundreds* of thousands of dollars into banner ads, which turned out to have a positively abysmal click-through rate," said one San Francisco-based business-to-consumer Internet executive who asked to remain unnamed. "The whole banner thing seemed like a logical, good idea, but in reality did nothing more than get our name in the face of surfers intent on paying attention to other information. We switched to billboards along high-volume commuter corridors, and to print ads in a couple of key magazines, which had more effect in three months on building traffic to our site than nearly a year of banner ads."

In a September 1, 2000 article *The Wall Street Journal* reported that "Web advertising isn't working as well as everyone had expected."[3] For specific services that directly apply to a given site—such as the Driveway.com ads on three email sites, which offer increased storage space—banner ads make sense. For online advertising, however, companies are wiser working to be listed on appropriate portals and search engines, where people go to find them—essentially employing a "pull" as opposed to a "push" online strategy. Getting listed on Yahoo!, Alta Vista, Google, Lycos, Go, and the other major portals and search engines can be a time-consuming, intensive, and difficult effort, but ultimately can yield the most return in online visibility.

With so many possible advertising venues, how can effective decisions be made about launching a brand through advertising? The answer, at least in part, lies in first identifying the nonoptional areas of advertising versus those that are discretionary. Companies that produce consumable physical products (e.g., a soda can or a disposable camera) obviously have no choice but to put the URL onto the product itself; if the product is nonconsumable (such as a stereo, car, furniture, etc.), the URL is put on the packaging and on accompanying product materials (e.g., a manual). Companies that provide services have to place a URL onto literature, business cards, receipts, and anywhere else the company name is displayed or viewed.

So much for the *required* forms of advertising, which leaves the *optional* forms. There are so many ways to advertise a company today that it is tremendously difficult to determine which is the best, but defaulting to understanding the audience is *always* the best way to clarify the situation. This is where tying the execution stage to the information garnered in the discovery stage of branding can be so beneficial. Using the market research which took place in discovery, the team responsible for execution should ask consumers, clients, and others where they find information, what they read, and so on. For most business-to-business brands, homing in on a target audience, and avoiding a shotgun style of advertising, will always yield the best results.

Usually, the difficult part of advertising a Web brand isn't finding *where* to advertise it, but rather figuring out *how* it should be advertised. This is where the branding efforts of the four preceding stages will again pay off, by providing a checklist for advertising at both the visual and verbal levels. Recently, for example, SAP featured a wide-ranging series of airport billboard advertisements for MySap.com. Unfortunately, the ads gave literally no information about SAP or MySap.com, and unless the person seeing the ad knew what SAP was (and, in spite of being one of the world's largest private software companies in the world, most people haven't a clue as to what the company does), the ad was completely useless. It was unclear from the ad whether it was a consumer brand, a business-to-business brand, a service, a product, or anything else.

Unfortunately, branding errors such as this one are all too common after an overly ambitious agency pushes a concept beyond being useful for a corporate brand. With the widespread proliferation of Web brand ads, it's incumbent upon each company—unless it's already a household name—to ensure that the ads quickly and efficiently describe the company and what it's doing, and establish brand identity. There are just too many URLs and information noise for people to be forced to figure out enigmatic advertisements in addition to everything else they're doing on Internet time.

Ronald Chan, managing director of ZenderFang, a Singapore-based advertising and creative agency and former branding executive with major international firms such as Y&R, put it this way: "People are enamored of the technology of the Web, but they've forgotten about basic marketing principles. Ad agencies have added to the problem; lots of dotcom companies have come about and ads have been created, but they don't tell you what the company does. They've done the ad in absence of the brand."

"Traditional advertising is a sunset business," says Jovan Tay, managing director of Brandz (www.brandz.org), a Southeast Asian branding and marketing firm. "Clients have outgrown ad agencies that haven't kept up with the New Economy and the changes it brings. Many are not able to grow as fast and ably as the clients. It's essential that any advertising initiative—wherever in the world it takes place—positions the brand at the highest priority and then everything is more likely to flow naturally, whether it's the Web, a print ad campaign, or a big event. Those are the advertising agencies that will become the big winners in the years to come."

When a creative team presents advertising concepts, ask team members to explain how the brand will be integrated with their work. Watch for a good balance of brand personality versus brand character attributes, and remember the goals set in the brand-mapping exercise: Do the ad concepts reflect where the brand is going, or where it's been? Is the ad concept sufficiently exciting and engaging, but without going outside the bounds of the established personality parameters? Are the concept and pitch driven by the specific advertising venue or by a true understanding of the problem the company is working to solve for clients?

- *Advertising pros.* Advertising is the fastest, most immediate way to get a new brand known; it is highly controllable and can be very targeted, and there are a vast number of venues available. Properly executed ads are a great way to express a brand.
- *Advertising cons.* Advertising campaigns can be extremely expensive. They offer less credibility than PR, and it may be difficult to choose from the plethora of options for where the ad might appear. Certain venues can be less than effective (e.g., banner ads).
- *Web implications.* Advertising the Web brand usually means advertising *off* the Web but finding the most targeted audience. Certain forms of URL advertising are nonoptional—there's no excuse for *not* having a brand URL listed on a product (or its packaging or documentation), business card, or other point of exposure. For optional advertising, it's essential that the effort put into establishing the online brand and the company also be used in the creation of the advertising campaign, whatever it may be.

The New Event Horizon

There is an explosion of event opportunities today, with numerous Internet and ecommerce trade shows and seminars of all sizes taking place in all regions. Giant technology trade shows like Comdex in Las Vegas or CeBIT in Hannover, Germany, can be overwhelming even for medium-sized companies, and small shows seem to have little impact.

Launching a new brand at a trade show is tricky, and this option must be *very* carefully considered. A trade show launch usually means that physical property must be designed, built, and set up (which can be expensive and time-consuming); the right event must come at the right time in relation to when the company wants the brand to launch; the overall cost of travel, sponsorships at the show, time out of the office, company "trinkets" (also called "swag") and the booth space must be calculated. While one data point is to consider the "cost per lead," a number obtained by dividing the number of qualified leads the show generated by the total cost of the show, this figure doesn't yield meaningful information on how effectively the company image and identity were established.

Infinite Technology (recently acquired by Captaris Corporation), the wireless application protocol (WAP) company from Baltimore quoted earlier in this book, exhibits at a surprisingly high number of shows for a company of its size. Essentially this came about because the president, in the early days of WAP, went to great lengths to educate the market on the various technology aspects of WAP. When more and more WAP shows began appearing as the technology became more prevalent, the show promoters would ask the various exhibitors who they thought would be a good keynote speaker. Many of them mentioned Infinite's president, and as a result, he was invited to numerous shows around the globe. Today the company also puts up booths at many of the shows featuring WAP technology. For Infinite, events were a highly successful way to launch and to build the brand, the subbrands, and the company.

The good news is that, just like advertising, there are many, many shows from which to choose and at many price points. The difficulty is finding a show that is both appropriate for the company and its brand and also well promoted and attended. Usually relegating the full launch of a brand to a trade show isn't the best idea, even if there is also a company-sponsored event like a breakfast or party. The launch must still be surrounded by other forms of advertising, PR, and promotions, and it's important to evaluate the allure of launching at a trade show against the need to mount all the other marketing activities that will take place at the same time.

- *Events pros.* Many new venues are becoming available. Events are highly targeted; they provide unique opportunities to meet one-to-one with customers; and they can be great for locating potential partners and suppliers.
- *Events cons.* Events are expensive, and the timing must be exactly right. In larger shows, the company's effort may not stand out. Events take up significant amounts of company time and energy.
- *Web implications.* For certain markets, trade shows can be good venues for companies to provide one-to-one access to clients and explain technology and business models in depth. For consumer-based Web brands, the real advantage is in finding partners, giving speeches, and the like, as much as finding customers. For vertical markets, the big increase of shows means a better chance to network in person, followed by collaborative Web activities.

How Direct Is Direct Mail?

There was a time—the birth of spam—when everyone thought the Web was going to be the next stage in direct mail. The "age of spam" was short, however, as many companies realized it wasn't helping their image any to be sending unsolicited emails to unsuspecting victims. And, in some countries, such as Germany, the penalties for spam were (and are) quite severe. Mailing lists of people who had agreed to receive promotional emails became hugely valuable, and were listed as corporate assets.

The Web is inherently a one-to-one marketing opportunity, and it's easy to see how appealing electronic direct mail is to the direct-marketing mentality. Avoiding the cost of postage and printing alone is an appealing advantage. But getting junk email is *not* appealing to the average consumer, even those who willingly agreed to receive promotional information. The percentage of direct email that gets read, like the percentage of snail direct mail, is in the single-digit range.

Most businesspeople today receive dozens if not hundreds of emails daily, and have no time to read direct email advertisements. Consumers, however, are another story: the average home Internet user receives only a handful of emails daily, and is much more likely to at least glance at an electronic message about a new product, company, or promotion, particularly if there's clearly something in it for the consumer. The implication for companies using direct email is that the brand must be built not just in the email message but in the *subject* line of the email, in order to induce anyone to click through to the message, much less to an actual Web site.

In fact, for a brand being launched, either business-to-business or business-to-consumer, it's once again back to basics. The hard truth is that a snail-mail direct piece is likely to have a higher read rate than an email equivalent simply because it's not as easy to toss out. In the world of email, obvious junk mail (is there any other kind?) simply has to be clicked and discarded; physical junk mail at least gets a glance as it flies into the wastebasket.

Is it worth it to go to the expense of a direct-mail campaign to launch a Web brand? It depends on the type of business, the geographical distribution of the audience, and the promotion involved. The cost of reaching a large audience is likely to be more expensive via direct mail than it would be to run an ad in a newspaper or magazine. Finding accurate lists of direct-mail recipients, either online or offline, is difficult, at best. Direct email campaigns present additional problems. Email lacks the personal quality of physical mail (if the word "personal" can ever be realistically applied to any mass-distribution campaign). It is more difficult for the person receiving a personalized invitation for a new credit card, or being offered a coupon for a free meal for two at a restaurant in exchange for test-driving a new car, to resist the offer when it's made on paper: it simply appears more tangible.

Direct mail isn't going away as a viable consideration for launching or promoting a Web brand, but for most Web brands the "spam factor" means that it has limited application.

- *Direct-mail pros.* Distribution can be broad, and direct-mail campaigns are highly controllable.

- *Direct-mail cons.* Direct mail is expensive, and name lists can be inaccurate. It is a poor choice for the launch of a Web brand, or even for ongoing promotion. Direct mail reaches a known audience only, and does little to promote brand credibility.
- *Web implications.* There are much better choices for launching a Web brand than using direct mail. Efforts both in Asia and in the United States that used direct mail to promote online brands had a very limited success among consumer audiences.

Brand Pruning: Maintaining the Web Brand

History, once again, offers an important lesson for building a brand. During the first millennium, the people of the British Isles were already refining what would become a world-class reputation as wonderful gardeners. The process of "pruning" had come into vogue, the purpose of which was to "direct the growth energies of a plant into the channels desired by the cultivator. It is all about human control—a well-pruned plant yields more than a wild one. . . . [T]he skilful pruning of branches demonstrated his [man's] ability to create a profitable working partnership with God's bushes, vines, and trees."[4]

Pruning a brand and a company means essentially the same thing as pruning a garden: it's all about channeling energy and focus, with the intention of producing a more streamlined, attractive entity with a higher yield. Companies with poorly pruned brands are like badly maintained gardens, with weeds and stray stems, leaves, and branches twisting about untended, and with a limited ability to produce strong revenue. Old Economy companies—even technology firms—that have struggled to cross the threshold into the New Economy are often guilty of poor brand pruning, which becomes all too obvious when they attempt to migrate to the Web and find it difficult, if not impossible, to adequately portray their brands on the Web. This is even more important in today's Customer Economy, as it requires a profound dedication to providing clarity to clients and directly answering their needs without a cluttered product or service offering.

This is because brand pruning is not easy. It requires taking a hard look at the brand and its subbrands and making difficult decisions to abandon some brands—cutting off some limbs to ensure that others are strong—and to focus on core business. Many companies of the 1980s and 1990s spent time acquiring and merging, at the cost of building a splintered, poorly pruned brand which was producing revenue in various siloed spots but which was not, overall, a focused, properly channeled, unified brand. For houses of brands, like Kimberly-Clark, success came through focusing on individual brands and understanding the framework.

Pruning takes place once a brand is at cruising altitude, past the launch—and is typically the hallmark of broader corporate brands with multiple products and subbrands to offer. Simply looking at the home page of different established companies with complex product, subbrand, and acquisition histories can quickly reveal if they've done a good job pruning the brand. For the most part, if a site clearly directs site visitors to the information they seek and articulately explains what the company is about at a foundational, core level, it's a good bet the brand pruners have been at work with their shears. If the company presents a vague, needlessly complex home page, and site visitors leave the site with little more insight into the company then when they arrived, often it's because the brand hasn't been attended to. It's important to note that brand pruning has nothing to do with the navigational elements of visual or verbal articulation; it's not about how well the site was designed and built. More critically, it's about how the brand has been built and *is being taken care of.* It addresses and corrects a questionable brand framework and structure, and speaks to how a Web site can support or damage a corporate brand.

This is not to say that smaller, less complex brands don't need pruning—they do. Maintaining a brand means guiding the brand as it grows and ensuring that the brand doesn't become diluted or confusing to customers. Even a simple business-to-business service, such as a garment manufacturer needing to attract name-brand clothing designers, can create a site that is confusing and poor at conveying the company's focus and specialization. This is because brand pruning is, once again, all about focus, that is, ensuring that the messaging on the Web site home page immediately conveys the core mission and purpose of the company, or, in the case of a company that needs to have a high-end design on the home page, at least drives the site visitor to a one-click-away page that does have a great explanation.

The Web sites for Cisco, IBM, Daimler-Chrysler, Sony, and Philips, for example, are representative of very large companies with incredibly complex brand frameworks, all of which are powerful branding organizations with a mindful eye to keeping the brands well pruned. Going to the home page on such sites is a powerful, positive experience, and typically allows visitors to quickly drill down to the information they seek.

As companies grow in size and complexity, how can they ensure that they are keeping their brands well pruned? In public relations, companies that fail to commit to being responsive and informative to the press *at the highest level*—in other words, at the level of the president and CEO—cannot hope to ever truly establish a strong identity in the press. Similarly, a commitment to keeping brand maintenance alive and well must be made at the highest level. In addition, relegating brand management to individual product lines is rarely a formula for success, and usually breeds disparity and brand inconsistency. When the brand effort is fragmented, it is nearly impossible, even for the most skilled Web design firm, to build a cohesive, well-pruned Web site.

Ongoing brand commitment at the executive level is a top-down approach, and means that consistent messaging reaches every part of the company in a trickle-down effect. Companies where various products and subbrand managers are each responsible for building their own brands, and are expected to "bubble up" in the company to create the effect of an overall brand, *cannot* succeed in building a strong corporate brand. This approach will result in obscure, complex identities being reflected in the Web site, and few people, from the press to employees, will be able to figure out what the company does.

When this happens, don't blame the Web designers, but instead blame the lack of brand commitment and ongoing brand pruning. Essentially, brand pruning is a followthrough effort that affects the *key producing years* of the corporate brand. Many companies decide to change names, end up with declining profits, or are finally gobbled up by larger firms simply because they were unable to maintain their brands properly.

What are the core elements of brand pruning, with a mind to the Web site as the most visible point of exposure?

- A long-range, ongoing commitment to brand maintenance.
- A senior executive in the company with assigned responsibility as the brand watchdog.
- A brand team—internal, external, or both—chartered not only with creating new brands but exercising extreme prejudice in guarding the existing corporate, subbrands, and product brands and in integrating the brand issues with how they are reflected on the Web site.
- Putting into place regular brand research study, benchmarked against factors established in the framework stage. This is a realistic and effective way to help ensure brand awareness internally.
- An ongoing awareness of natural brand life cycles, understanding that all names, brands, products, marketing campaigns, and corporations go through dawn, daylight, and twilight years—especially given the accelerating brand cycles taking place simply because the world is running on Internet time. Few companies will be like Kikkoman (the soy sauce company in Japan) and still be in existence several *hundred* years after they were formed.
- Articulation of the brand in the company descriptive documents and proceedings: the annual report, the dynamic business plan, board meetings, annual meetings, and corporate presentations. This is a reflection of commitment, and helps ensure that the brand promise will continue to be fulfilled.

Ongoing brand pruning prevents having to overhaul the brand system and the Web site, and allows natural branding to occur. It's nearly impossible to cut the grass in a yard when it hasn't been cut for months, or to restore to glory a garden that has been neglected for a very long time. Similarly, a corporate brand requiring a weed whacker to get it cut down to size and functioning properly has already had a significant negative impact on revenue stream, identity, stock price, and corporate credibility. Building into a business model a plan for ongoing brand evaluation and maintenance is tedious and requires a lot of planning, but ultimately it keeps the weeds out of the garden and the yield higher, and makes for a much better landscape.

Rediscovery: The Key to Longevity

There comes a time in the life cycle of every brand when it's time to seriously evaluate whether the brand has come to the end of its natural life span. This may be the result of product revisions or acquisitions, or simply that market research reveals a decline in market interest or excitement about the brand. Perhaps the competitive environment has changed. Perhaps the soil has been worked in one area as much as it can be, and new fields must be cultivated—either geographically or by market. *Rediscovery* is so named because it implies not only a time for change in a company, but a deliberate initiative driven at understanding what's working and what's not, and then integrating that information forward into the discovery and framework stages of building Web brands. In many ways, rediscovery is about counting the corporate blessings.

Rediscovery also implies research. In today's speeded-up Internet environment, few companies are taking the time to really do their homework before building or rebuilding a brand. To a degree this is understandable because they are creating entirely new consumer and/ or business offerings, and market research can't yield qualified opinions from a market that's never seen what the company is about to launch. Right? Wrong. Good market research can provide qualitative forums in the form of focus groups, where executives and other business and consumer thought leaders can be interviewed at length. In the wake of the dotcom crash of April 2000,[5] venture capitalists began asking more frequently, "How do you know this will work?" Answers like "It's great technology" or "I've studied the market and been in it for long enough to know" no longer sufficed to yield the $10 million check. There had to be real market data and research backing up the plan.

Rediscovery, in the same manner as the start-up, serves to apply market research ranging from the brand beginnings through its life cycle to yield an understanding of which areas of the business—and perhaps the entire business—need redefinition or revision. Sometimes rediscovery leads to a renaming or other branding activity, but that's for later stages to determine. At this stage, it's sufficient to understand the brand as it is now and to know that change is on the horizon. Later research will help corroborate and validate that what's being seen on the horizon is real and not a mirage.

7

Branding the Internet Village

Loyalty, Service, and Partnership

Forsitan et nostrum nomen miscebitur istis.
(Maybe too my name will be joined to theirs.)
—Ovid, *Ars Amatoria* III, 339 AD[1]

The Internet Village serves the same purpose as has the physical village for all recorded time: It's a place where people come to meet, to trade, to build, to learn, to consume, and to exchange ideas. It's a collective experience in the true spirit of synergy, where the whole is greater than the sum of its parts. In a real village, there are two types of trade taking place: trade between businesses and consumers, and trade between businesses. The shopkeeper sells clothing and groceries to the villagers and residents of the community, while the blacksmith and the shipbuilder work directly with those *in* business. And so it is with the Internet, which has two distinct categories of commerce: business to business and business to consumer.

Literature by the ton describes the differences between these two types of Internet trade, pontificating about and forecasting the growth of each, the challenges, the pitfalls, and the myriad stories of success and failure. Much has been and will be debated over the years to come, and little is certain, with a primary exception: Building a brand is essential to success in either market.

Most experts do agree on one other point, that the online business-to-business market by far exceeds the business-to-consumer market in size, just as it does offline. Industrial services, finance, manufac-

219

turing, and production have always been bigger than consumer goods and services, and this is visibly reflected on the Web today.

As a result of branding being essential and business-to-business being so much larger than business-to-consumer, two branding tenets can be logically extrapolated:

1. As a general rule, bricks-and-mortar business-to-consumer brands stand a better chance of succeeding in the New Economy, simply because the economies of scale are not as great as they are for business-to-business companies. These brands enjoy significant momentum, and financial buffers allow them room to survive and thrive on the Web over the long term. The business-to-consumer pie is not as large, overall, and competition is wild and fierce. A few first-to-market success stories, such as Amazon.com, do not create a trend and, in fact, foster false hopes and a gold-rush effect when there's not all that much gold to go around.

2. The business-to-business market holds great opportunity for services and communication within the global community for new brands where the new brands do not compete head-on with bricks-and-mortar business models but instead coexist alongside them. It is inherently difficult for legacy industrial behemoths to convert business models and significant infrastructures to accommodate pure business on the Internet, yet they have no choice but to take brands on the Web seriously. Because the proverbial pie is so much larger, many small businesses can start up and build a brand and significant momentum before the large ones even become aware of their presence.

So does this mean that consumer start-up companies are doomed to failure and big companies will have a tough go of the Web? Not *necessarily*. Generally, however, it has been increasingly easier for business-to-business start-ups and increasingly difficult for business-to-consumer companies to succeed. Many consumer Web sites struggle to show a profit—or even revenue—while companies such as Hummingbird, Inktomi, and Commerce One, all pure Internet business-to-business firms, continue to be excellent, growing businesses in spite of rollercoaster stock performance. Other start-ups, such as Relera, a co-location firm based in Denver, have received significant funding and immediate attention—even in the wake of business-to-consumer firms failing and struggling to form a profit model. Co-location is the business of setting up the physical and IT infrastructure to host Web sites and application service providers (ASPs). Co-location is a unique business, combining building/construction, telecommunications, IT, and the Internet, and companies like Relera join Exodus and others in making a big business out of providing services for both business-to-business and business-to-consumer Web sites. In fact, companies with business in *both* business-to-business markets and business-to-consumer markets are, at least indirectly, becoming increasingly common. This type of corporate and brand diversity is traditional bricks-and-mortar behavior, and provides a form of economic load balancing, ensuring that when one area of business is weak, another can pick up the slack. With today's increasing focus on customers in the Customer Economy, the concept of who is the ultimate recipient of the product or service has risen in visibility and importance. This makes the divide between business-to-consumer and business-to-business less clear, and drives forward the concept of business-to-customer above all else—whomever the customer may be.

Frederich F. Reichheld, director emeritus at Bain & Company and a Bain Fellow, and Phil Schefter, a VP and leader in ecommerce at Bain's Boston office, coauthored a story in the July-August 2000 issue of *Harvard Business Review* entitled "E-Loyalty: Your Secret Weapon on the Web."[2] In the article, they argue: "Without the glue of loyalty, even the best-designed e-business model will collapse," and "Contrary to the common view that Web customers are fickle by nature and will flock to the next new idea, the Web is actually a very sticky space in both the business-to-consumer and the business-to-business spheres."[3] Companies like Avaya, the Lucent spin-off that is now a strong leader in the voiceover IP business (which will very likely replace conventional corporate telephone systems in the near future), are going all out to adopt a customer-oriented approach both offline and online. This approach embraces the tenets of the next generation of the New Economy—the Customer Economy.

"We've heard New Economy pundits argue that the Internet has overturned all the old rules of business," the *Harvard Business Review* article states. "But when it comes to customer loyalty, the old rules are as vital as ever. Loyalty is still about earning the trust of the right kinds of customers—customers for whom you can deliver such a consistently superior experience that they will want to do all their business with you."[4]

At the same time, Reichheld and Schefter acknowledge that the Web "raises new questions and it places the old rules in a new context." This is where the inherent differences between etailing—online retail (consumer) business—and ecommerce come into play. Similarities exist, such as clients in both business to business and business to consumer want sites that are focused, fast, and easy, but at the same time, there are clear differences in how the two types of business achieve loyalty and return business. Business to consumer is primarily about driving *sales*, while business to business is primarily driven at producing *revenue*. An elusive difference, to be sure. But different factors come into play in each model. (Note that ecommerce is generally considered to be transaction-oriented business to business, although the term is widely misused and has been used inaccurately to describe both business-to-business and business-to-consumer models.)

People who enjoy the NetRadio.com experience, for example, who like how the Web site behaves and who listen to the music, will continue to listen because it's the easiest way to find and hear the music they want to hear, and they'll buy CDs when the impulse hits them, because it's easy. That's sales in its purest form.

"If there was any lesson to be learned from the success and failure of the first Internet land grabbers—and more significantly, from their predecessors in the Old Economy—it's that brands aren't built quickly and the surviving settlers are the ones who work hard at constructing a business rather than puffing up their chests to prepare for a showdown," said Rob Calem, freelance technology and business journalist for *Forbes ASAP*, *The Wall Street Journal Interactive Edition*, *House of Business*, and *The New York Times on the Web*.

"The first wave of Internet entrepreneurs focused on providing products or services to consumers (business to consumer). They hopefully spent the bulk of their bank accounts on 30-second television ads showing, for example, a gerbil shot out of a cannon or a sock puppet impersonating a pet dog. Slowly, though, the business-to-consumer market has been yielding to the old-timers, whose brands were already established by their years in business serving their customers' needs. Similarly, among the Internet companies focusing on the business-to-business marketplaces, the most successful will be those that establish their brands by meeting their constituents' needs, largely by introducing new efficiencies into existing business processes."

Conversely, when Commerce One or Ariba enters into a long-term relationship with a major automobile manufacturer, or when a company like Entricom signs a deal with a major "TelCo," sales are of course involved, but the result is more of a long-term partnership that yields long-term revenue. The business-to-consumer model is about getting customers to return to buy more things or services, while the business-to-business model often means doing things together for the benefit of all involved.

Further, just putting something online won't change a market reality. Singapore, for example, is a tiny but important country. In fact, the postal service guarantees same-day delivery. With a relatively small but crowded population of 3 million, virtually all of whom live in small apartments, going mall shopping is more than a simply functional experience: It's a chance to get out into an open, cool space (outside and in apartments it's way too humid and hot, all the time) and socialize. The series of malls on Singapore's Scott and Orchard streets makes the Mall of America look like a corner drugstore, and is literally swarming with people. As a result, it's no surprise that catalog sales have never been very popular or successful. "It's not like in America, where you drive long distances to the mall to buy things," one Singaporean mentioned at a department store counter. "Unless it's something really hard to find or rare, we don't want to wait in our little condos for something to arrive, when we can travel just a few minutes and find it in a store and at the same time spend time with friends." The Web-based business-to-consumer experience, in this case, is regarded no differently than a catalog sale and, in fact, is seen as an infringement on social life.

LocalBusiness.com is a portal providing regional news and information for business. Entering the LocalBusiness.com site, users encounter a listing of U.S. cities. Jeanne Lang Jones, senior correspondent for LocalBusiness.com in Seattle, believes there's a place for both business to business and business to consumer on the Web.

"Business to consumer is being abandoned much sooner than it should be. The Internet is moving so quickly from front to back office, there's lots of efficiency. The big suppliers are going to be online and they can pull the small ones in as partners or acquisitions, depending upon their brands.

"But trust factor and experience are big deals in business to consumer. It depends on the person, and it's not as much fun as going to a store. I alpha-tested homegrocer.com (that was bought by WebVan), and, even in alpha, I found it very pleasurable. They put flowers on the food, wore booties so they didn't track mud in my house. However, I still liked getting out to the store, and using them depended on how squeezed for time I was. I had come to trust and enjoy them, but I found, in reality, I didn't use them all the time— just as with any other store or service."

Jones had arrived at a fundamental reality for business to consumer: Just because people shop at a site doesn't mean they won't shop somewhere else. People buy from both Amazon and Barnes & Noble, depending on a variety of factors, just as they might shop at two different grocery or hardware stores. While in business to business many companies are entering into more exclusive agreements, in business to consumer customers shift around—which is why "eloyalty" plays such a strong role. Each online service wants people to shop with them as exclusively as they possibly can—just as any offline business does. While customers may go to both Kmart and Target, both stores want them to shop exclusively at their own store.

Loyalty plays a big role in both partner and customer relationships, which means that trust, setting proper expectations, delivery, and "the promise you keep, not the promise you make" must all work in harmony. For Amazon.com, it's the ability to deliver the new Harry Potter book to customers *the very day* it ships. For the occasional Singaporean shopper, it's the ability of an online business-to-consumer site to locate a rare item and underpromise and overdeliver. For Ariba, it's following through with a new potential partner who just happened to fill out the partnership interrogatory on the Web site and who 'gets a callback within a day. In either case, it's the beginning of what will hopefully be many years of eloyalty.

A sad commentary, perhaps, on our priorities, is the tendency of the pornography industry to be a leader in technological advancement—primarily as a result of its constant search for new venues and new ways to counter legal barriers. The VCR, DVD, and the Internet all hide not-so-closeted skeletons of porn beginnings, at least in the commercial, consumer realm. What's porn telling the world now, when it's becoming increasingly difficult to make money on the Web directly as a result of online sales? Many etailers are going belly-up, and the biggest in the business—Amazon.com—has yet to prove it is a good long-term bet. It's unclear how any of the portals can make money, given the poor performance of banner advertising and the wide range of options. The way pornography leveraged the Web was at first to provide free access to sites, and then to "up-sell" over time. Sites that were interesting built traffic, and sites that were not struggled and either were acquired, barely limped along, or disappeared altogether. The sites that continued to grow then began, relatively slowly, to require fees to "get to the good stuff." They weren't big fees, relatively painless to anyone who really wanted what they offered, but it began to build revenue stream, nonetheless. And they grew. And grew. And grew. The infrastructure behind major cyber-porn today exceeds that of Yahoo!'s total user base. This has major implications for portals; some continue to be threatened with financial doom on a daily basis, eking out a living and depleting their angel and venture capital coffers. Vertical portals provide incredible services for seekers within a given market and are a boon to inter- and intraindustry communication. Yet they aren't making much money from banner ads or other revenue schemes.

Inevitably, other companies will start to do what the porn industry has done, and perhaps a little like what the Costco or Sam's Club model has successfully done: charge a relatively painless, nominal membership fee and build volume. Lots of it. Then minimal margins don't hurt so badly, and the venture capitalists feel like they actually *invested* in something.

Over the next few years, there will be (no maybes about it) a shakeout within Web etailing and ecommerce businesses. Sites will be forced to require nominal membership fees from loyal customers—both business-to-business and business-to-consumer customers—who will be picky about where they spend their money. They won't pay fees to portals they don't like or don't use, and those portals will find themselves struggling to survive, ultimately being acquired or going out of business. But the portals and Web businesses which people like and use frequently will find that people don't mind paying a membership fee if they find what they want, when they want it—either in the form of products or services. The shakeout will be a form of "e-volution," with natural branding selection being the rule.

Other sites will take the proven approach of the controlled-circulation publication: magazines like *InfoWorld* have traditionally given the publication free to the entire reader base in return for completing a detailed questionnaire about purchase authority and behavior. This gives advertisers a highly targeted and qualified audience, so they are willing to pay higher ad rates. To ensure a highly refined audience profile, Web businesses will begin to qualify their audiences and restrict access to sites. This is, perhaps, the only way the Web banner will survive in the years to come: by advertisers saying "prove it!"

Brand loyalty will be a driving factor of the future of success on the Web. Portals that continue to underpromise and overdeliver will be bragged about by users, inspiring others, in the true spirit of viral marketing, to join. Vertical market portals, especially, will become required-membership locations for any company that wishes to be listed online or that wants the privilege of being able to search the invaluable portal database for information.

Pornography has succeeded in up-selling customers by providing them with what they want and by making access easy. Companies like Seattle's Flying Crocodile, the king of cyber-porn IT infrastructure, were laughing all the way to the bank at the height of the dotcom suicide days. And so it will be with mainstream ebusiness, both vertical and horizontal. Slowly but surely more and more Web sites will become gated communities, walled off by membership fees and access requirements, and only those companies and organizations providing well-managed, useful services for a highly qualified audience will be able to command membership fees and attract advertisers. The rest will fall by the wayside, either going out of business or slowly being acquired by the stronger, more successful firms.

Brand loyalty will be the key to companies being able to accomplish this next stage of Web survival. No consumers and no companies will pay a penny to a site which they don't like or find useful, which doesn't have stellar services and lightning-fast responsiveness, which lacks clear and lucid messaging and navigation, or which doesn't provide them with what they want. The more a site can provide for them, within a context that they like, the more often they will return—and the more they will want...and be willing to pay for. *That's* brand loyalty.

The Future of Online Selling

By the year 2003, the online shopping experience will be dramatically different from what it is today, driven by an increasing integration of consumer buying trends with online brand development: People buy online primarily for convenience. If it's easier to buy it online than in person, or if it saves time, then it stands a chance of working. Home food-delivery businesses, like www.Webvan.com, are all about convenience for people who don't have time to go to the grocery store: They are too busy working, they have a new baby, or myriad other reasons. But this doesn't preclude the reality that, when they have time, they may enjoy going to a real grocery store and squeezing the melons. Online prescriptions, such as from www.drugstore.com, will be increasingly successful because nobody really gets a kick out of going to the pharmacy, especially to pick up a prescription they need on a regular basis. But going to the bricks-and-mortar drugstore to compare shampoos, open the bottles and smell them, and choose from a panoply of choices that can be both seen and touched is an experience that simply can't be replicated on the Web.

Businesses that look for daily annoyance shopping and replace it with convenience also stand a chance. For example, NetFlix (www.

netflix.com), which rents online-chosen and then mailed DVDs with no late fees, and which lets users rent as many DVDs as they want for one flat fee, has the potential for outpacing Blockbuster, providing it maintains a profitable revenue model.

The Web Can't Create an Environment beyond Virtuality

Buying books online is convenient, especially when the buyers know what they want—at least generally. But it cannot replace, for example, the experience of going to a Barnes & Noble store, smelling the fresh paper and ink, having a Starbucks coffee, sitting in a comfortable chair, and browsing through a stack of books before buying them. Perhaps more important, it can't offer the convenience of returning a book at the counter. This is why a company like Barnes & Noble, and others like it, stand a better chance, long-term, of succeeding over Amazon.com, because the online brand simply extends and augments the company's bricks-and-mortar presence, and the two work together elegantly. The same is true of any in-store shopping experience: hardware, groceries, automobiles, clothing, and videos. The strategically positioned tables at Costco, for example, where friendly staffers offer samples of cooked-on-the-spot foods, are enough to keep people coming, in person, to the store. Again, however, this doesn't preclude the fact that people often see something in person and then order it over the Web later. The live and the virtual, for many consumer brands, must work in tandem. To put things into reverse, is it conceivable that Amazon.com will open a bricks-and-mortar presence—and be good at it? If it could replicate the enjoyable experience (with its own twist, of course) of Barnes & Noble, would people feel as comfortable and as attached to the brand in person as on the Web? Will there be a reversal in trends—or at least a balancing phase—where online brands will attempt to increase their chances of long-term success by "going offline?" It seems inevitable, at some level.

Combining in-person, live, and on-location experience with Web access in one manner or another may be the next stage of survival for some major online brands that today are pure technology. In Amsterdam, for example, there is a travel agency associated with KLM where people can go and sit (or stand) at terminals and surf the Web to travel sites. The location looks like an Internet café (without the coffee), with floating travel agents helping the surfers. It costs nothing, but provides a way for students and tourists to make travel arrangements in person without paying to get online—and it gives the virtual brand a physical presence, thus making it more memorable and sticky.

The Barriers to Acquisition Must Be Minimized at All Costs

Ease of returns, clearly stated shipping policies and costs, ease of entering credit card and shipping information, ensuring confidence in a secure transaction, and the ability to get online with a live person are essential to customer retention. Amazon.com has done a great job of this with its one-click purchase model, and so have Expedia.com and Travelocity.com. Sites that require people to enter their personal information every time they place an order simply won't be tolerated. Electronic wallets help in this effort, but are limited to precious few sites and have yet to be adopted consistently and broadly.

For low-cost, easy-to-find items (like kids' school clothes or notebooks), it doesn't make sense to buy them online except in rare circumstances. And it really isn't that much fun for the kids or the parents.

Sears and Spiegel have done well with their catalog sales over the years because their regular direct-mail catalog is fun to look through and easy to use. Readers can flip instantly through dozens of pages at a time to see how a garment or other product looks. The full-color, high-resolution images in a magazine are far superior to the images on a computer screen, and it's much easier to browse pages of a catalog than pages of a Web site. Major catalog brands also have to be online, of course; the online catalog will generate sales, but it won't replace their traditional catalog business. Rather, it will complement it. For example, it will be easier for people to browse the pages of the catalog, find what they want, and *then* order it online—the ordering experience is easier online, and the browsing experience is easier in a catalog. This is something the pure technology brands will be hard pressed to offer, and why the bricks-and-mortar consumer brands will, ultimately, prevail—particularly in areas where there needs to be a massive selection catering to a vast number of sizes, colors, and other physical attributes of the products.

If It's Hard to Find, Find It on the Web

After listening to new music on www.netradio.com, listeners can then order what they want with a simple click—much easier than going to a CD store and staring at the sea of plastic cases and wondering what's new and interesting. Or consider purchasing a greenhouse kit. Greenhouses are generally hard to find locally, but a number of greenhouse dealers can be found online, making it easy to compare, select, purchase, and have the rather bulky and heavy items delivered. Without the Internet, buyers would have to search for likely catalogs, or make numerous calls to gardening stores—which don't typically even have greenhouses in stock.

Rare and out-of-stock items are usually a natural fit for the Web—just ask eBay. If the item being sold can be found only in a handful of places around the world, the Web obviously is the prime venue for sales. Rare wines, jewelry, out-of-print books, antiques, custom cars, stamps, and other items that would be difficult to find on a simple shopping trip all have a place on the Web, either in auction sites, from online dealers, or in electronic boutiques. Such sites are often hard to locate, however, and typically require some portal searching—which behooves those sites to ensure that their brands are listed and known to the major portal sites. Even sites with really wonderful items for sale that neglected to list themselves with portals are likely to remain largely unknown until word-of-mouth marketing starts to work—and depending on viral marketing is a very slow and often suicidal marketing strategy. People will always search longer for hard-to-find items, but the objective of all online brands needs to be as visible as possible. Just as the more frequented shops in a tourist city are those which have good locations and which are listed prominently in the Yellow Pages and on popular tourist maps, sites which let themselves be known both online and offline will be busier.

Sites that offer focused specialty items benefit greatly from descriptive URLs, allowing people to finding them logically. For example, www.littlegreenhouse.com is a site devoted to, guess what, greenhouses. For someone looking for a home greenhouse, this name is memorable, unique, and descriptive. As long as the company doesn't expand into hardware supplies or home furnishings, this brand will work perfectly.

Consider the Geographic Realities of Selling Online

Kozmo.com had taken advantage of urban markets by delivering rental videos within major cities, right to the consumer's door. They also brought snacks and magazines. The customer dropped off the video the next day at various strategically placed drop boxes around town. But, given that videos are low-margin, low-cost items, putting this type of service into play in a wider suburban or rural area would not work. For online grocers, it makes sense because the purchases are larger, with more margin—and minimum purchase requirements are tolerated by customers. Localization, however, is a *huge* issue for retailers that want to sell outside the United States. The level of online purchasing confidence and comfort is low in many countries—even in countries with a relatively high connection rate.

Focus on Building Brands, Not Sales

Even for models like littlegreenhouse.com, the experience consumers have on the site—from selection to ordering, to delivery and customer service—can dramatically alter customer perceptions and affect their desire to return to the site and tell others about it. Having a great product is simply not enough. For smaller, boutique sites, as well as large consumer sites, encouraging viral marketing is essential. Offering incentives in return for giving friends' email addresses, such as Amazon.com does, or the "Refer a Friend" offer on the AT&T global site (www.att.com/global), not only provides essential email names and contacts, it encourages people to feel so good about a site they will recommend it to others—the essence of viral marketing.

Don't be afraid to at least consider charging a minimal fee for a truly worthwhile site—or part of one. Some sites may wish to experiment with the controlled-circulation model, charge an "entrance" or membership fee to see premium or rare items, or charge a membership fee that brings with it the benefit of strong discounts (the Costco model). Paying such fees may make people feel they *must* return to the site and shop, because they've paid for it. But beware: The minute a site begins to charge for membership, consumer tolerance for lack of service, unresponsiveness, limited selections, and unavailability drops dramatically.

Partner or Perish

It was not immediately evident in the mid-1990s how partnerships would help business-to-business companies in the New Economy. The term "business development" was new and lacked definition for the average organization, and most partnerships lacked meaning and substance. Today the difference is dramatic. Companies have made it on the Internet through partnering and combining their brands to provide complementary solutions. As soon as it became evident that the Internet and business represented an interdisciplinary opportunity, with specialists ranging from information technology and enterprise resource planning (ERP)[5] to Web designers and content managers, companies began to partner with one another to create well-integrated intranets, extranets, and Web presence. They also found they could be more powerful in business by working together than by being in absolute competition. The automobile industry, for example, was characterized by nonexclusive agreements with competitive auto manufacturers that sourced parts from the same companies. This, in turn (to simplify it somewhat), led to mergers galore, such as the Daimler-Chrysler megadeal.

These partnerships came about, in part, because the companies were able to work together online and could communicate easily and quickly via the Internet. Then along came fast-growing companies such as Ariba and Commerce One, pure technology Internet companies whose business model was driven by partnerships in business and the need to make those (and other) alliances smooth and operational. Firms such as IBM, Oracle, Mitsubishi, Compaq, Microsoft, Siemens, BP, Sony, and scores of others quickly jumped on the partnering bandwagon, signing agreements in emerging areas where they realized they could not mount their own initiatives quickly enough to remain competitive.

According to Guy Hicks, vice president of corporate communications for SDRC, a major business-to-business software developer based in Cincinnati, Ohio (www.sdrc.com), "A primary feature and benefit of Web messaging is how it creates a new dimensionality in branding. SDRC creates software that allows our customers, such as Ford Motor Company and Boeing, to collaborate throughout the product life cycle, from new product concept, to development, to marketing and product enhancement. The Web is especially vital in our business since it helps magnify the benefits of partnered offline communication efforts, especially as we continue to recognize and practice new levels of communication and collaboration."

Hicks emphasized that the Web will "never be a singular marketing tool, but its unlimited dimensionality greatly extends traditional communication mediums. It further creates opportunities to fully utilize partners and globalization, which were somewhat constrained with the other communication tools. Marketing on the Web is all about natural presentation and creating believability, while continually redefining 'forced' dimensions."

The Agony of the Legacy

Many companies that had traditionally been "isolationist," working to do everything themselves with a disparate group of suppliers—a key difference from companies that took the partnering route—have become much less visible in the New Economy and are finding themselves in a state of decline. What differentiates companies struggling to emerge from Old Economy cocoons from those that have already spread their wings and flown? Often they cling to the notion that being a sales-driven organization is a positive model and fail to fully grasp the value of marketing and brand as more than an ad and a name. They are not committed to developing a public image beyond a very tight and vertical focus, and they resist high-profile alliances with other companies, preferring, instead, to cling to their isolation. Companies that continue to keep a low profile even though the Internet age is upon them, and which rely for visibility on very basic, simplistic marketing campaigns and Web sites lacking real brand cohesion, will begin to lose market share and revenue instead of gaining them as the Web takes hold of their markets.

Instead of clearly facing the New Economy and the Web head-on, they attempt to redeploy existing products. The result is a lackluster Web presence—and no partners. Too late in the game, they attempt to build additional services and products that they believe will make the company appear to be Web savvy, but these efforts often have exactly the opposite effect—like a middle-aged executive getting his nose pierced. The momentum of companies that try to go it alone, instead of through a broadening infrastructure of partners and networks that can provide key Web-enabling technology and global business acumen, begins to wane. Starved for revitalization, employees begin to jump ship, and the companies head down the road to obscurity. This is "the agony of the legacy" effect which many Old Economy "big-iron" companies face today in a variety of market sectors, ranging from technology to transportation.

IBM, in contrast, has avoided this agony by very early on adopting both a partnership and New Economy plan with its introduction of the ebusiness concept. Essentially, IBM was responsible for the use—and, admittedly, in some cases, overuse—of the "e" as an identifying factor in brands which had effectively come of age in the New Economy. But the "e" was only a surface indicator. What lay *beneath* the "e" was what really mattered, and IBM reconstructed its business model from the inside out. Through a process of rediscovery, IBM executives completely repositioned the company—for example, in many cases referring to its mainframes as "servers," which is what they were being used for in the Web world—and developed a solutions focus not on how they could "push" hardware and software on clients, but rather on how they could work with clients and *partners* to clearly and quickly understand client needs and provide a customized approach to solving them. As the largest consulting firm in the world, IBM was able to provide solutions, create new technology, leverage old technology, and, at the same time, partner with companies that could provide them with significant development efforts they couldn't achieve themselves within a competitive time frame.

Branding plays a tremendous role in these partnerships. Companies that have clearly established a brand and can articulate it well stand a much better chance of being considered and accepted as a viable partner. Today's obsession with "corporate dating" offers many opportunities for established brands, and the choices companies make about whom to partner with are influenced strongly by their perception of how hard potential partners have worked on establishing a sound business and an enduring brand. As the saying goes, "Water seeks its own level," and this is true of partnerships: partners look for ways in which they are similar. They look for philosophy, size, revenue, and brand strategy. When there is a strong disparity in corporate size, the relationship often becomes strained. The smaller firm may feel that the bigger one is taking advantage of it, and in some cases that the larger firm is simply trying to take over (although clearly this is a viable exit strategy for some firms). A smaller company with a strong, established brand is in a much better position to be a true business partner, as opposed to simply a convenient supplier, with a larger firm. And a larger firm lacking a clearly articulated and well-established brand stands a poor chance of attracting good partners of any size.

Size Does Count

Jacque Solt, formerly a marketing executive with Hewlett-Packard and now with her own company, TechStrats, is a business strategist and go-to-market specialist helping companies of all sizes optimize brands and build market share. She advises that launch strategies differ depending upon brand maturity: "Migrating a big company to the Web is nearly the opposite of a small company coming into the environment, where they're trying to set themselves apart as much as possible. As a large company, you must rely on the brand equity you've developed over the years because it provides stability and trust in a constantly changing Web market. You must utilize current market perception and brand equity, and build from there.

"Further, you must use *more* of a descriptive brand identity for a mature, bricks-and-mortar company. If you already have a name, but then add another, nondescriptive name, things get confusing awfully quickly. For example, if Microsoft decided to develop a news station on the Web and call it Microsoft 'Wow,' it would confuse people because it would stray from the corporate descriptive model, and vary from what people *expect* to understand. Large companies have no choice but to be true to form.

"It's like the difference between being a teenager and an adult—while adults are more established and enjoy more privileges, they also have responsibilities and can ill afford to behave or act inconsistently.

"On the other hand, a start-up needs to cause conversation and 'buzz.' If an established company can create buzz *and* be descriptive, it's optimal, but rare and incredibly difficult to achieve. For an established company, it's always better to default to the descriptive rather than completely creative. They have to follow the tenets of quality, stability, and being natural and believable . . . all the while avoiding redundancy with established and widely communicated corporate messages. Does that mean noncreative and boring? Not at all—just cognizant of the entire package. If your company is known for quality, it becomes the backdrop for your brand creation. Communicating quality is not an issue—regardless of the Web business targeted.

"For a big company to energize its brand on the Web, they have to understand themselves and its audience, create a market strategy with an identity to attain high levels of visibility, and utilize highly compelling tactics that complement but also push the corporate culture and brand identity."

Branding the Experience versus Experiencing the Brand

The changes in twenty-first-century business demand an increased emphasis on personalization and immediacy—for both business-to-business and business-to-consumer models. These dynamics, which are integral to the Internet economy, underscore the fact that companies' greater profitability will be gauged on how well they talk directly to their audiences, on a one-to-one basis, and also how quickly they provide audience members with the particular service or piece of information they happen to be after at a particular time. The winners in the New Economy will undoubtedly be the ones that grasp the primary importance of these two elements and continually exercise them in all their promotional and messaging efforts.

How do these truths affect branding today? The legacy tactics of the sales approach, promoting a particular brand to encourage usage or purchase and hopefully yielding brand loyalty, is being quickly replaced with the the ebrand promotion model, where the whole *experience* the brand offers, rather than inherent traits of the brand itself, is promoted. Brand awareness, readability, fit-to-concept, and memorability are still critical elements to building a brand strategy, but, with ebranding, just as important is what happens once an individual arrives at the site. Is the content applicable? Is it easily navigable? Is there access to ancillary services or information that enhance the experience and keep the user at the site? In fact, Microsoft has rebranded the newest versions of Windows and Office with "XP," for "experience," emphasizing that working with Microsoft is more of a brand experience than it is a functional or performance-driven activity. This kind of brand strategy, designed to capture the minds and emotions of customers, is seeping into every maturing business model that is deployed on the Internet.

Many legacy companies lack experience in directly communicating to individual audience members; the Web provides the mechanism with which to do this, on an ongoing basis—which is why stickiness continues to be the primary yardstick for measuring brand effectiveness online. It's true that ebrands live on eloyalty, but perhaps not to the same degree that legacy brands do. This is partly because online business is still in its infancy, but also because the experience is the primary criterion upon which competitive ebrands are judged. The fact that Yahoo! is a memorable name and cuts through the portal clutter is very positive, but if Excite or Go offered an *enhanced* experience, Yahoo!'s name differentiation would become less important.

Further evidence that experience is *the* branding factor on the Web is the rather short amount of time needed to deliver brand extensions. The fact that Amazon has not yet registered a profit (as of this writing) is more a function of high infrastructure costs, both online and offline, than the costs of making believable its extensions into many additional product offerings besides books. As long as the experience of purchasing one of these other items, for example, a home-repair tool, parallels the book-buying experience, Amazon's extensibility is highly credible. Yahoo! can quickly broaden its scope with auctions and sports, for example, because it offers high credibility in an enhanced online experience, regardless of content or service.

Leveraging the Past: It's All about Bricks *and* Clicks

What are the characteristics of legacy versus New Economy brands? What factors—both tangible and intangible—are indicators of companies that have effectively integrated the demands of the Internet age, but are still effectively leveraging their business heritage? Think of five or ten firms that were market leaders a decade ago. Which of them has succeeded in retaining their leadership in the New Economy?

For the medium- to large-sized company realizing that change is inevitable, and indeed that it is most likely already taking place, a set of key factors contributes directly to the company's ability to succeed in moving forward. The factors speak directly to how the brand is perceived, both online and offline, and how new business tools and behaviors integrate with traditional ones. In building and extending brands in the context of the New Economy, consider the many aspects and perspectives of the corporate experience and brand, and how they can be converted into renewable, energetic, and productive resources to ensure the company's longevity and competitive prowess.

Factor 1: Products and Services

Which are the primary, dominant product and service components of the company? Which are not and perhaps ripe for pruning? What hard decisions must be made to move the company forward and to ensure profitability? No matter how visually stunning or witty the brand names, if the brand experience—how products and services perform and are delivered—is not a positive one, customer retention will be increasingly difficult. As the company grows, acquires new brands, develops new products and services, and perhaps merges with other firms, has the fundamental framework remained intact?

Factor 2: The Use of Knowledge as an Asset

The company's information and knowledge "consumers"—whether employees, clients, or partners—need to be engaged in the production process with feedback and input, information, and ideas. Further, the company needs ways to manage the information resulting from increased collaborative efforts among all those who become involved with the brand, and to use that information in ongoing corporate developments and branding. How quickly the company manages information intake, storage, and access must be in Internet time, so the information can be recycled, used, and integrated into rapidly evolving product and service developments.

Has the company begun to catalog, archive, and make accessible the various efforts of information hunters and gatherers, as well as producers, globally? How is it keeping track of and recording corporate information history so that future generations can benefit from successes and failures?

Factor 3: Becoming Virtual

Has the company become increasingly virtual, developing realistic and fair approaches to the New Economy work ethic and business culture (sensible telecommuting, online access for everyone—intranet, extranet, and Internet—the creation of a corporate "community" online, clustered groups of networked teams throughout the world, and so on)? Is the IS/IT department in harmony with the rest of the company in terms of standards, architecture, new technologies (such as handheld devices), telecommuting, operating environments, Web access, etc.? How has it addressed legacy systems versus new technology?

Has the company gone digital in every way possible—memos, reports, telephones, white boards, blueprints, photos, models, designs, graphic arts? Surprisingly for those deeply immersed in the Internet age, many Old Economy companies still exist and are still trying to determine—or maybe *not* trying—what to do about becoming digital. Does technology intimidate the average executive in the organization, or does the average executive embrace it? What implications are there when of two merging companies one is highly adapted to the virtual world and the other is not?

Some companies wear a resistance to the New Economy like a badge. Take, for instance, Berkshire Hathaway, Warren E. Buffett's company. Buffett, a self-proclaimed technophobe who, on his Web site, at www.berkshirehathaway.com, encourages people to "drop me a line—not email, though, I haven't made it that far." In spite of being a multi-billion-dollar success story, the company still uses the Web site only as a virtual brochure. Could its brand be more successful, and its clients be better served, if it embraced rather than resisted the Internet age? For a company steeped in tradition and legacy values, would that constitute forced instead of natural branding? The answer to that question has nothing to do with a traditional company's assessment of the value of resisting technology, and everything to do with how best to serve its audience in the way they would most *like* to be served—namely, and increasingly, on the Web.

Factor 4: Internal Brand Matters

The steps a company takes to ensure brand consistency, and whether it employs a top-down brand discovery and framework process, make a big difference as to how employees embrace the brand and how they can articulate it. Are they involved? Do they understand the brand? Can they give the elevator speech? Does the human resources department educate new employees about the brand, and give them the basic points of the elevator speech along with the benefits packages? How has the company addressed the New Economy free-agent mentality, where turnover rates are higher and employees no longer assume life-long employment? Are there sufficient employee incentives to ensure strong recruitment and staff retention? How has the company dealt with employees' increasing skepticism of stock options as a viable alternative to cash? Does the corporate brand support loyalty from new generations of employees, or does it speak more to a twentieth-century, industrial work ethic?

Factor 5: Organization

How is the company organized? Is it a flat, nonhierarchical structure, with direct access of "everyone to everyone," or is it clinging to the traditional hierarchical model, with deliberately aloof management? Companies today are shedding middle management and feeling liberated as a result. This doesn't always mean widespread layoffs, but rather a shift to a more knowledge-based infrastructure that benefits the brand's appeal and accessibility.

In the definitive New Economy Web self-service model, can customers, employees, partners, suppliers, vendors, and stockholders use the Web to obtain information and answers and make business decisions without having to speak directly to a person in the company? Today, how a company addresses customer relationship management (CRM) has a direct effect on how its brand is perceived. Systems put into place to integrate marketing, the sales force, and customer service and relations have a direct impact on revenue, profitability, and brand endurance.

Factor 6: Global, Not International

Giving thought to fully integrating global business into the company culture is a big change for companies that traditionally looked at international business with an "us and them" perspective. Understanding that how a brand is perceived and marketed at a local level must be a part of corporate brand consistency, and framework is essential in quickly being able to ensure that everyone involved with the company anywhere on Earth is onboard.

According to Christopher Wünsche of DeekelingKommuniKation in Frankfurt, Germany (a division of BBDO), "Most business-to-consumer online Web sites have an informative, entertaining, or—increasingly—commercial approach. Online shops still mostly sell products of well-known brands, using the impact brands have created over time. Consumers tend to show loyalty to brands, not to online shops. The reasons for preferring one online shop against another is price or convenience or something else, but not the product itself. Business-to-business approaches on the Web have to deal with the same difficulties as in classical communications chains: goods and services are normally more complex and thus more difficult to explain and the value per item is higher. But as the business-to-business market is not as purely brand-driven as the business-to-consumer sector, manufacturers may use the advantages of the Web to present and promote products on virtual marketplaces to clients they would have never reached through classical media."

Factor 7: Moving Ahead

Has the company determined how to combine its progressive structure and well-articulated brand? Has it put into place tools to allow the exploitation of new horizons of multimedia information and knowledge, as well as previously unimagined ability to access resources, people, and information? It's a big job for any company, business to business or business to consumer. However, in spite of moving at Internet speed, bricks-and-mortar companies enjoy a legacy of tradition that, if used properly, can be a long-term asset and advantage—providing the brand is given highest consideration as the flag bearer marching into the New Economy.

8

The Global Web Brand

We have learned to be citizens of the world, members of the human community.
—Franklin Delano Roosevelt, Fourth Inaugural Address, 1945[1]

While nearly half of the world's population has yet to make a single telephone call, the World Wide Web is nonetheless a global phenomenon, and there's hardly a culture it hasn't touched in some way, shape, or form. Far beyond the Web, brands penetrate the Earth to the point of endangering cultural diversity—what *Colors* magazine refers to as "monoculture"—with McDonald's, Marlboro, Coca-Cola, Nestlé, and Microsoft found everywhere from Bangkok to Paris.

Global brand extension combined with the Web is profoundly affecting the world. Travelers to London, for example, are startled by the amount of *purely local* Internet businesses advertising in the underground, on buses, in publications, and on virtually every centimeter of free space available anywhere. Many Americans, upon going to London, are surprised to see so many non-U.S.brands well developed and implemented on the Web: for example, www.orange.co.uk (a United Kingdom–only telecom site), www.lastminute.com (reservations for theater, travel, etc.), or www.qxl.com (a United Kingdom and now pan-European auction site). After all it is an English-speaking region, yet—the American Web brands to which they're so accustomed are nowhere in sight.

FIGURE 8.1   EasyEverything.com's Internet café in
Amsterdam, featuring 650 HP workstations.

EasyEverything.com, for example, is a London-based company
that has more than 30 Internet cafés in Europe and is now taking hold
in the United States. The Amsterdam EasyEverything, in the Munt-
plein, features 650 flat-screen terminals and keyboards, along with
universal serial bus ports and headphone connections (see Figure 8.1).
The low cost (about $1 for anywhere from 20 minutes to 4 hours),
along with EasyEverything's distinctive name, orange-colored image,
and easily franchisable business model, give it a good chance to become the McDonald's or Starbucks of the Internet café world.

"The brand proposition of the 'Easy' company is all about combining low cost with good value," said Ivar Gribnau, manager of business
development and marketing for Benelux for EasyEverything.com. "We
believe in an honest, open concept, and I think building a brand like this
is only possible when you have good and clear corporate statements.
For us, being low-cost is unique in the Internet café market, because we
make use of the latest technology at a great price, which has been readily
recognized by customers and the press. We underpromise, and overdeliver."

The World Wide Web

The entire globe has become enamored of the Web, and what it has to offer in communication and access to amazing amounts of information. It's even become a problem for some of the more restrictive governments, such as China, the Middle East, and even Singapore (where pornography is strictly forbidden). Powerhouse business countries like Germany, the United Kingdom, the Netherlands, and Canada all have high levels of dotcom start-ups and business and personal Internet connections, and virtually every company addresses the issue of building and extending its brand online. Governments like Brazil have acted early to grease the technological wheels, viewing the Web as a way to raise the socioeconomic standards of the country. In fact, 7 million people filed their income taxes on the Web in Brazil in 1998.[2] Dotcom advertising appears virtually everywhere in the world today: on the sides of buses in Hong Kong, inside any metro in the world, on cybertour pamphlets being given out in the London underground, on billboards in Rio de Janeiro.

But global Internet branding is not without its challenges. Connection speeds vary globally, with the United States, Norway, and Germany at the forefront in both business and home access. Businesses in South America frequently must endure slow connections, while in the Netherlands it's not uncommon to find ISDN connections in private homes. This variation makes it difficult for companies to know what to expect when they are building Web sites to be accessed by individuals or businesses in different regions. They can either take a lowest common denominator approach by simply making the sites very sparse and quick to load, or accept that certain areas will have to cope with longer load times. For sites with a significant amount of information to display—especially true of consumer and business portals—this can be a daunting problem. A slow connection can be detrimental to the overall brand experience on the Web, and can keep customers away for the foreseeable future if they spend more time waiting than surfing.

New Economy Imperialism

Localization is a significant issue. According to Global Reach,[3] 51.3 percent of the Web is accessed by English speakers; by 2003, and as the size of the overall pie continues to increase, only 32 percent of the Web will be accessed by English speakers—a whopping 68 percent using other languages. These statistics are confirmed, within an acceptable margin of error, by other global research firms, such as IDC. According to data reported in a September 2000 article in *World Trade* magazine, Norway, Singapore, the United States, Sweden, and Canada have the highest home connection rates, all ranging between 40 and 50 percent of the total population.[4] Interestingly, according to the Global Reach statistics, although Japan's home connection rate is not as high, Japanese is second to English (although by a *very* distant margin) as the language most used online. This may be because a smaller percentage of the Japanese population speaks English, in contrast to so many European cultures where English is almost universally understood or to multilingual areas of the world such as Singapore, where most people speak English and Chinese, plus other languages such as Malay or Thai.

This has very real implications for any company building a brand on the Internet intended to go beyond its immediate region. The Web has been very anglicized, and has had a dramatic impact on the global proliferation of the English language. Culturally, as well, American business standards have both been assumed and pushed upon those using the Web for personal and especially business purposes—not always with a positive impact. The world, however, is beginning to push back.

The business implications of localization are also affected by the business climate in a particular region. For example, while the Internet is popular in Japan, it has been very difficult for Web start-ups to incubate and launch there simply because the government imposes very high registration charges on new businesses, preventing the garage-band style of U.S. and European start-up businesses which have so widely populated the Web in the Western world. The Japanese business climate is experiencing some global warming, however, as it increasingly adapts to working with other cultures. For example, traditionally, Japanese businesses have been highly *physically* segregated, not sharing office spaces; now there is a trend where dotcoms are beginning to locate in common facilities—an unprecedented change in Japan's business culture.

Simply because a large online population exists in a given area or speaks a given language isn't a complete green light to begin building a brand, and caution is advised on all fronts. Finding qualified research firms in a specific region is a necessary and important step for any company building a Web brand on foreign soil, as is building a strong human presence.

"People are wary of American companies in Britain," said Will Clarke of Insight Marketing and Communication, a major British high-tech PR firm (www.insightmkt.com). "It's an 'us and them' factor, and very often a 'dotcom' means it's a U.S.-run operation. When we see the dot-co-dot-UK it means it's a British company, and even though it's a longer URL, there's cultural relevance and meaning for it. For a British company that wants to build a global brand—say, for example, British Petroleum (BP)—using the UK extension would be ineffective, although they should *also* own it as a redirect within the UK. But for certain UK-only brands, the UK extension is an asset."

The American push has also had an effect on how development resources are being treated worldwide. In September 2000, the BBC broadcast an interview with N. R. Narayana Murthy, chairman and CEO of Infosys Technologies Limited (www.inf.com), the largest software company in India, a country which has gained the reputation of being the world's richest source of software development talent outside of the United States. In the interview, Murthy said American companies—even New Economy leaders—are employing Old Economy tactics in foreign areas like India, where they simply come to the area, open an office, and recruit talented developers away from existing Indian firms. Instead, he complained, U.S. firms should be *partnering* with existing Indian companies and benefiting from a stronger global penetration with a highly localized, formal association.[5] Because the Internet is inherently a one-to-one communications vehicle with power to reach the masses, the importance of localization cannot be overemphasized: the more localized a Web site is to the culture, language, currency, interests, business practices, and even laws of a given region and user, the stickier the site becomes, and the more powerful the brand.

Legally, the Internet represents a snakepit of dangers for business, as well. For example, the term "love" can appear in multiple Web site names depending upon what country and extension it has—.com, .de, .net, .sg, .co.uk, .br, .dk., .nl, and so forth—and each must be registered separately. Yet very few companies have registered their URLs in more than a handful of countries, despite the fact that it's much cheaper and easier to register a name than to defend one. In his book *e-Commerce Law & Practice,* published in Malaysia, Julian Ding states: "The Internet is a landmine for the unwary and caution must be exercised. The United Nations Commission on International Trade Law has issued a model law for Electronic Commerce which may be adopted by member countries. It remains to be seen whether the UN's initiative would be universally accepted. The adoption of the Model Law would, to an extent, support the call by the U.S. on the need for uniformity in e-Commerce."[6]

One way to address this problem is to follow the lead of some of the bigger but largely national companies, such as British Airways. Anyone from the United States who is interested in them simply clicks on the U.S. area on the www.britishairways.com site, or types www.britishairways.com/usa. The argument can be made that there is some nationalistic pride involved when companies that want to build a site specifically for their own country, or to emphasize that they are from a given country, choose a country-specific URL. Perhaps www.britishteapots.co.uk is better than www.britishteapots.com; nonetheless, if the company's intention is to *sell* teapots, then it had better own *both* URLs.

A person attempting to get onto Expedia.com while in Munich, for example, must be aware that the browser in a German office doesn't *allow* www.expedia.com to be entered. It automatically diverts to www.expedia.de—although it *does* allow www.expedia.co.uk (why?). This is a problem because Expedia requires users to log in for given countries, which means that a U.S. user cannot log on to the German Expedia and check his or her itinerary.

Especially from a business-to-business standpoint, it's also important, if not critical, to understand that being global on the Web means much more than building armchair business relationships. Ironically, perhaps, in spite of global email connections and Web sites, personal relationships must be built and nurtured face to face. This means that people doing business around the world must *travel* around the world. And the business behavior of the executive in a one-to-one relationship, and how that executive represents the company, must accurately match the company's brand at the office and on the Web, and the one perceived by its customers.

The Coming Global Wave

While many American companies—both technology and nontechnology—admit that global reach and global branding are essential, they are first focusing on North America to "get it right." Many multinational firms have English-only sites that are limited in global scope. But by 2003, globalization will be essential for staying ahead in what will be a hard-run race. The companies that today are preparing for this wave, thinking about how they can be more global, and especially using their Web sites as tools will be in a strong position to win as world Internet markets heat up and begin to tip the scales on revenue opportunities. Today, well over 60 percent of Microsoft's revenues come from non-U.S. sources; this percentage will be common within a few years for many global brands of all types, a trend that is greatly reinforced by the Web. It's common for well-established brands to manipulate and prosper by leveraging the "economic tidal effect," emphasizing business in a strong economy while de-emphasizing it in a softening one (or vice-versa, depending on the business and strategy).

The same is true for companies *outside* the United States lured by the big-bucks opportunities they see in America. "It used to be most of the business we saw was U.S. companies coming to Europe," said Insight's Will Clarke. "But now we're beginning to see a reverse trend of European companies wanting to launch and extend their brands in the U.S." The success of non-U.S. brands such as Nokia,

Ericsson, Volvo, Mercedes, and even consumable products like Mentos candy (from the Netherlands) has only been reinforced by the companies' efforts to localize their Web sites for the U.S. market.

Business-to-business companies now have unprecedented access to making their names known to U.S. companies: Take, for example, the garment industry. Supplied by medium-sized Asian companies, big U.S. and European clothing brands have relied on a wide variety of manufacturing services from Asia for many decades. It's not unusual to encounter Thai or Chinese companies making 50 or more percent of their revenue from U.S. brands that outsource their garments globally, like Nike. How do these firms, going forward, become known to new business? Through word-of-mouth, certainly, but increasingly over the Web.

A buyer at a company like Nike might get on the Web, go to a portal, and type "garment manufacturers in Thailand" into the search engine, and see what comes up. In the past, finding Thai garment manufacturers might have involved numerous phone calls, faxing the consulate or country's business development department, and other time-consuming search methods. The buyer would then have had to contact various companies, probably facing a language barrier, before being able to begin to develop a relationship. Today, instead, a list of manufacturers comes up on the search engine, the ones that look appealing are selected, and initial emails are sent to the companies selected. What would have been a several-weeks-long project is done in a few hours.

What this implies, however, is that those companies in Thailand (or wherever) that can be located by using a search engine have built Web sites that accurately portray their businesses, brands, and business practices, and communicate in English (or German, or whatever) to whichever target regions they would like to have contact them for business. It further means they must follow up on email inquiries sent to them, employing someone capable of really understanding what is being sought and answering carefully and quickly. Finally, it means the companies must have located and listed with the key search engines in target industries as well as in general engines (e.g., Google or AltaVista) in the given target regions. The corresponding revenue opportunities for these companies far outweigh the cost of development, and the cost of *not* having a Web site will become increasingly devastating over the next few years.

The Global Web Brand

A common misconception today is that once a company's Web site is up, the company is global. Sure, the Web site can be accessed from anywhere in the world, but just having a URL no more makes a company global than having a phone number, a brochure, a fax machine, a physical address, or even an office in another country—it simply means that access to that company can be gained via the Web. What makes a company global is how the business model and the brand approach the global marketplace, and how they communicate with it. Simply hanging the URL shingle isn't enough to either attract or retain site visitors and potential clients from anywhere; the Web site must be fully integrated into the company's overall business strategy. And if that strategy isn't global, the Web site won't be either.

The Old Economy legacy model of companies split into "U.S." and "international" business is a thing of the past, and sticking with such models is like waving a big red flag proclaiming that the firm really *isn't* global and that any issues other than those taking place in the United States are of secondary importance. If a company has designs upon being, or already is, a global brand, the Web site must reflect this by *immediately* addressing key localization issues and providing instant access to those areas of the site that have been designed for specific languages and cultures. Simply listing the location and phone number of a regional office in London or Tokyo won't do.

The implication of this New Economy standard is that companies must prioritize their key target regions; it doesn't mean that every language and culture in the world must be addressed. If, for example, a typical business-to-business firm plans to conduct 50 percent of its business in the United States, 45 percent in Europe, and 5 percent in the rest of the world (ROW), and if Europe is prioritized further into 40 percent United Kingdom, 35 percent Germany, and 25 percent Scandinavia, there's no real reason in the short term to localize the Web site beyond German and, perhaps, British-English (most businesspeople in Scandinavia speak, read, and write English). It does, however, mean that any pricing needs to address at the least the dollar and euro currencies and perhaps the individual regional currencies, and ensure that people from these regions can access *live* businesspeople in their own time zones. It also means that news and information about the company needs to be localized.

"The problem U.S. companies have in Europe is it's very diversified as to cultural views, language, and business practice," said Corinna Voss, managing director of Munich-based HBI (www.hbi.de), one of Europe's largest independent high-tech PR firms. "Tag lines, for example, if they're too American, are difficult to understand. They have to be easy to understand in order to work in Europe. Some European companies working internationally, like NSE, a German company using the tag line 'Thinking Ahead,' or Netherlands-based Philips using 'Let's Make Things Better,' write them in English because in German or Dutch it wouldn't work at a global level. . . . English is just much more common.

"By the same token, however, these same companies, and companies in the U.S. trying to work in Europe, have to understand two primary points: localization and consistency. What I see very often is companies with a coherent, established brand in the U.S. that lose control over their brands in international offices. Something as basic as the business cards look different from country to country—colors, shapes, designs—and it looks bad to the press, customers, and everyone if the company hands out a set of differently branded collateral. This happens far too often, looks very unprofessional, and doesn't help an international brand in the least. Now imagine, if you will, if something so basic as a business card can't be made consistently within a company. How can they hope to ensure consistent regional messaging and brand identity in key regions on the Web?

"Companies *must*, on a regular basis, involve the leading international executives in branding. They need input from the top managers, and then they have to apply that to the Web, to collateral, to trade show 'stands,' and to templates for presentation. In a press presentation, four different PowerPoint presentations, all of which look different from the art on the Web site, look really bad. It says the German team doesn't understand or isn't involved in the process; sometimes the 'international' team doesn't even realize branding is important and doesn't give a damn if their stuff looks different— because they think theirs looks *better*. But it is embarrassing for everyone to give a press presentation and show different, disconnected information from the same company."

Voss views this as symptomatic of a disparate brand strategy and framework: "The U.S. may, in fact, not see the importance of *involving* their regional offices in branding, which is a real mistake. They frequently just give the basic parts and pieces of the brand, but don't bother to explain how everything fits together. It's critical that companies help their people around the world to understand the connection between appearance, brand, and sales. . . . especially for young companies. 'E-branding' is pretty successful in Europe, particularly for companies that go to the trouble of working with their staffs around the globe to involve them in the branding process, and then to build a brand off and on the Web that meets their needs."

Luc Levi, director at Wisse Kommunikatie/Worldcom in the Netherlands, complements the statements of Voss with a cultural angle: "One of the most important things to think about is that language is very different here from the U.S. I don't mean just words— the *style* is different. In the U.S. everything is 'bigger and better,' and the U.S. uses far more superlatives. You see it on the Web, in press releases, and everything. When American companies use the Web and localize it, they need to localize the *language* and the *cultural* aspects of the language and information as well. Saying 'We're the biggest, we're the best,' etc. won't and doesn't work here—it never has. That's a cultural business turnoff, it doesn't sound credible, and everybody starts to laugh. Readapt. Localize. If you *are* truly the biggest—like Microsoft—you can maybe get away with it, although even *they* have developed a credibility problem. In Holland, even Bill Gates has to be a little humble—we're not a highly ostentatious society.

"The Web is one of the most interesting vehicles to anglicize the world, and to create a world language. But, then, why does Xerox have a Dutch site specifically for the Dutch—even though they know the Dutch all speak English? Of course, not everyone can do this."

Levi believes American companies need to work harder to understand local cultures before they simply blast into the region with a Web site and a revenue plan. "When an American company moves into another country, they need to look at how those people express themselves. Americans always 'boost' themselves and exaggerate, by being 'better,' 'bigger,' and so on. This needs to be taken into account for a site that is international, whatever the language, because most cultures react negatively to that kind of brand 'promise.'

"After World War II, when Americans came to Europe, they realized Europeans weren't exactly like them. In the same manner, when the Japanese invaded the American and European markets with their cars, they *failed* to realize Europe wasn't like Japan . . . which is why Japanese car brands never really became a big auto threat in spite of, perhaps, better products. Americans should learn from that and not make the same mistake with the Web."

A Global Marketing Legacy Reveals All

U.K.-based Terry Connor is somewhat of a bricks-to-clicks brand himself. One of the most colorful, outspoken, and creative international marketing consultants in Europe, his presence dates back to the wild advertising world of London in the 1960s, where his work with global agencies like Benton & Boles, Foote, Cone & Belding, and Bates included such accomplishments as launching Heineken Beer and Camay soap throughout Europe, and being involved with IBM's climb to European prowess. Later, moving into IT, he directed global networking hardware brands like Allied Telesyn and now consults with U.S., European, and Asian companies such as Com21, Foundry Networks, and RackSpace, and globe-hops like most people go to the supermarket. There are few people in IT today who have as much global branding and marketing perspective and sense of reality, and who aren't afraid to say it directly to a client. Meeting in the Royal Lancaster hotel in London's Hyde Park, Connor had very pertinent advice for companies seeking visibility and business in the European market and beyond.

On the Big American Cultural Faux Pas

"You can't treat Europe as one territory, even *within* countries: the north and south of every country differs, just as it does in the U.S. There's a *huge* difference in doing business and building brands between Milan and Rome, Nice and Paris, Munich and Berlin. The biggest mistake Americans make in launching their firms here is to treat Europe as one big culture—it's killed many, many fine businesses and products and vastly elongated their ramp to success.

"The problem with the Web is that it allows this same mentality to be taken to the next level—putting up one Web site for literally dozens of cultures and languages, for example.

"Suppose your company required employees to wear a uniform, and so you had to differentiate yourself with ties, socks, shoes, and shirt, as well as your personal identity, such as hair, complexion, and ultimately your personality and behavior. *This* is the approach companies should take in Europe, providing corporate consistency with localized, individualized personalization on the Web, in person, and in marketing materials."

On Creative Implementation

"Take, for example, trade shows and advertising: In general, and that's a very liberal 'general,' the following countries all have differing levels of tolerance in creative implementations:

- In Germany, you must be serious, although to a lesser degree in southern Germany (e.g., Bavaria).
- In Italy, you can be zany.
- In France, there's a mix of zany and serious works.

- In the UK, you can be off the wall.
- In the Netherlands, you can be wild but serious is also well received.
- In Scandinavia, it's back to serious.

"The same applies to the Web. German Web sites tend to be more serious, with fewer photographs, artwork, and images but with a high degree of sophistication in design. There is always much detail in the text and content. Conversely, Web sites in Spain and Italy are *much* more frivolous, with many graphics, cartoon images, photographs, silly fonts, and the like—which the Latin cultures really love and are able to effectively combine with business issues and implementations."

On PR

"American press releases tend to combine several stories, which, in Europe, would ideally be broken into separate releases but often are not. The average editor 'bins' 80 percent of the press releases on-the-spot . . . and the more multipurpose each one is, the more likely it won't be read. Furthermore, U.S. PR people don't realize that, in Europe, the heavy-duty reliance on the analyst community isn't as pronounced as in the U.S."

Rules for U.S. Business in Europe

"There are four primary rules for doing business and building a brand in Europe:

1. *Culture.* 'When it's an asset, play upon your culture; for example, "Wrangler" jeans or "Marlboro" won't have any appeal if they're localized into Polish. But when it's meaningless—say, for example, if you're Amazon.com or Commerce One, being American has no real value, so you must adapt to the local culture or deal with lots of barriers to entry.'
2. *Language.* 'As with culture, it may be advantageous to put up a

Web site in English, if it's primarily for show—as with an image site that's not intending to make sales or build business partners. But in Germany, for example, an English business-to-consumer Web site will not work because the average German doesn't speak English that well—and he or she is certainly not going to feel good about putting a credit card number on an American site they have a hard time understanding. For a business-to-business site, doing business in Germany requires building relationships— which will always be easier with a localized presence. Simply having an English site will make Germans—or any other culture, for that matter—suspicious that there really isn't a localized presence, but rather a remote-controlled U.S. imperialistic one.'

3. *Business practices.* 'Every region of Europe has its own business practices, ranging from how you communicate, to the structure of meetings, to how you treat women. It's vastly different between Germany, the UK, France, Italy, and *wildly* different if you get even further, such as into Eastern Europe and the Middle Eastern countries. This is why we see so many advertisements in places like China or Saudi Arabia which make little or no sense to us, and why the Web sites in those regions can be equally as enigmatic. To hope to build a business in a given region, companies must become versed on the business practices and realities of that area and then apply them. I don't care if it's simply a Web site, there's no use doing it without first understanding how business is done in that place—and nobody can give you that information except a native of the region who also knows your business. The term "best practices" for many companies is a joke, because it only means a homogenized way of doing business in one place and in one way—when, in reality, effective global business practices are an elegant integration of corporate messaging and consistency with a high degree of localized presence and sensitivity. How this is reflected on the Web, which can be the first encounter a potential customer or partner experiences with a brand, is as important as knowing how to offer a business card in Japan or what to wear to a business meeting in Hamburg.'

4. *Research.* 'The importance of researching the European market before attempting to launch here—for anything from an office to

a Web site—is vastly underestimated. How can anyone hope to know how a brand is doing, or how business goals are being set and accomplished without setting a benchmark? So few companies do real market research in Europe, it's tragic. Most companies that actually *do* research find out some fundamental facts, like that a simple Web site can't be an office for you. You mustn't just have a façade. In order to have a real brand, you have to have people to back it up. Until you put into place a proper infrastructure, you're throwing your money out the window. If you don't get it right at the beginning, you've blown it. Plus, it's *far* less expensive to keep an existing customer who will give you repeat business than to win a new one. First impressions count, and you can blacklist yourself quickly. Amazon did untold brand damage here by being unable to fulfill its orders for weeks and shipping books from the U.S. It defied the Web's promise of immediate gratification, and so, unless they needed something they simply couldn't find, most people here avoided it and now have turned to other European booksellers online that have become popular. But they could have averted this with some simple up-front market research. The company may, in fact have done some [research], but it certainly didn't get rolled in to what they rolled out.' "

Finally, Connor also has advice for European companies launching brands in the United States or elsewhere, where the same principles apply, in reverse: "In 'Coming to America,' brands also need to know how to play upon their culture if it's an advantage, while others must not. If a brand represents a high degree of style, for example—such as Gucci, Ferrarri, Heineken, or Braun—these can be used as a strong asset. On the other hand, does the average American really need to know or care that EasyEverything.com is a British company? Not really. The cultural and style issue, very often, is much more well adapted to physical consumer brands such as clothing, automobiles, food and beverages, and so on, than to a Web-based service.

"I did consulting work for Inalp, a Swiss IT company, that exhibited at a major European trade show. They wanted to use a Swiss 'Alphorn' and a fake cow dispensing beers, along with women in the booth wearing traditional Swiss clothing. I told them being Swiss didn't offer a shred of value for a pan-European trade show, and did nothing to boost their image as a major computer firm. Instead, they put on a proper international booth with a sophisticated, business-oriented image, and they did phenomenally well. Had it been a different show, a different industry, a different type of company and product, or a different region, I might have advised them differently. You have to know your audience *and* yourself."

Examples abound of how branding and the Web are converging at Internet speed around the world, and the one common denominator seems to be that an established brand has a better chance of being successful.

Asia

Great Eastern Life is a major insurance company in Singapore, and Asia overall. Formed in 1908, it's a well-established corporate Asian brand. Many of the people the company is targeting today are under 30, well educated, and connected to the Internet, and although they want a brand they can trust with something as important as insurance, they don't want than to deal with a stuffy, stodgy, bureaucratic insurance company. According to Yeow Hwee Ming, senior marketing manager for Great Eastern Life, "When I first joined Great Eastern, I found the company had lots of history but many 'sacred cows.' One of those is the logo. The existing logo is a lion with the statement 'supremacy,' which dates back to the beginning of the company. While there are many strengths, not the least of which is the connection to Singapore of the lion, with the new Internet world, it is less meaningful for younger people—especially those who have Internet savvy. Plus, the lion is very British and looks like a lion of the Crusades. This symbol is very common in Singapore, a remnant of the British colonial days. So, while 1908 reflects history and an established image, to our younger generation—who are critical to our future—it also looks old. This is one of the first areas of our brand we seriously examined: how the logo looks, how it can be changed, and where it appears—on the Web, in advertisements, on the buildings, and so on."

But the most profound impact Yeow Hwee Ming is having on Great Eastern Life is in his unique integration of a new marketing concept, a tag line, and the company's URL. "Our previous tag line was *'We Take Care of You for Life.'* This sounded to me and us like a manufacturer's claim, somewhat industrial; overall, we hadn't paid attention to our core brand structure, strategy, and positioning. The new tag line, 'Life Is Great,' represents three things, all of which are essential to Singaporeans: financial independence, health and well-being, and building and bonding relationships. More importantly, we then extended the tag line to become the actual Web address of the company—don't you think typing 'www.lifeisgreat.com.sg' feels better and is easier to remember than 'www.gelife.com.sg?' Based on our feedback and research, 'Life Is Great' is neutral but holds limitless marketing and brand identity opportunity, including strong emotional appeal. Then the association comes naturally. 'Life Is Great' really adds to the emotional attachment, and neutrality is *important*, because Great Eastern Life is all about being a company, while 'Life Is Great' is all about 'you.'

"We've also taken away the 'supremacy' statement. A lion is naturally a symbol of leadership and supremacy, so saying the word is redundant."

Yeow Hwee Ming has taken a very realistic, forward-thinking approach to how the Web is being integrated with traditional as well as emerging Asian culture. "In Asia, what's different about Web branding is that if you're not a bricks-and-mortar company, it's going to be very tough to make a name for yourself that becomes a successful business. Here, the Barnes & Noble business strategy is what works: bricks to clicks are much easier, and, in general, in Asia overall it's significantly less effort and risk for an established brand to extend to the Web than for a start-up to make it."

Tan Kin Lian, CEO of NTUC Income, another of Singapore's biggest insurance companies, has taken a grass-roots approach to building market among Singaporeans, and is also highly concerned with building a brand, both offline and online, with all age groups. In a meeting in his offices in the executive suite of NTUC Income in Singapore, he shared: "We have a list of 100,000 people, mostly Singaporean, who receive regular email from us. This is driven at both building revenue *and* brand. We build revenue by presenting new and different 'products,' and we help build brand by keeping people attached, engaged, and seeing that our Web site and company are interesting and that we have good products and services.

"We view building our business as a three-stage process, and it moves from online to in person. We may have gotten the person's name from the Web site, a seminar, an ad, or another place. The first stage is to first make contact via email to create an interest but not to offer a solution. With a response from the person, we then offer more substantive information about what we're offering to lock in the interest. The third stage is to make a sale. We're using Old Economy marketing methods—create interest, offer, and sell—and applying them to the Internet—and, ultimately, creating a personal relationship with the client even if it began on email.

"We look upon the Web from two strategic directions, one being our intranet with agents and staff as a very efficient way to do business and process; we've already integrated our clientele and service infrastructure with cutting-edge business-to-business practices. The other part of our strategy is driven at building upon our well-established brand: we have good programs, you can trust us, we have good prices, and 'I like NTUC.' That's what will keep us competitive in the New Economy."

David Croasdale, director of Newell Public Relations in Hong Kong—one of the largest high-tech firms in the region, with clients like Yahoo! China and Cisco—points out that the actual number of connected consumers versus connected businesses in Hong Kong is vastly disproportionate, although the number of connected ones is growing. Further, as everywhere else, business to business is potentially an exponentially larger market in China than business to consumer. However, "Companies must realize they need both English *and* Chinese brands—meaning frequently acquiring *two* names. Further, there are significant cultural and linguistic issues for this market. For example, the number '8' is a very good-fortune number in China, and the number '4' represents bad luck, even death. As a result, many phone numbers have 8s but not many have 4s. Older buildings in Hong Kong don't even have fourth floors. Because English and Western letters and words don't translate well into Chinese, Web sites often use *numbers* as names. For example, www.136.com is a popular site in Shanghai. If you look at www.

register.com you'll see that many numerical sites are owned by Chinese or Asians."

"It's all about building a Web site with business value," said Basskarin Nadir, a Singapore-based marketing adviser. "For portals and other businesses designing a Web presence, branding is a first step, which is a shift. It used to be considered only after several years, especially here in Asia, but now companies aren't just selling themselves, they're selling their *brands*. For big companies, they try to look at the Internet as a delivery channel, and making it transactional has been a big issue—in other words, anything more than brochureware. This is affected significantly by the regulatory environment in which they operate—a big issue that U.S. companies often forget when attempting to build a brand *outside* the United States. The Singapore-based www.debtdomain.com is an example: To what extent can they do online banking? They can't cannibalize existing accounts because of regulations, so the question becomes, 'Can the customer work with me on the Web or will they want to go to a banking office in-person?' and puts this very real issue of loyalty into play—which is being quickly diluted by the Web and is unavailable for Internet-only brands."

Of course, this now has significant implications for banks in Singapore that have been waiting for the governmental tide to shift so they could begin to deploy their online banking images and extend their brands online. The task is still, however, for them to meet the challenge of continuing to build a personal relationship with clients and at the same time building their brands and emotional appeal online.

Asia is a place to go to get things—such as manufacturing, parts, or even development talent; Latin America is, as yet, largely untapped and believed to be somewhat financially risky, although it is beginning to be viewed as a promised land of the Internet. Europe, however, is seen as highly viable, and the most approachable offshore brand destination. Europeans, in turn, view North America as their first brand destination outside of their own continent.

Europe

For the vast majority of companies based in the United States, when they think of global branding, it's Europe that comes to mind first.

Paul van Schaik is a partner of the Human Capital Group of Deloitte & Touche in Utrecht, the Netherlands. In an interesting way, his view of the Web and how it affects the professional recruiting business in the Netherlands and the rest of Europe echoes that of NTUC in Singapore.

"For us, the Web isn't an end in and of itself; rather, it's simply another communication and marketing tool. Ultimately, however, we have to make contact in person and build a personal relationship— this is what keeps people. At this point, to recruit senior executives for a big firm there are only small chances you'll get them on the Web here. Believe it or not, many senior executives still don't have a PC on their desks. They're part of a generation that's not connected, and they have secretaries typing their letters. However, the next generation has laptops, PCs, palmtops, and all kinds of connections, and they're coming on quite quickly. The Web is becoming increasingly popular for finding both jobs—although not, perhaps the top-level ones—and for finding recruiting firms. And while there will *always* be people who need to be contacted personally, for middle management there's no reason not to use the Web.

"There is much development taking place on the Web in our industry, and in Europe. Many companies have well-defined Web sites, although some don't and haven't realized what it can do for their brand identity. We haven't reached the ultimate Web sites yet."

Van Schaik believes, however, that the well-established bricks-and-mortar brand stands a better chance against the increasing glut of start-up job sites throughout Europe: "A well-established brand is a big advantage. You don't know who these start-ups are, and we have the lead. For something as critical as finding a job and being given recruiting advice, who's simply going to rely on a start-up with no name, no apparent experience, and who knows what kinds of contacts? Again, it boils down to relationships, both with those finding a job and the employers seeking them.

"But you can't ignore the *personal* side of business, in spite of a growing Internet culture. Sure, we have a good brand name, and there are many others. But a big part of the reason there are customers is because *I'm* a brand, also: People want me, no matter which company I'm in, so there's a personal brand in addition to the corporate brand. It's like having a doctor—no matter what clinic they may work for, you may very well want to follow him or her to that clinic. And that's something you can't build on the Web."

Jean Gomes is managing director of dPa Corporate Communications (www.dpacom.com), a well-established brand development and marketing communications firm located just outside London, specializing in high-technology firms such as Sony, Amdahl, Nokia, and Sun: "We believe companies need to focus at least 10 percent, if not 30 percent, of their traditional brand development investment on continuous brand-perception tracking and board-level challenge sessions that get the senior team to face the realities of what the market thinks of the company's brands.

"As the importance of the concepts of brand take hold in the boardroom (although certainly not universal in Europe), consultants now face a turning point in their careers—to acknowledge the realities of being strategic business consultants, or remain as tactical advisers who bundle up marketing communications projects. If experts are to consult at this level, they need to know more about financial models, sales processes, demographics, research, and perception analysis. As reality of a true 1:1 brand experience on the Web begins to be fulfilled, the implications of the whole strategic and operational activities of a company become inextricably bound in the brand consultant or manager's 'remit.'

"Globalization also means brand advisers need to understand more about the technical aspects of segmenting and targeting audiences through Web technology. Advances in that technology are happening weekly and can make the delivery of new services to a remote market a viable or essential investment today, when only last month they were uneconomical.

"We believe that, in terms of brand development on the Web, the biggest issue facing major brands is the fragmentation of attention in media. Throughout television and print advertising, megacorporations were able to establish national and global brands. The multichannel TV/Internet converged environment provides literally endless choice and need for niche advertising as well as niche product positioning. Consumers no longer want to buy mass-market toothpaste or orange juice, but are increasingly choosing niche brands they feel are especially right for them. Brand managers need to embrace the implications of this for established mass-market brands, or run the very short-term-reality risk of going out of business. The evidence for the decline of mass generic brands is seen in the recent bottom-line performance of giants like Procter & Gamble. dPa's solution to this challenge is the concept of the brand as a sustainable feedback loop with the customer, employee, and other stakeholders. The product will and must change. The brand will and must adapt in the knowledge economy."

Gomes believes Europeans love successful U.S. brands with a track record, but also resent the arrogant assumption that one particular style of marketing is right for everyone. "Thinking global and acting local" is rarely applied successfully. "A successful adaptation of an American Web brand requires a market feedback loop which helps to transpose the core brand values onto local needs. The loop needs to be continuous to ensure that the brand doesn't revert back to the U.S. model after the initial local input. We frequently find ourselves helping to 'unpick' the complexity of intercountry miscommunications about the suitability of messaging and techniques for local conditions. Often brand models have been imposed on a sales structure very different from U.S. sales structures, without any thought to the implications. Added to that, the differences in sophistication and preferences of European cultures are radical: What is perfectly acceptable to the French may be anathema to the Spanish."

Gomes says three things must dominate any American branding effort in Europe:

1. Concentrate on content.
2. Understand the marketing channels, especially the new media ones.
3. Differentiate based on rare qualities, for example, mineral water from the royal spa in Bath, England. Water is water, but there's only one British royal family.

Christopher Wünsche, Managing Partner with Deekeling-Kommunikation (a division of BBDO) in Frankfurt, Germany, is an expert in corporate brand development with clients such as Cognis, Boston Consulting Group, Deutsche Bank, Epson, Goldman Sachs, Toyota, Deutsche Telekom, and Viterra. Wünsche believes "corporate branding is the key factor for corporate success in the New Economy, for four reasons:

1. *Globalization.* Internationalization and globalization mean new competitors in home markets and expansion into new markets. Competition gets more and more intensive. To differentiate a company in times of exchangeable products and services, 'the corporate brand is the most valuable yet least tangible asset' of a company, as Jack Welch, CEO of GE aptly said.

2. *The World Wide Web.* The World Wide Web accelerates the corporate branding process dramatically. New names, new companies, and new competitors come across the borders and find a borderless marketplace. 'New' brands, like Yahoo!, Amazon.com, and others show they can be built with a speed unimaginable merely five years ago. As the Internet is a new and additional channel for corporate communications as well as a distribution chain, an online and offline presence must be linked in terms of content and message as well as in design and colors, typeface, and forms. An excellent example of linked online and offline marketing is Lycos Europe, where the black labrador retriever appears in all the media used to communicate the company's services. Current studies show that the degree of knowledge and brand recognition may differ significantly when the name and logo of the Web site are covered. Only the use of brand-specific design elements over all forms of communication guarantees high brand recognition.

3. *Mergers and acquisitions.* As the merger wave penetrates ever more deeply in Europe, and especially in Germany ('corporate Germany' is currently reorganizing itself), the reasons to merge with or take over other companies change. Not only are acquiring new businesses or market share, and regional diversification, the primary areas of focus, but buying brands as a means to access new customer groups has become increasingly important. Brands as a source of trust, and therefore customer retention, are a key factor for growth.

4. *The service and information age.* As modern economies move more and more away from industrial production to producing intangible goods like financial services, software, or IT, as well as virtual services sold by or in the Web, brands become even more important. Services can only be sold by branding, as nobody has the time to really learn about the advantages and details of a given service. The brand as an 'anchor of trust' involves building the client relationship before the actual sales process starts."

Even entertainers are cognizant of their fragility *sans* brand. Marie Frank, a teen idol in Denmark whose global popularity is growing (her music was featured in the recent movie, *Love & Sex*) said, "I think the Web is really important, and it was really hard when I didn't have it. People wanted to know how to write to us. It's one place where things can be channeled. It was a great relief to finally have our site up. After I won the fall Grammies in Denmark, there was a substantial increase in the number of people contacting me both in Danish and in other languages, and it was primarily being done through the Web. I think the Web will get more and more important, and one day when my contract runs out, the Web will become even more important: It will be an important part of a business for me and will allow my 'brand' to exist beyond that of the record company. Also, the film my song is in—*Love & Sex*—has a Web address, which also features my song. All of these ways are helping me become better known, and they're all on the Web."

When building a brand in Germany, or anywhere in Europe, Wünsche advises clients that building an online brand there is much the same as building a brand anywhere else: Raise the degree of knowledge, provide a clear core promise (value proposition) of the brand, build homogeneous core messages, create a constant visual appearance, and be highly consistent. The key is continuity, continuity, continuity, combined with a little innovation from time to time. "The core task of branding in the Web is to get into the relevant set of links," says Wünsche. "Whoever wants to be in business continuously with clients must be saved in the 'favorites' list. Therefore, the corporate name should be the same as the URL. Traditional brands often have the advantage of being known and take profit from the trust already established."

Latin America

High-tech companies like Acer—the PC manufacturer—have long known and enjoyed the benefits of focusing early on the Latin market. With a fraction of a percentage of the U.S. PC market, in the 1990s Acer entered key Latin markets like Mexico with concentrated marketing and brand-building initiatives. Acer's efforts to build a strong channel in those markets gave it a *significant* share of the market, well into double-digits—simply because it focused on the Latin market, nurtured the channel, delivered upon the brand promise, built personal relationships, and maintained a consistent, long-term presence.

Companies building brands on the Web have a real opportunity in Latin America if they follow the rules of the friendly business missionary, and work to build relationships—which is a key element, because the biggest complaint by Latin American executives is that Americans, especially, want to fly into town, do a deal, and leave—something completely alien to the Latin business culture. Building a relationship with a Latin American—and, certainly, differences exist among countries, so this is a slight generalization—means first building a *personal* relationship, which is becoming more difficult but nonetheless essential in the age of electronic communication. Latinos want to talk about family, interests, culture, and so on, and have several meetings, before business can really begin. How can this happen if they only know a company by its Web site?

This is one reason the Web sites in Latin America are frequently more lively, colorful, and graphically oriented than those of the colder northern nations. Companies building brands on the Web in Brazil find they must be friendly and approachable first, in order to create a real emotional bond to the business. The advertising is more frivolous, and the culture as a whole puts a lot more emphasis on "fun" than, say, Germany or even the United States. While the Latinos *respect* American business efficiency, they aren't likely to give up their long lunches or their reliance upon a good balance of style with function.

Bill Hinchberger is an American journalist in Brazil who has been producing a Brazilian portal—www.brazilmax.com—directed at non-Brazilians interested in the culture. He has a deep understanding of how Brazilian and Latin culture overall are becoming increasingly integrated with global brand and Web practices—as well as how Latin American cultures and businesses compare with one another, and, specifically, with Brazilian culture. (Brazil, by far, has the highest volume of business transactions in Latin America.) Hinchberger recalled: "At its recent launch party in Miami, the New Economy magazine *Punto-com/Ponto-com* distributed a booklet entitled 'Similarities in Conducting Business between Latin America and Brazil.' The contents: 10 blank pages!

"An inside joke but one with a serious message. Despite the best efforts of Simon Bolívar and his contemporary heirs, Latin America remains pretty much an exogenous concept. As MTV Latino learned early on, Mexicans don't care much about Chilean music—or vice versa. The only time most Brazilians think much about the rest of the region is during regional soccer tournaments. Regional free trade is breaking down some long-standing barriers, but more among businesspeople and the intellectual elite than among average citizens and consumers.

"Thus, consideration one of building a Web brand and business in Latin America: define your public, learn their cultural idiosyncrasies, and appeal to them. You may need to focus branding efforts on each society or, depending on your 'product,' certain subsets of each society. That means understanding the places where you want to do business—via first-hand experience, education, local partners, locally hired staff, or paid consultants."

He also emphasizes the importance of building local credibility: "For starters, get the language right. I've seen way too many awful translations on Web sites. And if you want to alienate a potential customer, just get the language wrong. Contract or hire excellent native-language translators and copy editors, and check and double-check their work before it goes out. Roberto Civita, CEO of the Abril Publishing Group, said that he believes the keys to brand success on the Net are the same as those offline: building consumer confidence and establishing credibility.

"There will be some interesting business-to-business opportunities in industries that are already important to the local economies, such as agriculture and food processing, petroleum, and mining. Business-to-consumer opportunities trail here both for the same reasons as abroad and because of the low Net penetration and the lack of confidence in online credit card transactions.

"Successful Web-based brands in Latin America will be the ones that identify lucrative niches, use powerful content to attract potential consumers into a virtual community, and serve that community's needs as people and as consumers. Beyond that, I think all of the consulting companies and advertising agencies are feeling their way around. Some are using spin-off subsidiaries, some are developing in-house business units, and some are even jumping into the world of incubators. But few locals can really claim success in branding online. The leading countries in Latin America where Web brands are taking hold are, as you might guess, Brazil, Mexico, and Argentina, for the same reasons as always: these are the strongest economies. Of these, Brazil has the most sophisticated and cosmopolitan business community."

Miguel Perrotti, a São Paulo–based high-tech executive and entrepreneur, believes thoughtful analysis and strong partnerships within and outside of Brazil and Latin America drive any and all success in the New Economy. "I invite my Internet-age compatriots to reflect on the nature of the New Economy: its companies, its brands, its implications, and the profound excitement it inspires. It's not about succeeding in 'bits and bytes' or patting myself on the back. It's not about conquering new territories. In IT, especially, the statement 'we come, we see, we conquer' rarely holds true. As entrepreneurs—as we've all become—we must be able to *actively* reflect: be able to understand, in depth, what is happening moment to moment, not what happened decades ago, a few years ago, or what might be happening in a few years. In fact, the future is as unreal as the past, and we know that predicting the technological future is about as accurate as determining weather trends. We have to really *think* about business, and understand all the various factors we know to be true, and leverage them against current and dynamic business conditions. Only then can we begin to believe we are creating a competitive edge. Only by using the power of thinking, and not simply firing off revenue and sales plans and going after every possible business opportunity together, no matter what it is, can we succeed as brands in the New Economy.

"Think about the Brazilian IT market and how it is changing, for example. Think about the effects of entrepreneurial myopia. Think about political and regulatory attitudes. Think about our role in this new world, which, I'm sure, businesspeople have thought about at various times over the last several thousand years when a major development occurred—whether in shipping, culture, invasion, or resources. A New World? Maybe. A new way of doing things? Maybe not. I invite others to share not just the New Economy, but an entirely new panorama of life with me, as a partner in thought, business, and success. As a Brazilian, what I *have* learned—even up to my neck in Internet issues and business—is that it is much better to think together than to struggle separately."

Global Business-to-Consumer Branding: Bricks and Mortar Win

Outside the United States, the world is, realistically, a few years behind in its romance with the Web. It still is in the enamored stage, in love with the *idea* of consumers having access to all kinds of information and purchases. However, in spite of the global dotcom explosion, certain realities need to be faced—ranging from Singaporeans simply wanting to get out of the condo to many citizens, worldwide, being still doubtful about the security of their credit card numbers being placed online. These factors have made it difficult to know where and when various business-to-consumer business models will work.

Wisse's Luc Levi points out that many regional brands stand a better chance of capturing the trust and long-term online loyalty of customers if they are already an established bricks-and-mortar brand: "A lot of companies don't use the Web to build a brand, but rather as just a brochure—which is an Old Economy mentality, although it can actually do quite well. We have a company in Holland very successful with traditional catalog sales, and they say they're doing well online, now, as well. Wehkamp.nl made their name in catalog sales, or 'post order' as we call it here, and seem to have successfully transitioned, primarily because they are a bricks-and-mortar company that had more momentum. They're very well known, a typical mail-order brand, and while maybe they're not very exciting, everyone knows them, trusts them, and they've done well.

"I have the feeling that a lot of Old Economy companies use the Web just because they have to be there; they haven't used it really to extend their brand but rather have only used it as another form of collateral. On the other hand, there are some new companies doing things differently. There is a new company called www.cigarline.nl. They're a mail-order business-gift firm; while they advertise in traditional media, they're a pure online company. Companies like this perhaps stand a chance if they can last long enough to establish a brand, but it won't be the quick climb to success of the typical American dot-com etailer."

Global Brands Moving Forward

As in the United States, global Web brands will entertain and serve consumers with a wide variety of products, services, information, and people-to-people connections. However, also as in the United States, it's the business-to-business brands that have the best chance of making it big and growing into multi-billion-dollar businesses and which must ultimately create and maintain the strongest and most formidable brand structures and frameworks. One strong common denominator for multinational Web brands as well as regional business-to-business brands is that the business world has a much lower tolerance for poor execution, unresponsive service, and confusing organization either offline or online.

"Business-to-business will work everywhere for one reason," said Luc Levi. "It's not the new acquisition, but the account servicing and retention that really count. The Internet offers you the ability to cut down on both time and paperwork, which helps keep track of customers and accounts automatically. The Net is and will continue to be a fantastic way for existing customers to do business. It provides an unprecedented opportunity for existing vendors who are known or who are working with established vendors to communicate, do business, and grow revenue together. Ultimately, it's all about profitability: You can have an initial success, but there has to be a revenue stream which continues to produce over a limitless time period—otherwise the original idea has no inherent value, by definition. That means there must be a solid business model with a well-framed brand structure, capable of extending in service, product, and time. And building that takes a concerted, methodological effort at all levels of the company, in all regions."

HBI's Corinna Voss echoed Levi's statements, citing one of the biggest recent success stories in global Web business-to-business branding: "Ariba is a start-up, but they have many big, multinational clients, such as BMW, and an entire management and company that reflect stability. In fact, BMW selected them *specifically* because of that. If you're going to work with companies like BMW or Deutsche Bank, you absolutely *must*, and I cannot emphasize this too much, you *must* reflect stability."

What are some key considerations for building a strong, global business-to-business brand? Consider these points:

- *Management.* The executive team must have a clear perception of the market, wherever and whatever it is, and what the company plans to achieve. They must have a brand and business road map if they hope to garner business, partners, and even agencies. "We'll turn down companies that don't seem like they know where they're going," said Voss.
- *Deliver a solution, not a product.* Ordering a pair of shoes online is one thing, but dealing with BMW, Sony, General Motors, or BancoBrasil requires a *real* solution and plan as to how to build a marketplace. Does the solution integrate with SAP and other enterprise resource planning solutions? Is it localized? Does the company have the ability to manage the business it is going after? Will it be able to keep the promise it makes, and continue to build a natural and believable brand?
- *Manage customers and brand, not the technology.* Technology has

become a commodity, and there's not a company without a spectacular technological infrastructure, or at least a plan for one. Managing and building a brand, however, is far more difficult and rare, as is managing and servicing customers beyond their self-service experience on a Web site. "We're all living interconnected lives, with more interdependencies, more links and ties—and doing so at a faster pace, with less margin for error," commented Alan M. Webber in *USA Today*. "And customers are not only demanding—they're more demanding then ever before."[7] It's not always about what goes *right*, but what goes *wrong* and how it is handled, which can make or break a brand. Says Webber, "Service recovery is all about immediate, instinctive, real-time response by on-the-scene human beings. And it's all about companies that have the right kinds of policies that let their employees do the right thing and do it without question."[8]

- *Integrate business-to-business and business-to-consumer.* Many business-to-business markets also serve the business-to-consumer markets, which means that the ultimate consumer will look at the *image* of the brand, while the partners, vendors, and business-to-business clients will look more at the *management* of the brand—both in terms of the people on the team and how the brand is structured. The bricks-and-mortar companies stand the best chance of building their brands online globally, provided they manage the brands well and extend them to the Web in a believable fashion—and they also have the most experienced and mature management teams. Yet, as in the case of Great Eastern Life, they must leverage their legacy with the youthful opportunities provided by the Web, effectively integrating image with management.

Online, Offline

Online branding is not an end in itself. It must be supported by a physical corporate infrastructure, an image presence outside the Web—even if it points people to the Web—in the form of advertising, PR, and other marketing communications venues. Further, these venues must be consistently executed, no matter what region of the world in which they appear, and they must be clear and easy to understand for any culture. Finally, they must be localized, where appropriate, to speak directly to the local business community. It's not only consumer brands that must localize; in fact, business-to-business brands have even more need for localization because they frequently have a much more complex brand framework and much more complex messaging.

Building a brand in North America is challenge enough for many companies, yet few would claim international business isn't essential to their future. Conversely, a company such as Wavetrend (www.wavetrend.net) shares virtual headquarters in South Africa, the United Kingdom, and the United States yet has fewer than 100 employees. Boasting large multinational clients, Wavetrend provides wireless identification products and services to protect all types of assets and intellectual property. Some companies choose to begin internationally, while some (more typically) focus on a specific region and then build out. Which model is more effective? Certainly, the single-region model is easier, but not necessarily more effective in terms of being able to compete and provide services to larger clients that are, by definition, highly global.

The bottom line? Building a brand that involves the Web—especially in the business-to-business market—requires addressing the nonlocal side of the business. The perception that the Web is instantly global is simplistic. Building a global brand doesn't happen just because the audience can access it from anywhere. Building a global brand requires careful planning and understanding of other markets that may use it. It requires relationships, localization, channels, and cultural sensitivity—just as much for clicks as it always has for bricks.

9

Beyond the New Economy

The wave of the future is coming and there is no fighting it.
—Anne Morrow Lindbergh, *The Wave of the Future,* 1940[1]

It takes only a telephone to catch a glimpse of what lies beyond these glorious, golden-era days of the Internet age. The AT&T Digital PocketNet® service-compatible phone, marketed by AT&T Wireless and featuring Web access, is a lesson in what's to come for all types of brands, ranging from giant multinational firms to tiny start-ups.

Even before turning on the phone users can see both the AT&T globe logo and the Mitsubishi or Ericsson logo (several hardware models are or have been available) emblazoned on the handset. As the phone powers on, three more corporate names flash on, RSA Data Security Inc., Tegic Communications Inc., and Phone.com, all of which presumably provide various types of supporting software and network infrastructure for the phone's operation. Clicking the phone's Web access reveals a further bevy of brands: Barnes & Noble, eBay, DealTime, GiftCertificates.com, FTD.com, Mercata, Yahoo!, eCompare, BarPoint.com, Yellow Pages, Mapquest, Zagat Dining, E*TRADE, TD Waterhouse, Schwab, Ameritrade, CBS Marketwatch, eSignal, ABC News, ZDNet, CNET, the *Wall Street Journal, USA Today,* ESPN, Expedia, Travelocity, TRIP.com, and Hollywood.com, to give only a partial list.[2]

None of these brands was requested or put onto the phone by the user. They came already loaded, and either provide service for the phone's operation or are simply there for the user to access easily. But each of these companies has something in common: Each has struck a partnership of some kind with AT&T Wireless, and each is at least attempting to meet the challenge of representing its brand online on a tiny monochrome screen. At this point, at least, they can't be differentiated on the screen using color or graphics. They offer pure content and service. Users count on the phone working, on their connections and transactions being secure, on being able to find what they want, and on being able to connect when and wherever they go. With increasing technological convergence, such as that of the Internet, telephony, and personal devices, branding will take on new forms. These will include newer (and not always welcome) forms of advertising and marketing arriving on the digital doorstep of consumers—perhaps only because they simply are in the vicinity of a shop, attraction, or restaurant eager for their business. AT&T's PocketNet is but one example of a converged and wireless brand future; many forms of wireless handheld devices will continue to appear over the coming years, all loaded with brands of various sizes and shapes. If the New Economy is truly evolving into the Customer Economy, then the concept must focus on what will be *beneficial* to customers and further serve their needs rather than on simply finding new ways of annoying them. This chapter does not attempt to predict the technological future. Instead, it is meant as a glimpse into how *branding* is changing and continues to evolve alongside technology. As long as technology is largely about communication, and the vast majority of it is, then branding will remain its natural companion.

The Microsoft Auto Vision

Microsoft is giving serious thought to the form-factor issue as it develops new capabilities for various devices in locations such as automobiles. The folks in Redmond are working extensively with automobile manufacturers and car stereo producers to ensure that the Microsoft.NET initiatives make it into everyone's driving experience. According to Gonzalo Bustillos, director of business development for Microsoft's Automotive Business Unit, "The brand-identity issues are the same—building a personality and recognition—and the tools are the same. You're broadening the target and reach, and using Web tools, and via the Web, you've transcended your target audience. It's very powerful, with lots of responsibility.

"Responsibility is a big issue, especially when it comes to the automotive industry, where safety and reliability are tied together inextricably. Further, the safety and reliability implications are different from person to person; for some, it means the product will never fail for me, while others are thinking there's financial investment and the company is backing me up.

"We [Microsoft] debated on what it meant to browse the Web. Does it mean simply searching for published info? That's the old way. Is it browsing and investigating? That's not what you do in a car. The Web is essentially a cloud of communication—you don't have to browse the Web, you *use* it. This, in turn, affects brand implications—if I'm browsing via audio, what is the brand? Is it something I listen to? Is it something I see?

"Obviously, I'm thinking that the rendering mechanism is mostly visual, for example, Intel 'Inside' being 'seen' with a sound—even if I'm not seeing it, I can identify it."

Microsoft had to carefully consider the form-factor issues, as well as how devices interact. The company wants to tie together various "hubs" of information—a person's home, office, car—with a single device, such as an enhanced version of today's cell phone.

"In today's market, legacy brands are very important. Once the PC form factor changes and is no longer the center of focus, what will that do to branding? The branding schemes will have to change. They'll be using various technologies but the combination of audio and visual cues and tones will be increasingly important to branding. I'll still need to tell the consumer that all these devices talk to each other, powered by Microsoft.

"Alternatively, if I'm using a handheld device, I can connect but it's not seamless. How well connected things are has profound implications for branding, and that's the value-add Microsoft provides in a world of multiple devices."

But to marketing giants like Microsoft, building Web access into cars and further connecting people's lives is about much, much more than networking and technology. Microsoft must think about the business-to-consumer and business-to-business implications and how they will build their brand not only with drivers but with the many others involved with automobiles: "First we deal with suppliers, then makers, then dealers, then the consumers. The average lifetime of a car is 10 years. During that time, on average, $85,000 is spent on buying the car, gas, license, insurance, tires, maintenance, brakes, and anything else. Automakers get $15,000 to $18,000 of that for the car, but after the point of sale their revenue opportunities are limited. We want to provide great revenue opportunities at the post-sales level. It would be great if a car dealer could *really* know what a driver wants, and be able to provide it to them, value-added." Microsoft is looking to electronic devices in cars to do much more than simply let drivers order flowers or access their favorite song (although that's important, too). Do users want remote navigation? Sure. That already exists.

"There are some basic services people would *really* pay for, way beyond navigation—I don't get lost that often. *Diagnostics*, however, would be great. That way I know what's wrong with the car, specifically, and can go to the shop and be able to tell them knowledgeably what is wrong with the car, instead of thinking I'm getting screwed. It's all about returning power to the consumer."

Taking Eloyalty to the Next Level

The bar is continually being raised above and beyond Olympic levels for companies competing for differentiation and customer loyalty. They enjoy fewer luxuries than brands enjoyed in the past, such as physical contact with the customer and the ability to out-design competitors. All of a sudden, the market involves brand factors like those faced by gas stations: service, availability, emotional appeal, pricing, loyalty, return traffic, and, last but most assuredly not least, personalization *and* personal relationships.

Competitive differentiators will continue to take on various forms: What makes one brand different or more desirable will depend not only on "better," "simple," and "more," but also on niche components that tend to make more of a difference in a crowded eworld. An example in the offline world is a recent radio campaign by a leading gasoline retailer that used cleaner bathrooms as the differentiator. Presumably, the reasoning was that audiences were likely to pay more for gasoline and service if they believed that cleanliness and orderliness were high priorities of the retailer. With Web branding, atypical points of differentiation like this will be increasingly and vigorously explored to create those ultraimportant, ultrafine lines of separation.

Form factors are getting smaller, from handheld devices and Internet phones to in-dash Internet access in vehicles, and in the future embedded devices will provide Web access in everything from refrigerators to wristwatches. While many devices—such as the AT&T PocketNet—come preloaded with various brands, only a fraction of those brands will be useful to any one user, which means users must be able to personalize the phone. They not only want to see *only* the sites that will be useful to them, but they want those sites to alert them to information, as well as other sites, perhaps, that fit their personal interests and needs.

People also want to be able to speak with a human when they need to. They don't want to hear automated information computers, they don't want to have to click through an endless stream of automated choices without ever reaching the answer to the technical question they seek, and they do want someone to remember them and address them in a personal fashion. The OnStar System in the Cadillac Escalade (see www.cadillac.com and www.onstar.com) has achieved this level of personalization; human beings speak to the driver in real time, surfing the Web and performing services like making restaurant reservations. General Motors deserves strong kudos for having the technological foresight to develop OnStar. More services of this type (although, perhaps, not specifically the OnStar model, which can easily be—and has been, on occasion—overloaded) will become the standard, not the exception. Focusing on innovation in how technology and the human touch can be combined will become increasingly critical to brand success.

From a business-to-business standpoint, all types of partnerships will continue to drive the growth of corporate brands, as they have with the AT&T PocketNet and its power-on brands (Tegic Communications, RSA Data Security, and Phone.com) as well as the hardware manufacturer (Mitsubishi). Business-to-business relationships made this happen, and visibility through the PocketNet and in other venues will drive new deals. As a result, the distinction between business-to-business and business-to-consumer brands will be increasingly blurred. Both types of business may be visible in a single venue, and users will be able to access only what they need. (The average consumer, for example, really doesn't care about the power-on brands that appear on the PocketNet screen, but the business-to-business client does.) Corporations will have to consider how and where they want their brands to appear, and whom they need to reach either through targeted marketing or through a PocketNet-type of business-to-business knowledge filter.

Branding Tradition: John Deere

John Deere & Company, based in Moline, Illinois, known primarily for its 163-year-old "John Deere" name, is one of the most trusted, established, middle-American, "iron-belt" brands in North America. The company typifies what a highly traditional brand faces today as it integrates technology and the Web into its business.

Deere & Company is up against an especially tough challenge because it thrives in the heavy equipment and agriculture markets, which are as entrenched in Old Economy ways as any business, anywhere. Yet the firm continues to receive strong support and reviews of its Internet work, and positive reaction to how its brand is represented on the Web, including the introduction of a redesigned trademark that speaks directly to the agricultural and manufacturing giant's commitment to technology.

"On the Web, just as offline, we're trying to create a broader view," says Ken Golden, Deere's public relations manager. The company is working on "rediscovering" its brand in the best New Economy sense: the Web; global recognition and business; effectively using and integrating Internet, extranet, and intranet communication; integrating new areas of technology into its business; developing new business opportunities in nontraditional areas (such as heavy equipment for maintaining golf courses); and initiating dialogues with both traditional (business to consumer) and new (business to business) audiences.

"One third of our business is global," says Golden. "We're only beginning to emerge, at least in the branding sense, as to how that plays out. A big part is how we make use of the Internet and how we construct our product and get it to market—extranet, intranet, and Internet.

"We're viewed as the premier producer of agricultural equipment by audiences in North America, that believe we're the leader everywhere. But that's not the case: We need to extend to other parts of the globe; for example, in Europe we're third, and globally we have a challenge to extend the brand. As an organization, we're *very* global, manufacturing in 17 countries, and selling to 160. However, our *brand* is not as global as we'd like. Brand management is a strong part of that, and we need to extend it further."

The company's brand is strongly tied to agriculture, so much so that Wall Street has a hard time understanding how the legacy company has and is extending its brand into new markets. "The brand is so strong in that core area [agriculture] that we have to discover a way to not lessen, but rather to extend, it across a broader range of business and regions," says Golden. For example, the company's fastest-growing growing division is lawn- and grounds-care equipment, which is significantly different from agricultural products.

"Part of the effort in branding we're going through is to develop visibility as producing some of the most technologically advanced equipment in general—not just in agriculture. We want to get the point across on the Web that people are looking at our equipment as a much broader solution, and we want our new trademark and effort in branding to allow us to achieve a much broader brand identity."

Finally, the company is converting—although cautiously—to allow the dominant subbrand, John Deere, to become the dominant corporate brand (Deere & Company). It is in the process of acknowledging that John Deere is the brand most recognized and most extendable beyond its traditional boundaries.

So, What's the Big Idea?

In the book *Heroes.Com*, Louise Proddow describes what she calls the "big idea" in business.[3] Brand, brand loyalty, and brand leadership surround the entire concept, and represent the ultimate goal of the big idea as it grows and becomes reality. Proddow, a product marketing director at Sun Microsystems UK, says "Great dot-com businesses are founded on big ideas. . . . The big idea goes through all parts of the business."

With the advent of the New Economy has come the increased emphasis on personalization and immediacy—in other words, branding the experience instead of experiencing the brand. These two Web-world dynamics underscore the fact that corporate profitability will be gauged on how well companies communicate directly with their audiences, on a one-to-one basis, and also on how quickly they provide individuals with the particular service or piece of information they happen to be after at a particular time. The winners and most enduring brands in the New Economy will undoubtedly be the ones that grasp the primary importance of personalization and immediacy and continually address them in all their promotional and messaging efforts.

In many cases, the legacy tactics of promoting the inherent attributes of a particular brand to encourage usage or purchase of a product, the result being (hopefully!) brand loyalty are being de-emphasized. Instead, companies are promoting the individual *experience* an ebrand offers, rather than inherent traits of the brand itself. Brand awareness, fit-to-concept, and memorability remain critical elements in building a brand strategy, but with ebranding, just as important is the experience offered once an individual arrives at the site. Is the content applicable, easily navigable, and accessible to ancillary services or information that enhance the brand experience and keeps the user at the site? Increasingly, these factors will drive brand loyalty and corporate success on all physical and virtual platforms.

"Espeak" is a skill that everyone, from the legacy to the purebred Web company, is still developing.. The good news is that the skill will improve naturally as it becomes a highly competitive component of brand identity. Espeak is really plain old customer service in a fancy wrapper; the Web simply provides a new mechanism for delivering it, and on an ongoing basis. It's the stuff the stickiest Web sites are made of, and is becoming the primary benchmark of effective ebranding (it also corresponds directly to advertising dollars a particular site can command).

As the Web matures and companies become more clearly defined, established, and differentiated online, brand extension will become increasingly challenging, especially for commodity and easy-to-find items: "Why would I buy a garden hose from Amazon when I can get it from an online hardware store or from the store down the street, especially considering I need it today?"

The strongest attribute companies can leverage is personalization. Sophisticated, personalized branding has gone way beyond its embryonic beginnings seen in the "my" revolution online (my.Yahoo!, My.SAP, etc.). It's all about building a one-to-one relationship with *each* member of the audience, all the while growing much faster than through traditional communications media.

Mass marketing efforts offline are based on reaching the largest groups possible, at the best possible times. With the Web, it's crucial to form individualized marketing approaches that will have the effect of create an en masse return, but with audience members returning one by one, at their convenience. Moving from bricks to clicks means that every brand must speak one on one to each person it encounters, and allow that person to reply in kind. Today's economy, new or old, is smarter, more efficient, more demanding, and more driven by relationships than by brainstorms, and it is loaded with opportunity. Looking ahead, the winners will be the ones who are able to meet innovation with business acumen, and who view the world market more as a giant conversation than a battlefield.

The Web is arguably the most powerful business tool in human history. It is useless, however, in the absence of sound business principles and practices, and is most effective when used in the context of how people have worked for centuries. Companies that make the effort to build brands based on both bricks *and* clicks will be the first to enjoy the untold treasures this new millennium offers and will lay the foundation for future generations of business leaders and innovators.

Notes

PREFACE

1. John Bartlett, *Familiar Quotations*, 14th ed., Little, Brown, Boston, 1968.
2. "Briefing: Branding," *Red Herring*, January 2000, p. 172.

CHAPTER 1

1. John Bartlett, *Familiar Quotations*, 14th ed., Little, Brown, Boston, 1968.
2. "The Missing Link in Web Retailing," *Forbes Magazine*, Jan. 10, 2000.
3. Katie Hafner, "Are Customers Ever Right? Service's Decline and Fall," The New York Times on the Web, July 20, 2000.
4. David A. Aaker, *Managing Brand Equity: Capitalizing on the Value of a Brand Name*, The Free Press, New York, 1991, pp. 15–16.

CHAPTER 2

1. John Bartlett, *Familiar Quotations*, 14th ed., Little, Brown, Boston, 1968.
2. Chuck Pettis, *TechnoBrands*, AMACOM (American Management Association), New York, New York, 1995.
3. Online focus group comparison submitted by Chamberlain Research, www.crcwis.com.
4. Research pros/cons submitted by Chamberlain Research, www.crcwis.com, a Wisconsin-based market research firm.
5. To see more information on this survey, see www.nabiscoworld.com.
6. Information on this case study was provided by Ed Tomechko, former president of NetRadio.com, who drove the brand to what it is today.

CHAPTER 3

1. John Bartlett, *Familiar Quotations,* 14th ed., Little, Brown, Boston, 1968.

2. Quoted from www.bluelight.com in "The BlueLight Story" section of "About BlueLight."

3. "Many Companies Kicking the Bricks-and-Mortar Habit," *USA Today,* July 5, 2000, Section B, p. 1B.

4. Jakob Nielsen, *Designing Web Usability: the Practice of Simplicity,* Indianapolis, New Riders Publishing, 2000.

5. David Siegel, *Secrets of Successful Web Sites,* Indianapolis, Hayden Books, 1997.

6. Ibid., p. 232.

CHAPTER 4

1. John Bartlett, *Familiar Quotations,* 14th ed., Little, Brown, Boston, 1968.

2. *Frequently Asked Questions about PricewaterhouseCoopers,* July 1, 1998, www.pwcglobal.com.

3. Scale Eight corporate mission, www.scaleeight.com, August 2000.

4. The book *e-Brands* by Phil Carpenter (*e-Brands: Building an Internet Business at Breakneck Speed,* Harvard Business School Press, Cambridge, 2000) is one of the few really analytical and in-depth books available based on a series of case studies. The author understands branding and presents very detailed information about a select few Internet brand efforts and how the brands were built and managed.

5. "Naming Advice," www.naming.net/advice.html, WriteExpress Corporation, 1997–2000.

6. All of these tag lines were derived from ads in major horizontal publications such as *Forbes, The Industry Standard, Hemispheres* (United Airlines's magazine), and other prominent publications as well as airport signage and billboards. Vertical, industry-specific publications were avoided, specifically, because of the already targeted audiences reading those publications.

CHAPTER 5

1. John Bartlett, *Familiar Quotations,* 14th ed., Little, Brown, Boston, 1968.

2. "AP Style" refers to a grammar, punctuation, and reference style based on the *Associated Press Stylebook,* which is followed by many newspapers and other publications. *The Chicago Manual of Style* (14th ed.) is another widely used style guide.

3. In the world of venture capital, an angel is a wealthy individual who privately funds a start-up or early-growth company.

CHAPTER 6

1. John Bartlett, *Familiar Quotations,* 14th ed., Little, Brown, Boston, 1968.

2. Deborah Lohse, "Dot-coms scramble for good public relations," *San Jose Mercury News,* Aug. 28, 2000. The information was attributed to Holland Carney, president of the U.S. Western Region of Alexander Ogilvy PR.

3. Suein Hwang and Mylene Mangalindan, "Yahoo!'s Grand Vision for Advertising on the Web Takes Some Hard Hits," *The Wall Street Journal/WSJ.Com,* September 1, 2000, p. 1.

4. Robert Lacey and Danny Danziger, *The Year 1000: What Life Was Like at the Turn of the First Millennium,* Boston, Little, Brown, 1999, pp. 27–28.

5. Many observers believe the crash was driven by the fact that it occurred at the time when Americans submit their income taxes. The previous year had resulted in so much money for various entrepreneurs that, at tax time, they had to sell significant amounts of stock to produce enough money to pay their taxes, resulting in a one-time big selloff in the market.

CHAPTER 7

1. John Bartlett, *Familiar Quotations,* 14th ed., Little, Brown, Boston, 1968.

2. Frederick F. Reichheld and Phil Schefter, "E-Loyalty: Your Secret Weapon on the Web," *Harvard Business Review*, July-August 2000, pp. 105–113.

3. Ibid., p. 106.

4. Ibid.

5. Enterprise resource planning is an area of information technology providing a combination of technology and services required to allocate resources and operate companies, such as financial, administrative, and human resources integrated software tools. Firms such as SAP and PeopleSoft specialize in areas of ERP that keep corporations running.

Chapter 8

1. John Bartlett, *Familiar Quotations*, 14th ed., Little, Brown, Boston, 1968.

2. This figure was attributed to Sergio Otero, President of Serpro, the multi-billion-dollar consulting arm of the Brazilian government, in an interview in September 1999.

3. Statistics dated June 30, 2000. See www.glreach.com/globstats; www.glreach.com is a "marketing communications consultancy that assists clients in attracting Web site visitors worldwide from all countries that are online."

4. Michael J. Bauer, "The E-ffect of the Internet on Supply Chain and Logistics," *World Trade*, September 2000, p. 74, table titled "People with Internet access at home, percentage of population." The figures were attributed to Economist Intelligence Unit.

5. Interestingly, about a week after the interview aired, Infosys announced a strategic global relationship with Microsoft and support for the Microsoft.NET enterprise server platform. Murthy undoubtedly had an ulterior motive in making these comments, but they still have value and meaning.

6. Julian Ding, *e-Commerce Law & Practice*, Sweet & Maxwell, Asia, 1999, p. 33.

7. Alan M. Webber, "When Things Go Wrong, Best Firms Recover Quickly," *USA Today*, August 24, 2000, p. 15A.

8. Ibid.

Chapter 9

1. John Bartlett, *Familiar Quotations*, 14th ed., Little, Brown, Boston, 1968.

2. These various services and brands change as license agreements and partnerships change. Also, special promotions appear on the phone from time-to-time.

3. Louise Proddow, *Heroes.com*, Hodder & Stoughton Educational, London, 2000, pp. 178–179.

Glossary

B2B/B2C (business-to-business/business-to-consumer) Conducting of business directly to another business or directly to consumers.

Brand attributes The expressions of a brand, pursuant to its personality, that can be modified moderately or dramatically with time.

Brand continuum The ability of a brand to extend itself as naturally and smoothly as possible to subbrands.

Brand equity The inherent positive or negative values associated with a brand over time.

Brand extension The extension of a corporate or parent brand into new brand areas or subbrands.

Brand gap A brand disparity created when Old Economy messaging is not recreated in New Economy venues.

Brand hump The milestone marking when, after a brand has been launched, it is easily matched to its core offering.

Brand mapping The plan of action that coordinates known factors with the ultimate goals of the brand.

Brand-name convergence The maturation process of a name, ultimately carrying it to encompass the promise of a brand.

Brand personality The inherent, nonchanging characteristics of a brand's makeup.

Brand process The systematic process that underlies solution branding, consisting of five phases: discovery; framework; verbal articulation; visual, sensory, and physical articulation; and execution.

Brand pruning The channeling of a brand's energy and focus, while stripping away ancillary messaging that gets in the way of a streamlined and growing brand promise.

Brand research Involving target audiences to help ascertain levels of established equity and also to validate the believability of a proposed brand or brands.

Brand strategy The art of extending a brand's promise consistently and seamlessly, while maintaining and enhancing its core believability.

Brand the experience versus experience the brand The advantages of personalization and immediacy associated with the online brand experience (branding the experience) over the Old Economy legacy practice of promoting purchase of a branded offering (experiencing the brand).

Branded house versus house of brands The premise of having one, universal promise which supports multiple subpromises (branded house) versus individual promises, without the universal promise and parentage (house of brands).

Branding hierarchy The elements involved in a top-down branding strategy, where umbrella-brand promises lend credibility to parent brands and/ or subbrands and their more specifically oriented promises. *See also* Parent brand; Subbrand; Umbrella brand.

Bricks-and-mortar firms The offline, physical, often Old Economy form of companies, as opposed to firms in the online, virtual world.

Competitive differentiation Comparing of similarities and differentiators among a particular competitive set of brands.

Core messaging The brand's primary associations, which complement and support additional, or secondary, associations.

Customer Economy The natural evolution of the New Economy, by which the technological innovations of the New Economy combine with a new emphasis on how masses of customers can be served uniquely and individually.

Cyber-squatter An individual who purchases a URL for the sole purpose of selling the name at an inflated rate.

Data mining Process of extracting knowledge from information.

Delta syndrome A Web phenomenon in which a single brand-name element is used for multiple URLs.

Elevator speech A short but comprehensive description of a company and what it does, based on a set of established points and customized to a given recipient, given in the time it would take to ride an elevator between a few floors. The elevator speech is best cast as a set of points to be used in a wide variety of situations with an equally diverse set of potential audiences, as opposed to a memorized short speech.

Experience the brand *See* Brand the experience versus experience the brand.

Forced branding *See* Natural versus forced branding.

House of brands *See* Branded house versus house of brands.

Hybrid neologism A made-up name that consists of two or more dictionary words or combining forms, such as Microsoft or Widevine. *See also* Neologism.

Ingredient branding The practice of including one brand promise within another for the purpose of establishing a greater total promise (e.g., Intel Inside).

Integrated branding The complete and consistent communication of a brand across all media.

Name analysis The process of weighing the viability of potential brands against a select group of criteria.

Natural versus forced branding The art of extending a brand based on established elements of believability (natural branding) versus extending a brand from undeveloped or underdeveloped premises (forced branding).

Neologism A coined word, such as "Acura" or "Epicor." A neologism is often created to further improve differentiation and optimize chances for being trademarked.

New Economy A commonly accepted term denoting the effects of the Web on the pre-Internet economy.

Parent brand A brand under which other brands reside.

Physical branding A brand's three-dimensional presence; industrial design.

Rediscovery The stage in the life of a brand's maturation where it is vital to understand what is working and what is not; the rediscovery period is often followed by creating a new brand or adjusting the primary brand.

Retroversion The inclination to integrate new technology with some dated standards in hopes of enhancing quick adoption and higher sales.

Subbrand The most specific level in the brand hierarchy; subbrands (e.g., Cadillac Seville), are subsumed under an umbrella (General Motors) or parent (Cadillac) brand.

Tag line The statement which complements a brand name, acting as a segue between the corporate brand name and the message; often used in conjunction with a Web site headline, with the tag line being more strategic and the headline being more tactical.

Umbrella brand A brand, like Microsoft, that encompasses an extremely broad set of parent brands and/or subbrands. *See also* Parent brand; Subbrand.

Vertical markets All the markets specific to one industry.

Virtual campus A group of Web sites, all under an umbrella brand, which are sometimes modeled after a physical infrastructure.

Wallflower brands Brands that have something to offer but which are undermarketed and so not very visible.

Index

About the Authors

Serge Timacheff is a strategic communications and branding expert with The Garrigan Lyman Group, a branding, strategy, and creative services firm based in Seattle. A former global corporate communications executive with Logitech and Attachmate and senior editor at *InfoWorld*, Timacheff has written hundreds of technology/business articles and several books. He has presented speeches and keynotes on branding in multiple countries, and has appeared on CNBC and in numerous other print and broadcast interviews.

Douglas E Rand is the leader of The Garrigan Lyman Group's office in San Francisco and a seasoned professional in brand strategy. A former managing director with the image and identity consultancy Addison Whitney, as well as a broadcast journalist, Rand has directed hundreds of branding initiatives for such clients as GM, Microsoft, 3M, Epicor Software, Siemens, and Hoffmann-La Roche. He also is a frequent speaker at events and workshops on effective brand management.